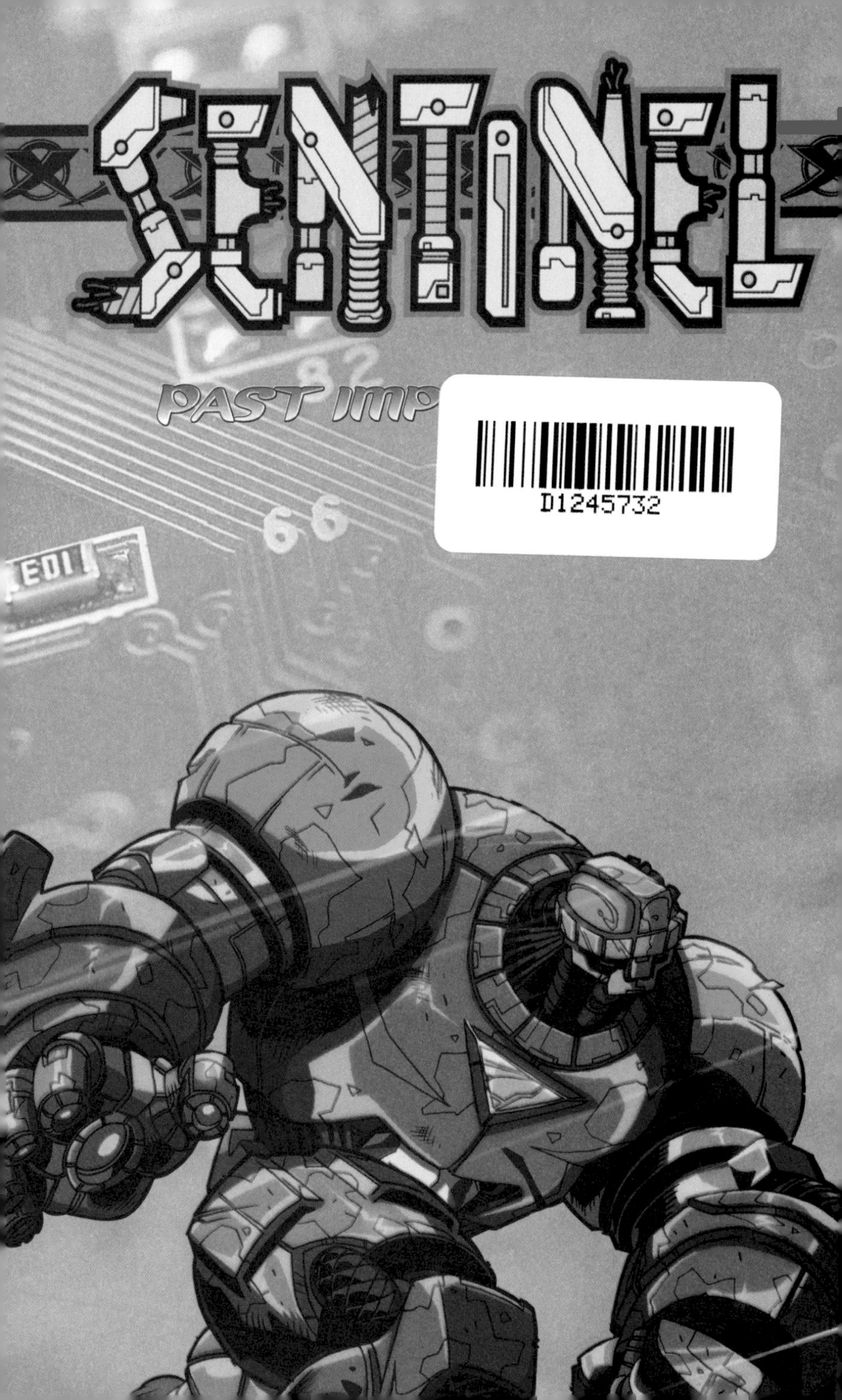
SENTINEL
PAST IMP

SENTINEL
PAST IMPERFECT

WRITER: : SEAN MCKEEVER

PENCILS AND INKS: JOE VRIENS & SCOTT HEPBURN
COLORS: KEVIN YAN & UDON COLORING WITH ESPEN GUDETJERN
& JOE ENG WITH GARY YEUNG [ISSUE #3]
UDON CHIEF: ERIK KO
LETTERS: VIRTUAL CALLIGRAPHY'S JOE CARAMAGNA & DAVE SHARPE
EDITOR: MOLLY LAZER
EDITOR EMERITUS: MARC SUMERAK

COLLECTION EDITOR: JENNIFER GRÜNWALD
ASSISTANT EDITOR: MICHAEL SHORT
SENIOR EDITOR, SPECIAL PROJECTS: JEFF YOUNGQUIST
VICE PRESIDENT OF SALES: DAVID GABRIEL
PRODUCTION: JERRON QUALITY COLOR
VICE PRESIDENT OF CREATIVE: TOM MARVELLI

EDITOR IN CHIEF: JOE QUESADA
PUBLISHER: DAN BUCKLEY

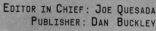

PREVIOUSLY

Sophomore Juston Seyfert was the constant target of bullies at Antigo Senior High until he found the battle-ravaged remains of a Sentinel -- a government-built weapon designed to hunt down mutants -- in his father's salvage yard. Using his strong technical skills, Juston helped to put the mechanical marauder back together, and then had it pretend to attack Antigo Senior High in order to scare the bullies and make himself look the hero by stopping the robotic rampage!

It worked.

Not knowing that the attack and rescue were all carefully orchestrated by Juston, his classmates and the entire community rallied around him. But the truth of the matter has weighed heavily on Juston, who realizes that the property damage and the psychological aftershocks of the attack have made him anything but the hero he'd hoped to be.

Since that day, Juston has tried to atone for his mistake by using the Sentinel under the cover of night, doing everything in his power to help others -- while also steering clear of the Commission on Superhuman Activities, a law enforcement agency concerned with federal crimes involving mutants and other enhanced humans. CSA Agent Brian Rinehart had his suspicions that Juston was controlling the Sentinel. A mutant himself, Rinehart was attacked and killed by the Sentinel, but not before he was able to deactivate the Sentinel with an energy blast.

With the Sentinel captured and the only person connecting Juston to the Sentinel gone, it seemed to Juston that his troubles were over. However, another CSA agent named Walsh began to put together the same puzzle pieces as Rinehart and planned to have the Sentinel's hard drives sifted through for evidence. Knowing that the CSA would discover his secret, Juston reactivated and recovered the Sentinel, deciding to run away and use the Sentinel's DNA detection skills in search of his mother, who'd abandoned his family a decade ago for reasons unknown.

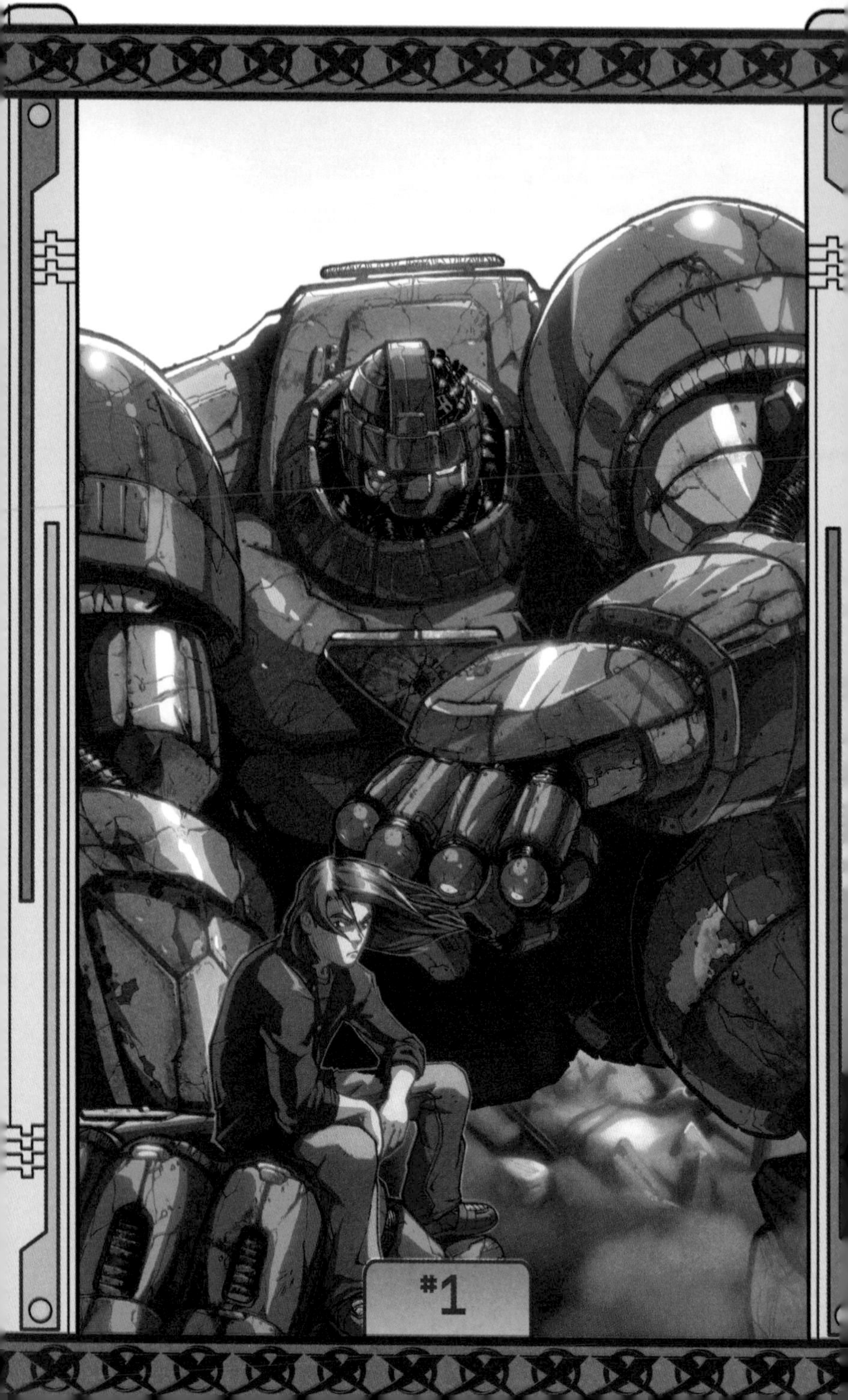
#1

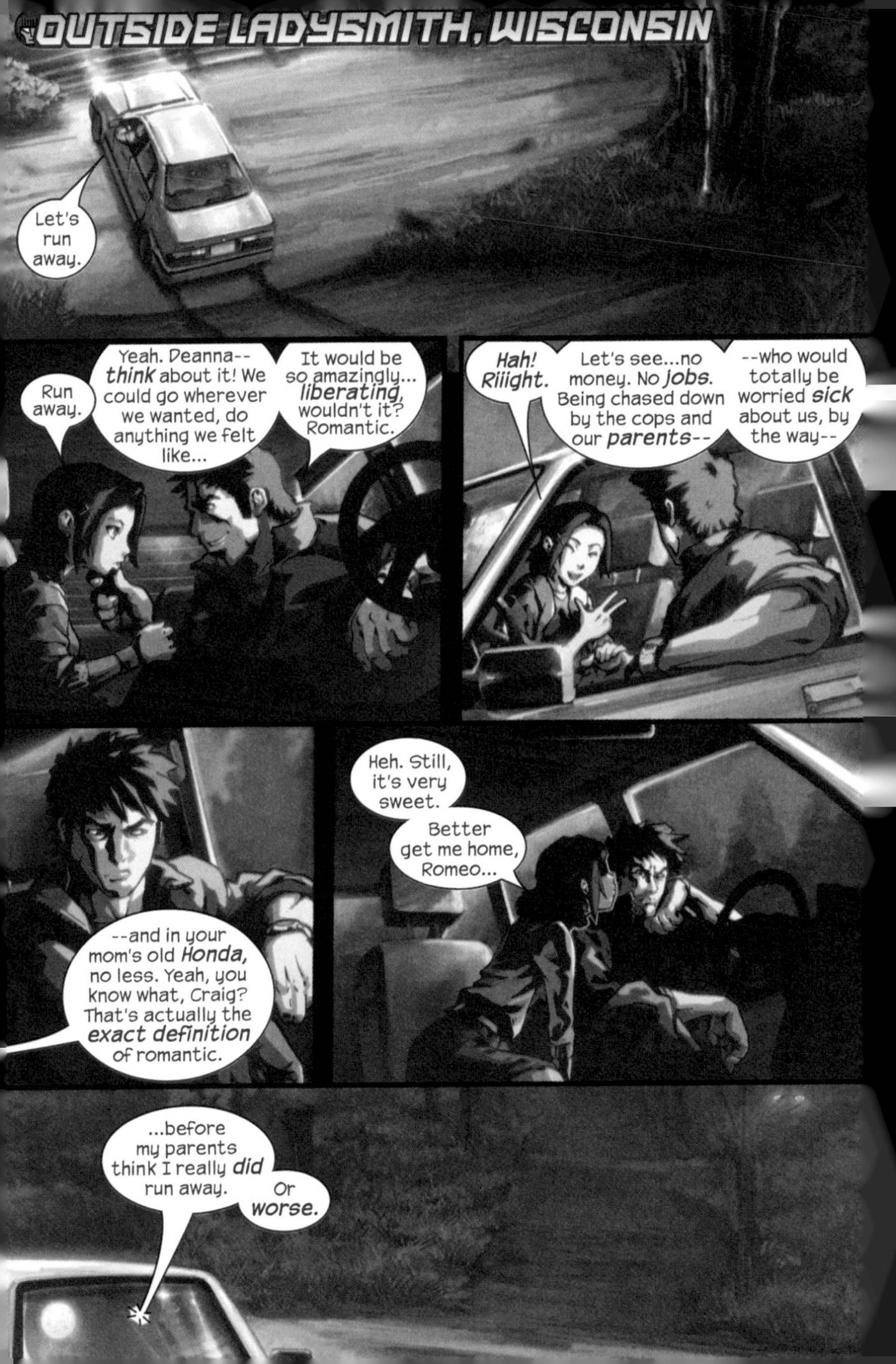
OUTSIDE LADYSMITH, WISCONSIN
Let's run away.
Run away.
Yeah. Deanna--think about it! We could go wherever we wanted, do anything we felt like...
It would be so amazingly... liberating, wouldn't it? Romantic.
Hah! Riiight.
Let's see...no money. No jobs. Being chased down by the cops and our parents--
--who would totally be worried sick about us, by the way--
--and in your mom's old Honda, no less. Yeah, you know what, Craig? That's actually the exact definition of romantic.
Heh. Still, it's very sweet.
Better get me home, Romeo...
...before my parents think I really did run away.
Or worse.

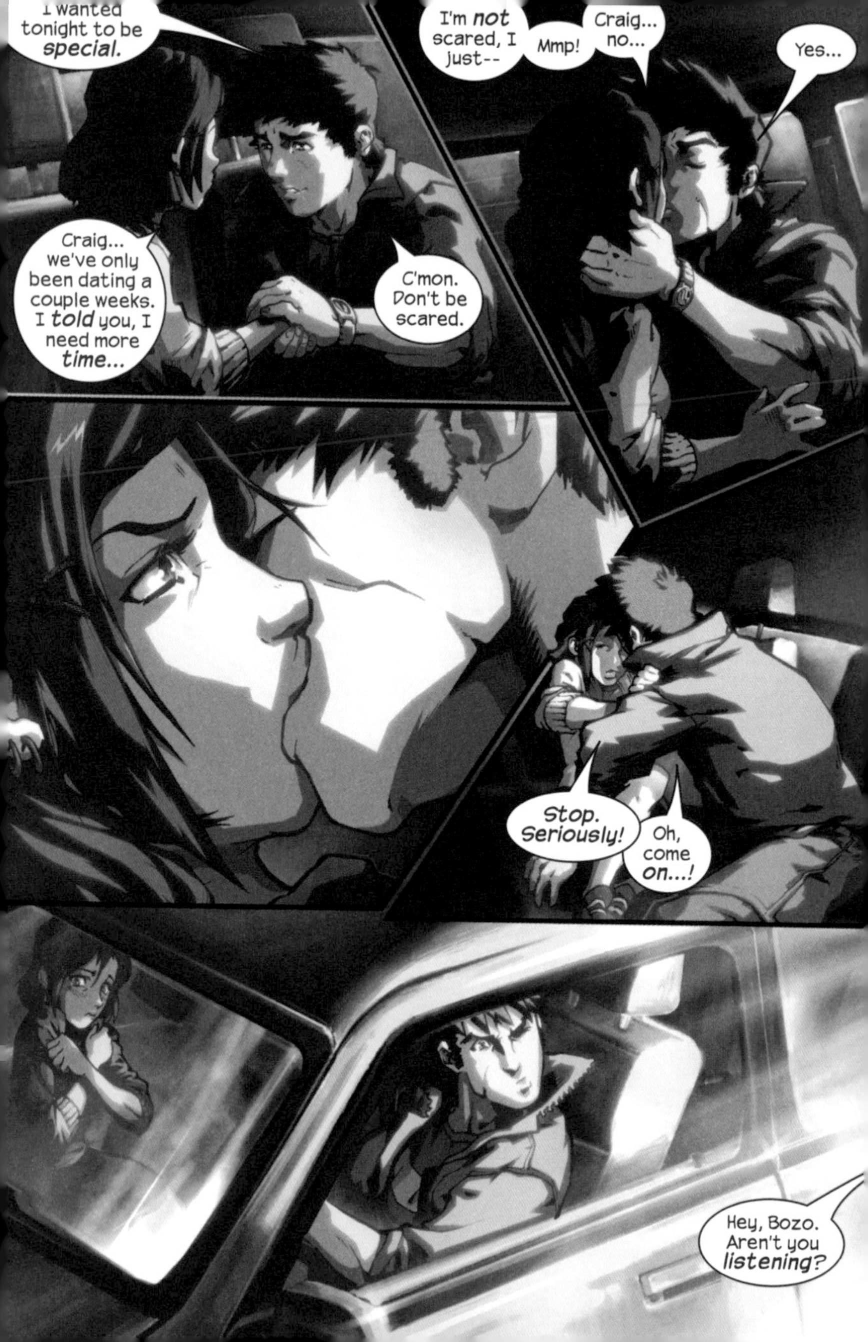

I wanted tonight to be *special.*
Craig... we've only been dating a couple weeks. I *told* you, I need more *time...*
C'mon. Don't be scared.
I'm *not* scared, I just--
Mmp!
Craig... no...
Yes...
Stop. Seriously!
Oh, come *on...!*
Hey, Bozo. Aren't you *listening?*

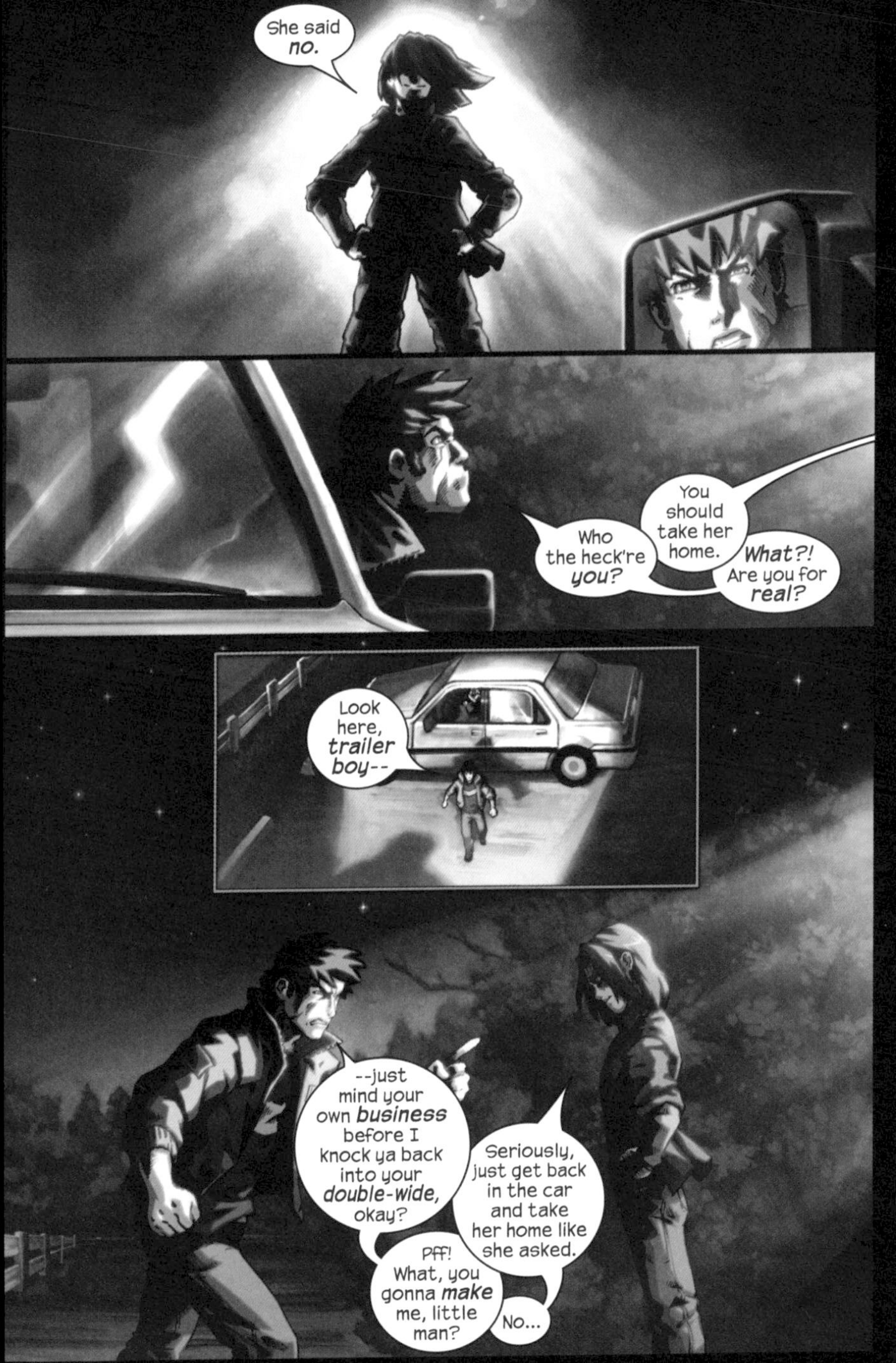
She said no.
Who the heck're you?
You should take her home.
What?! Are you for real?
Look here, trailer boy--
--just mind your own business before I knock ya back into your double-wide, okay?
Seriously, just get back in the car and take her home like she asked.
Pff! What, you gonna make me, little man?
No...

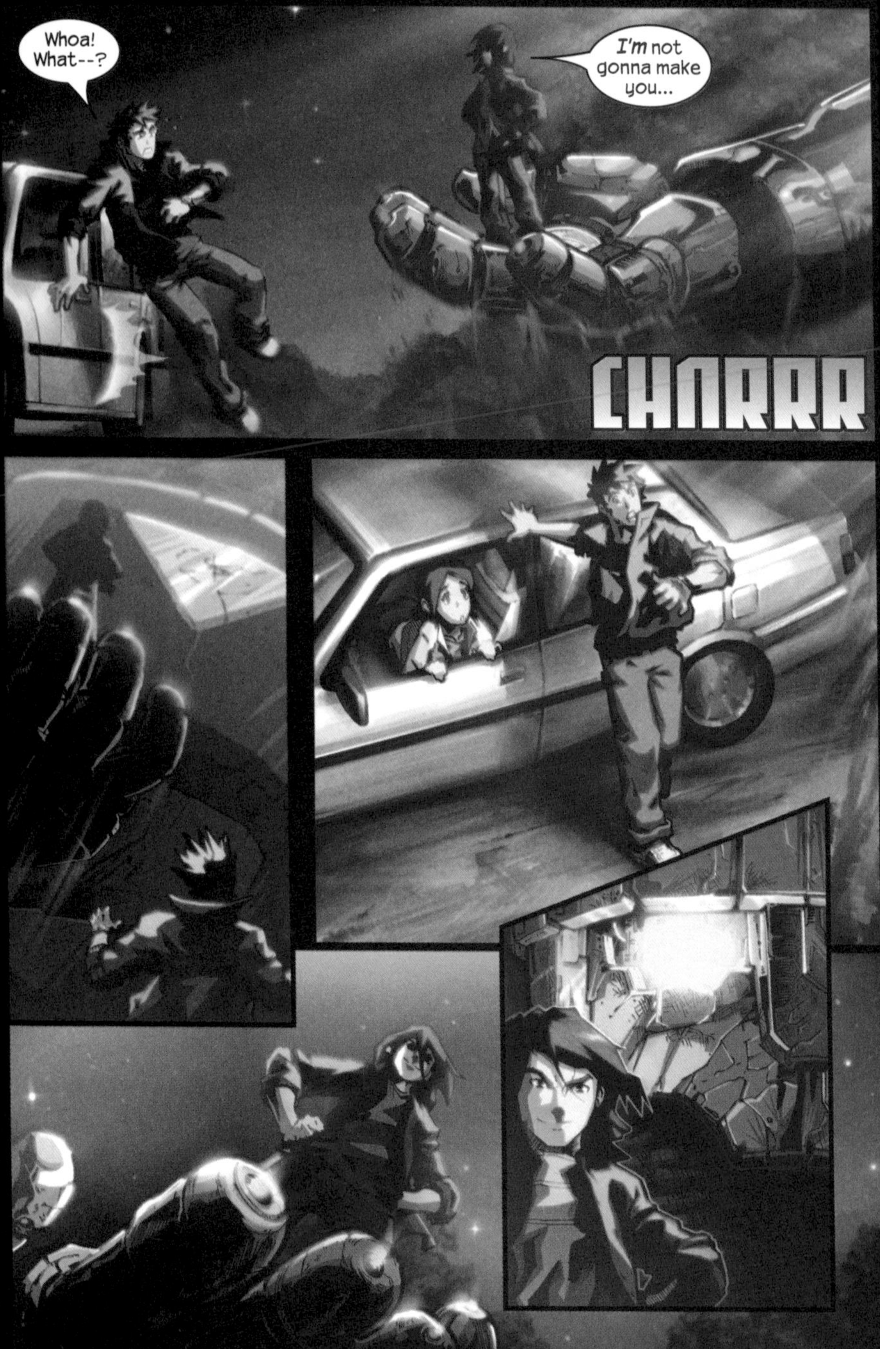
Whoa! What--?
I'm not gonna make you...
CHRRR

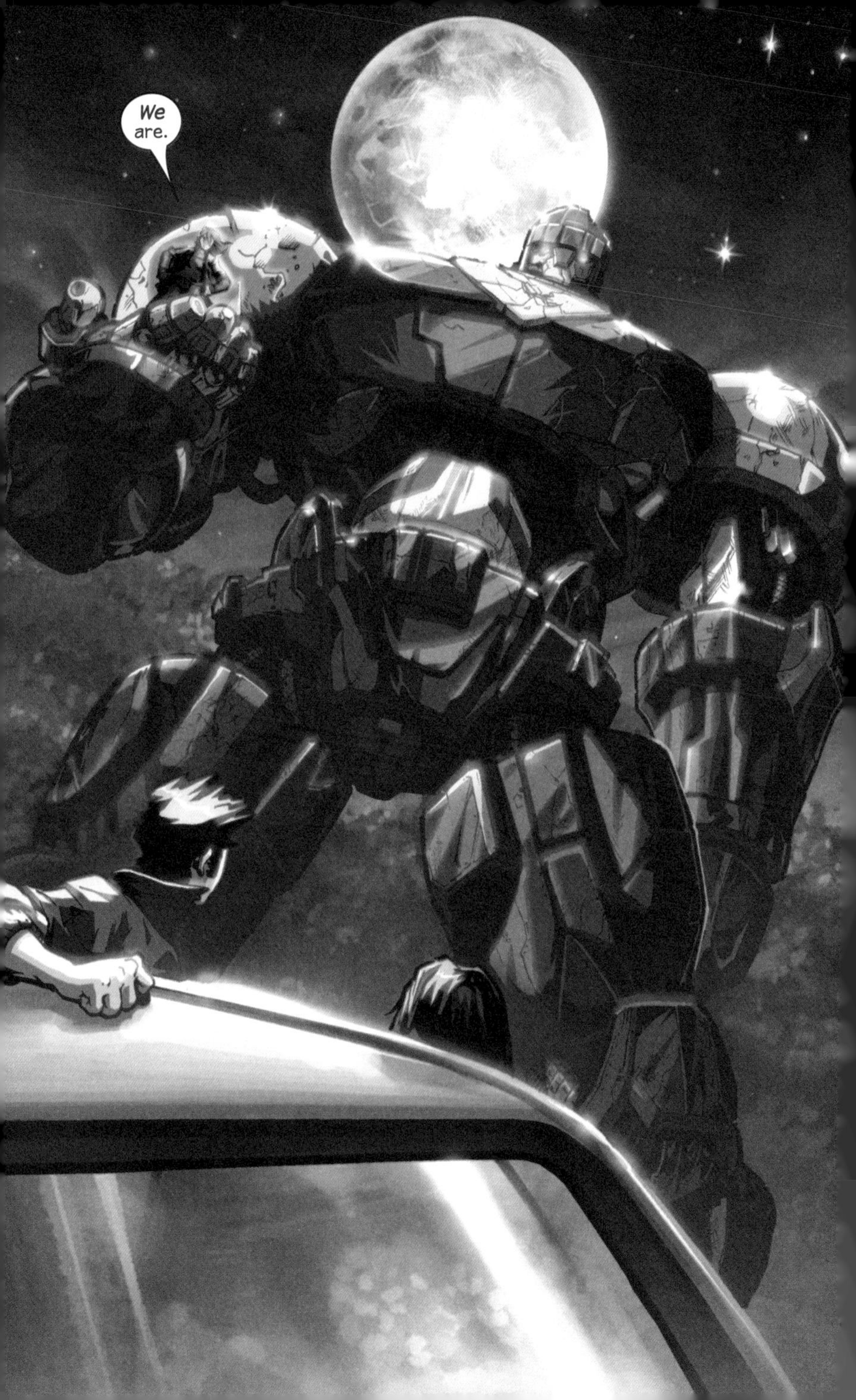
We are.

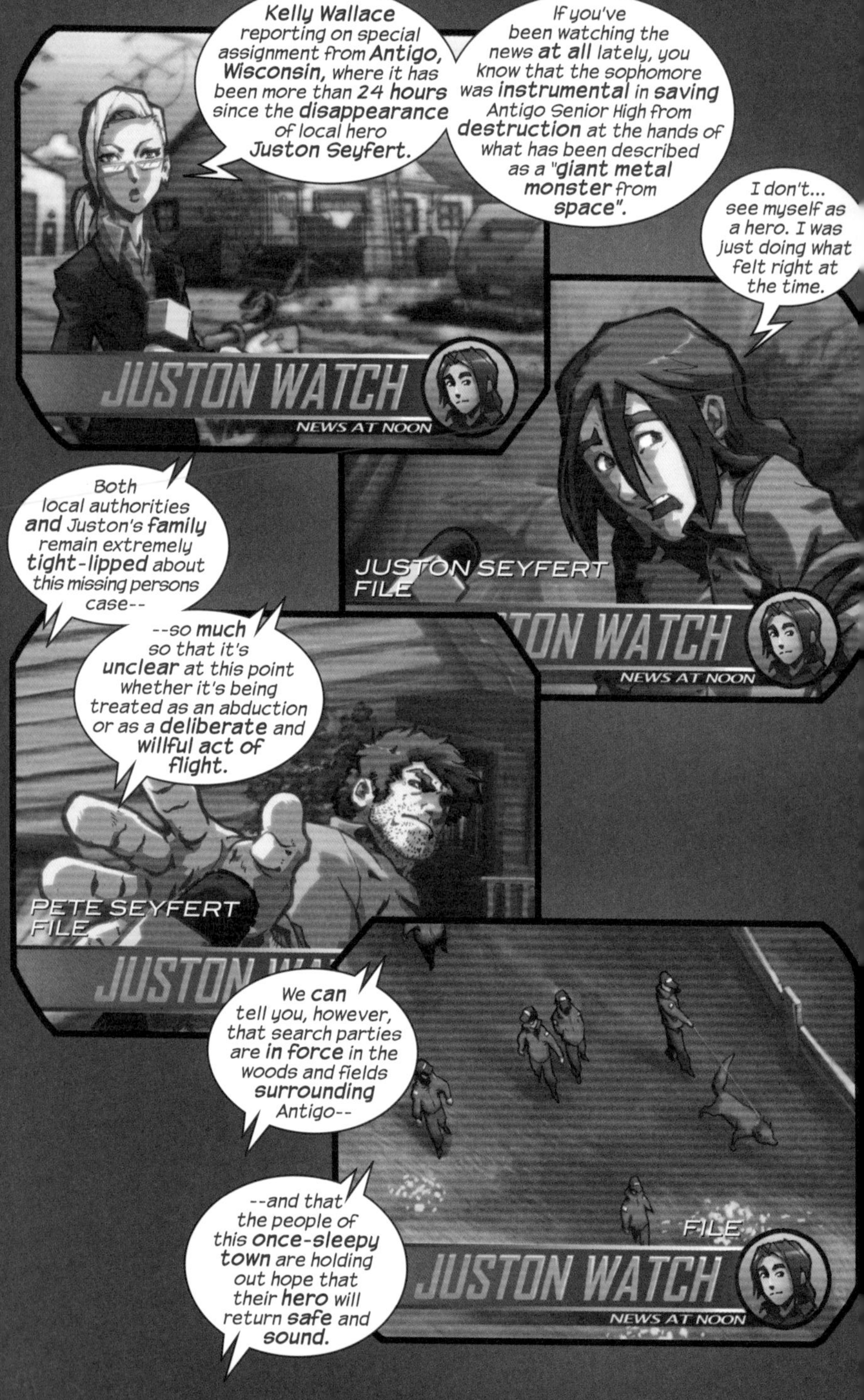
Kelly Wallace reporting on special assignment from Antigo, Wisconsin, where it has been more than 24 hours since the disappearance of local hero Juston Seyfert.
If you've been watching the news at all lately, you know that the sophomore was instrumental in saving Antigo Senior High from destruction at the hands of what has been described as a "giant metal monster from space".
JUSTON WATCH
NEWS AT NOON
I don't... see myself as a hero. I was just doing what felt right at the time.
JUSTON SEYFERT FILE
Both local authorities and Juston's family remain extremely tight-lipped about this missing persons case--
--so much so that it's unclear at this point whether it's being treated as an abduction or as a deliberate and willful act of flight.
NEWS AT NOON
PETE SEYFERT FILE
We can tell you, however, that search parties are in force in the woods and fields surrounding Antigo--
--and that the people of this once-sleepy town are holding out hope that their hero will return safe and sound.
FILE
JUSTON WATCH
NEWS AT NOON

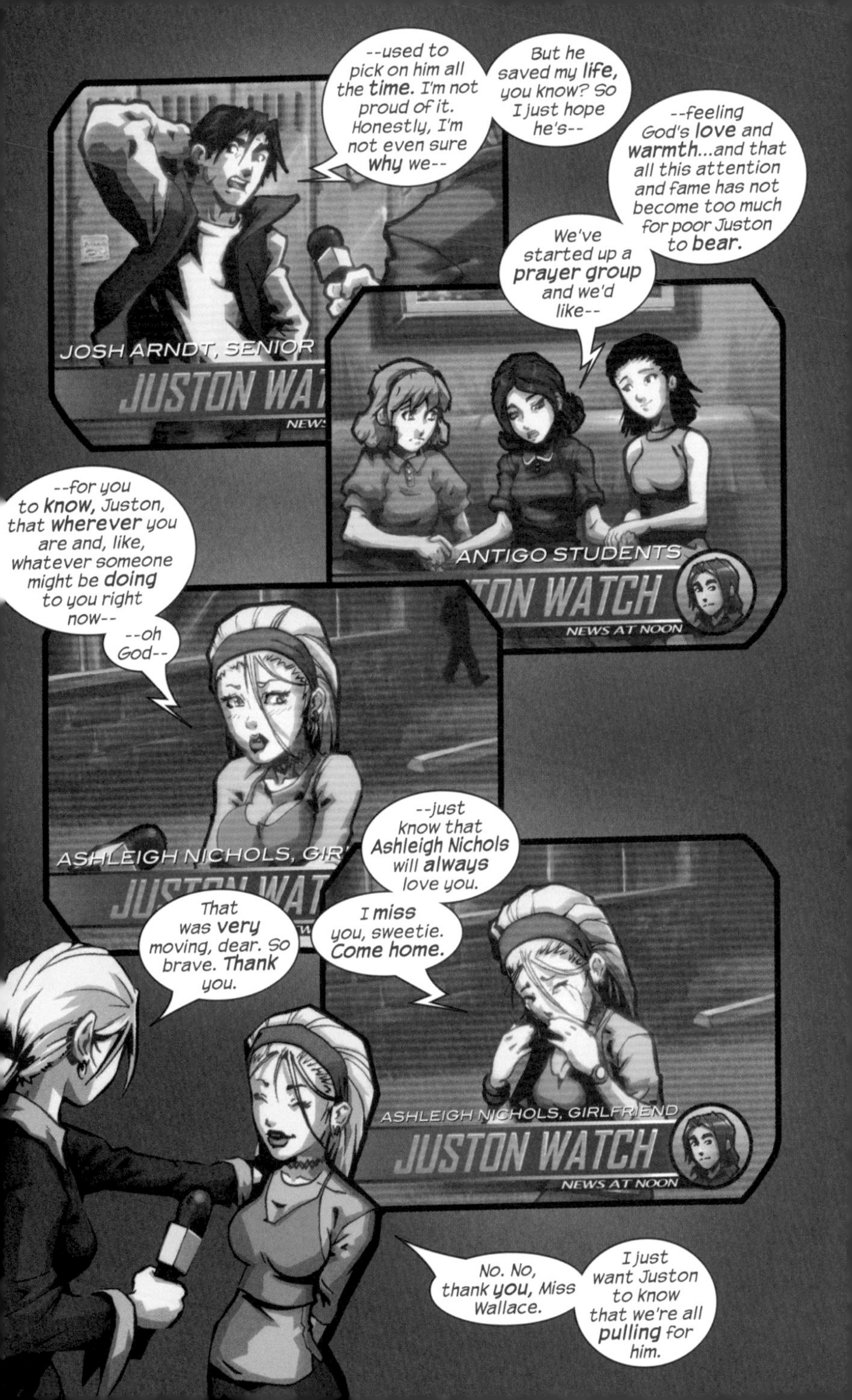
--used to pick on him all the time. I'm not proud of it. Honestly, I'm not even sure why we--
JOSH ARNDT, SENIOR
JUSTON WATCH
But he saved my life, you know? So I just hope he's--
--feeling God's love and warmth...and that all this attention and fame has not become too much for poor Juston to bear.
We've started up a prayer group and we'd like--
--for you to know, Juston, that wherever you are and, like, whatever someone might be doing to you right now--
ANTIGO STUDENTS
NEWS AT NOON
--oh God--
ASHLEIGH NICHOLS, GIRL
--just know that Ashleigh Nichols will always love you.
I miss you, sweetie. Come home.
ASHLEIGH NICHOLS, GIRLFRIEND
JUSTON WATCH
NEWS AT NOON
That was very moving, dear. So brave. Thank you.
No. No, thank you, Miss Wallace.
I just want Juston to know that we're all pulling for him.

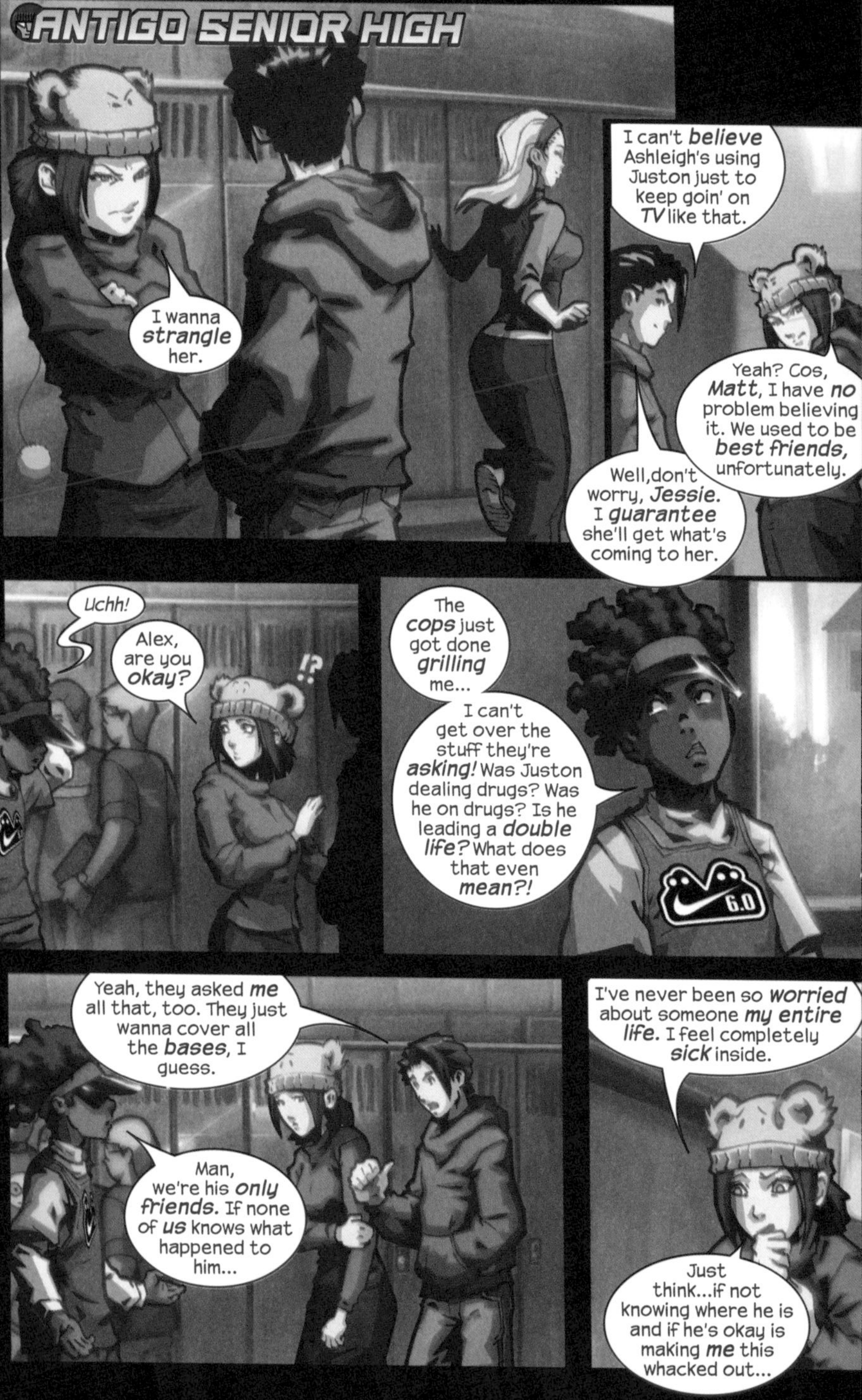

ANTIGO SENIOR HIGH
I wanna strangle her.
I can't believe Ashleigh's using Juston just to keep goin' on TV like that.
Yeah? Cos, Matt, I have no problem believing it. We used to be best friends, unfortunately.
Well,don't worry, Jessie. I guarantee she'll get what's coming to her.
Uchh!
Alex, are you okay?
!?
The cops just got done grilling me...
I can't get over the stuff they're asking! Was Juston dealing drugs? Was he on drugs? Is he leading a double life? What does that even mean?!
Yeah, they asked me all that, too. They just wanna cover all the bases, I guess.
Man, we're his only friends. If none of us knows what happened to him...
I've never been so worried about someone my entire life. I feel completely sick inside.
Just think...if not knowing where he is and if he's okay is making me this whacked out...

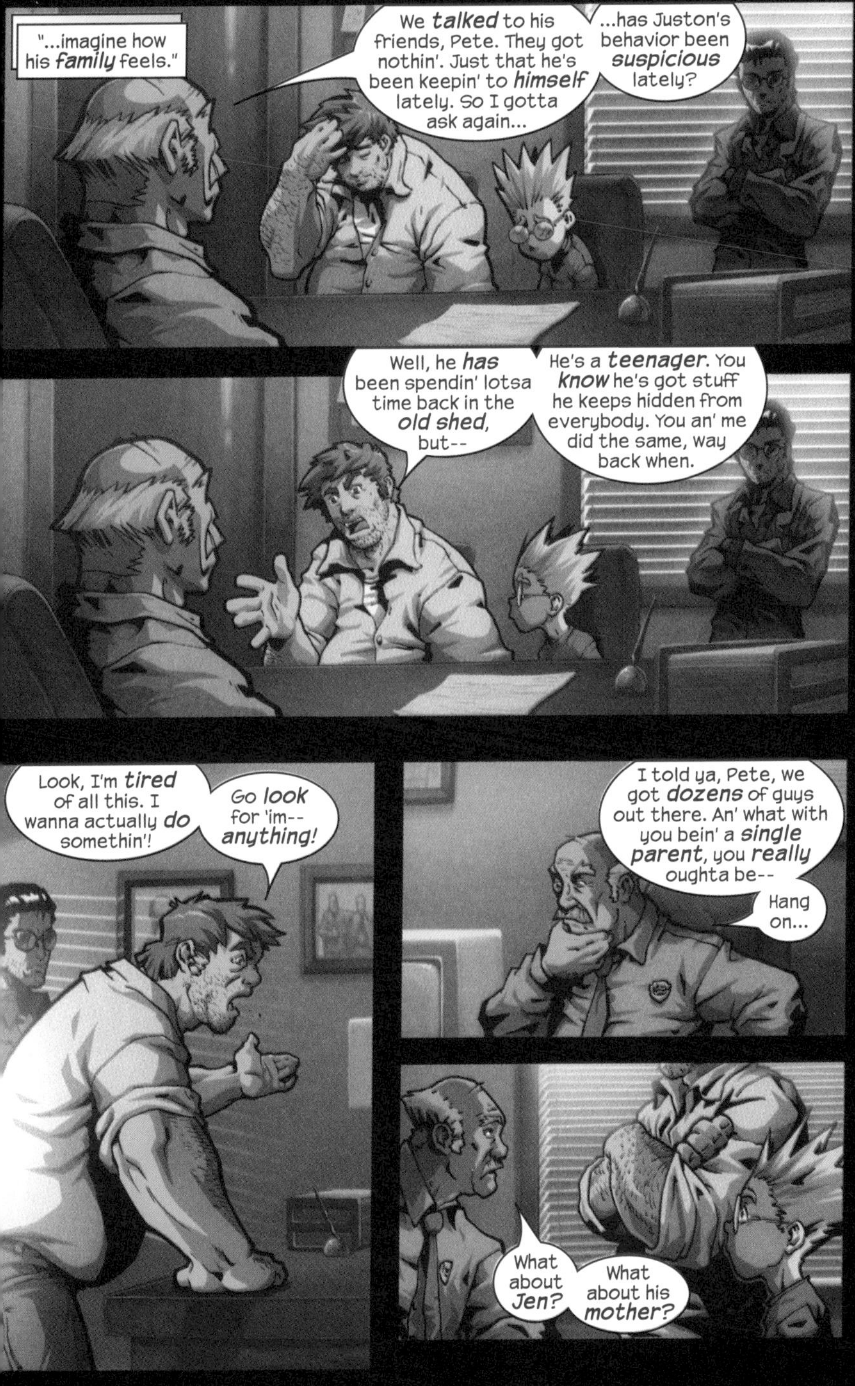
"...imagine how his *family* feels."
We *talked* to his friends, Pete. They got nothin'. Just that he's been keepin' to *himself* lately. So I gotta ask again...
...has Juston's behavior been *suspicious* lately?
Well, he *has* been spendin' lotsa time back in the *old shed*, but--
He's a *teenager*. You *know* he's got stuff he keeps hidden from everybody. You an' me did the same, way back when.
Look, I'm *tired* of all this. I wanna actually *do* somethin'!
Go *look* for 'im-- *anything!*
I told ya, Pete, we got *dozens* of guys out there. An' what with you bein' a *single parent*, you *really* oughta be--
Hang on...
What about *Jen?*
What about his *mother?*

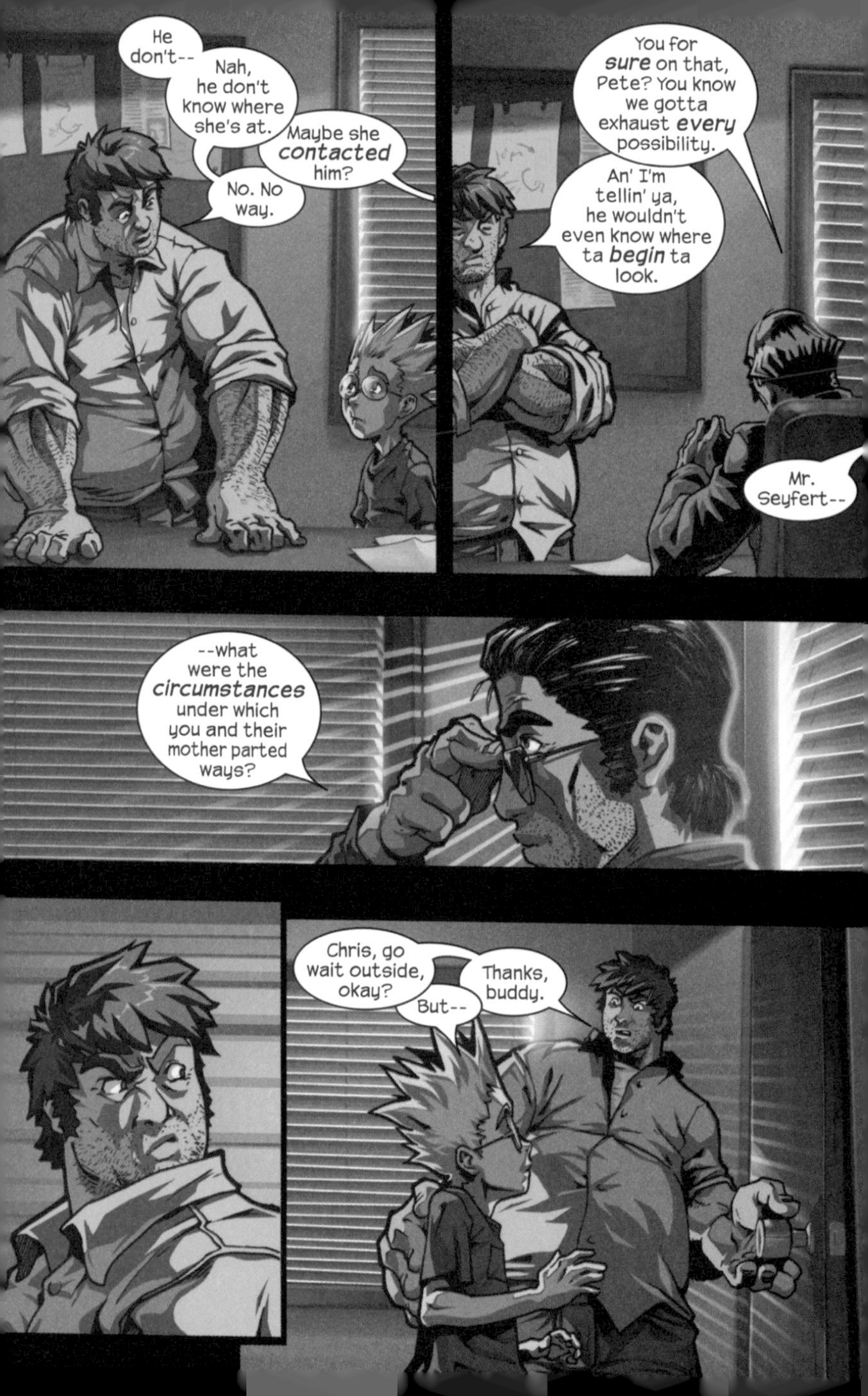
He don't--
Nah, he don't know where she's at.
Maybe she *contacted* him?
No. No way.
You for *sure* on that, Pete? You know we gotta exhaust *every* possibility.
An' I'm tellin' ya, he wouldn't even know where ta *begin* ta look.
Mr. Seyfert--
--what were the *circumstances* under which you and their mother parted ways?
Chris, go wait outside, okay?
But--
Thanks, buddy.

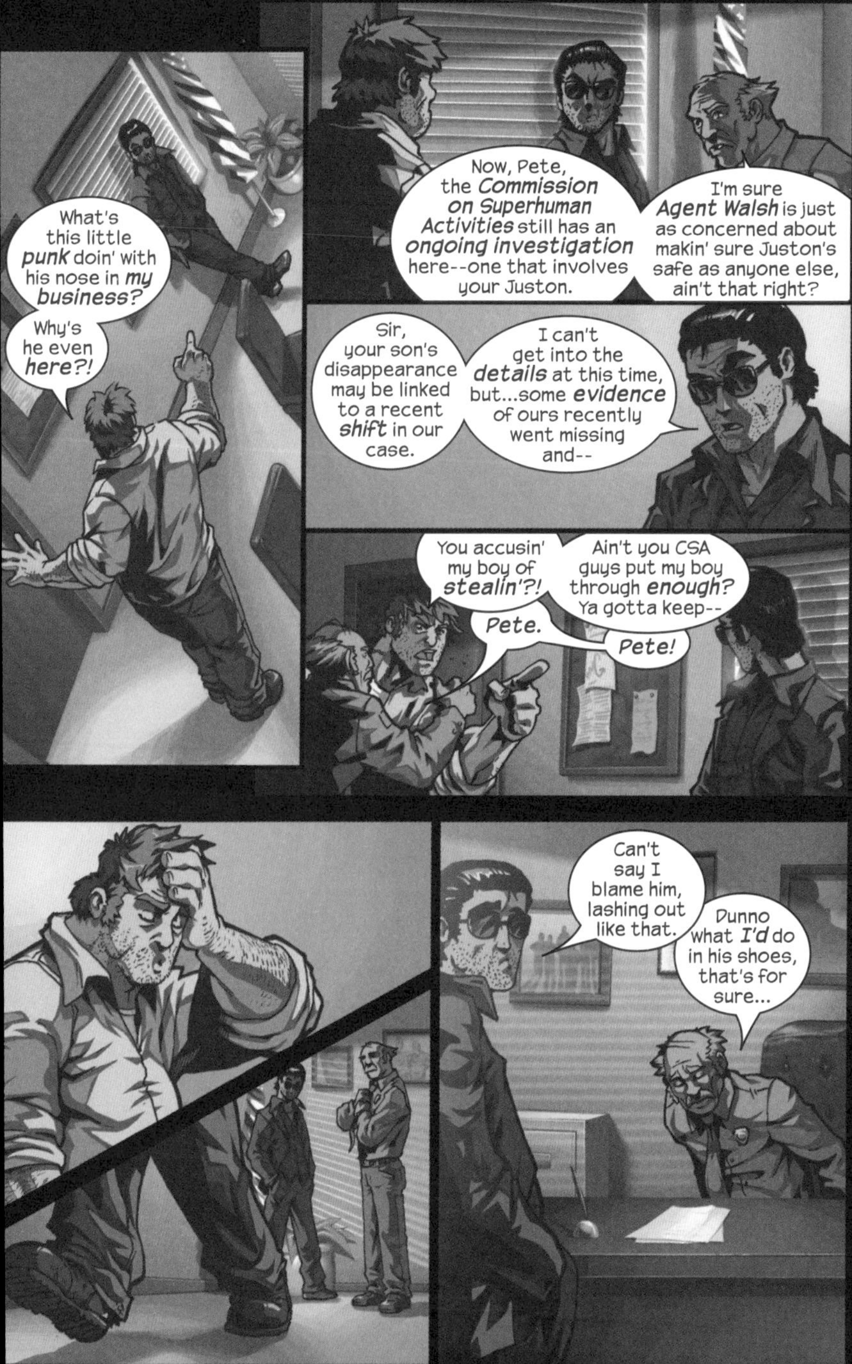
What's this little punk doin' with his nose in my business?
Why's he even here?!
Now, Pete, the Commission on Superhuman Activities still has an ongoing investigation here--one that involves your Juston.
I'm sure Agent Walsh is just as concerned about makin' sure Juston's safe as anyone else, ain't that right?
Sir, your son's disappearance may be linked to a recent shift in our case.
I can't get into the details at this time, but...some evidence of ours recently went missing and--
You accusin' my boy of stealin'?!
Pete.
Ain't you CSA guys put my boy through enough? Ya gotta keep--
Pete!
Can't say I blame him, lashing out like that.
Dunno what I'd do in his shoes, that's for sure...

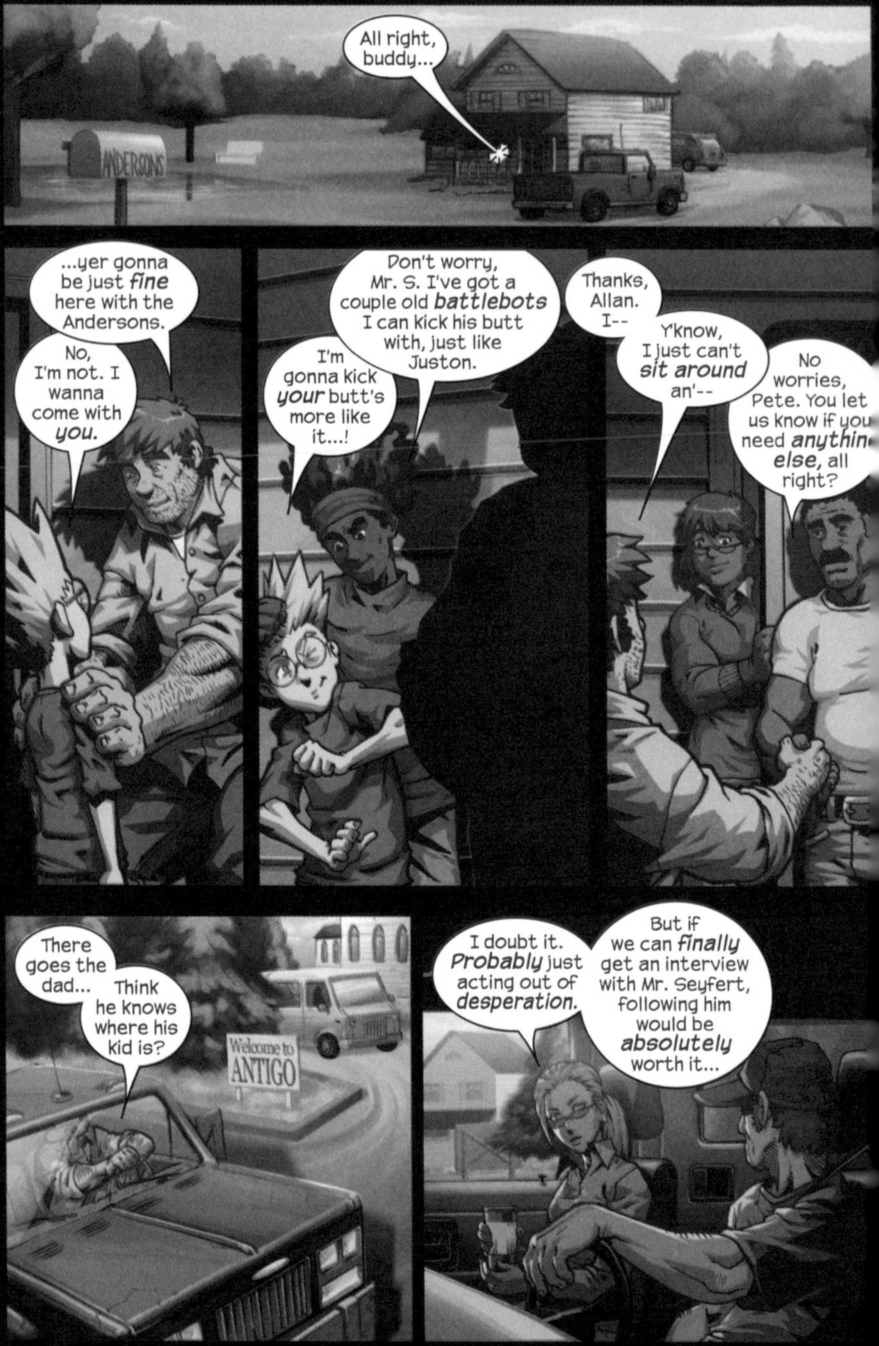

All right, buddy...
ANDERSONS
...yer gonna be just fine here with the Andersons.
No, I'm not. I wanna come with you.
Don't worry, Mr. S. I've got a couple old battlebots I can kick his butt with, just like Juston.
I'm gonna kick your butt's more like it...!
Thanks, Allan. I--
Y'know, I just can't sit around an'--
No worries, Pete. You let us know if you need anythin else, all right?
There goes the dad...
Think he knows where his kid is?
Welcome to ANTIGO
I doubt it. Probably just acting out of desperation.
But if we can finally get an interview with Mr. Seyfert, following him would be absolutely worth it...

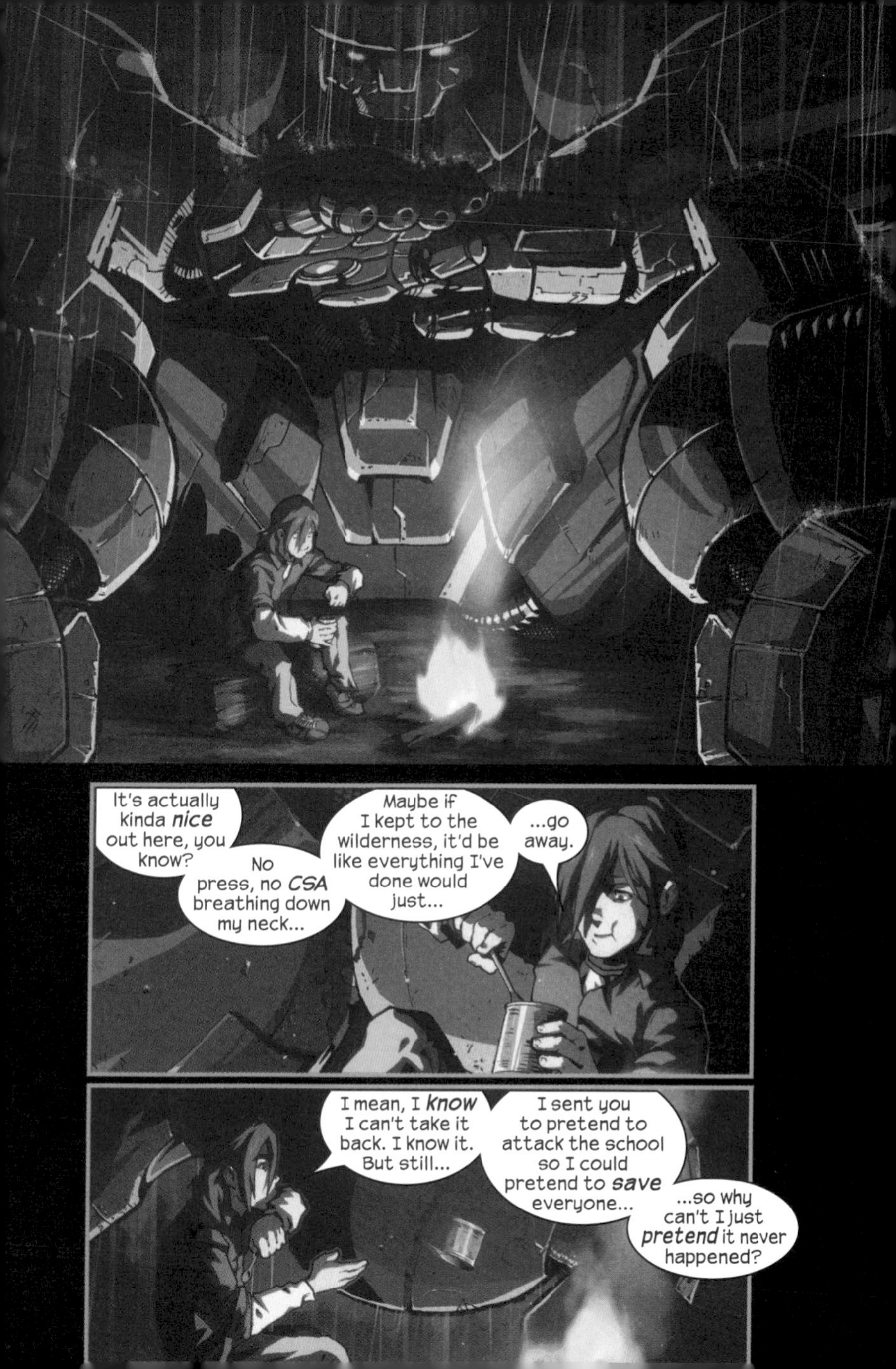
It's actually kinda *nice* out here, you know?
No press, no *CSA* breathing down my neck...
Maybe if I kept to the wilderness, it'd be like everything I've done would just...
...go away.
I mean, I *know* I can't take it back. I know it. But still...
I sent you to pretend to attack the school so I could pretend to *save* everyone...
...so why can't I just *pretend* it never happened?

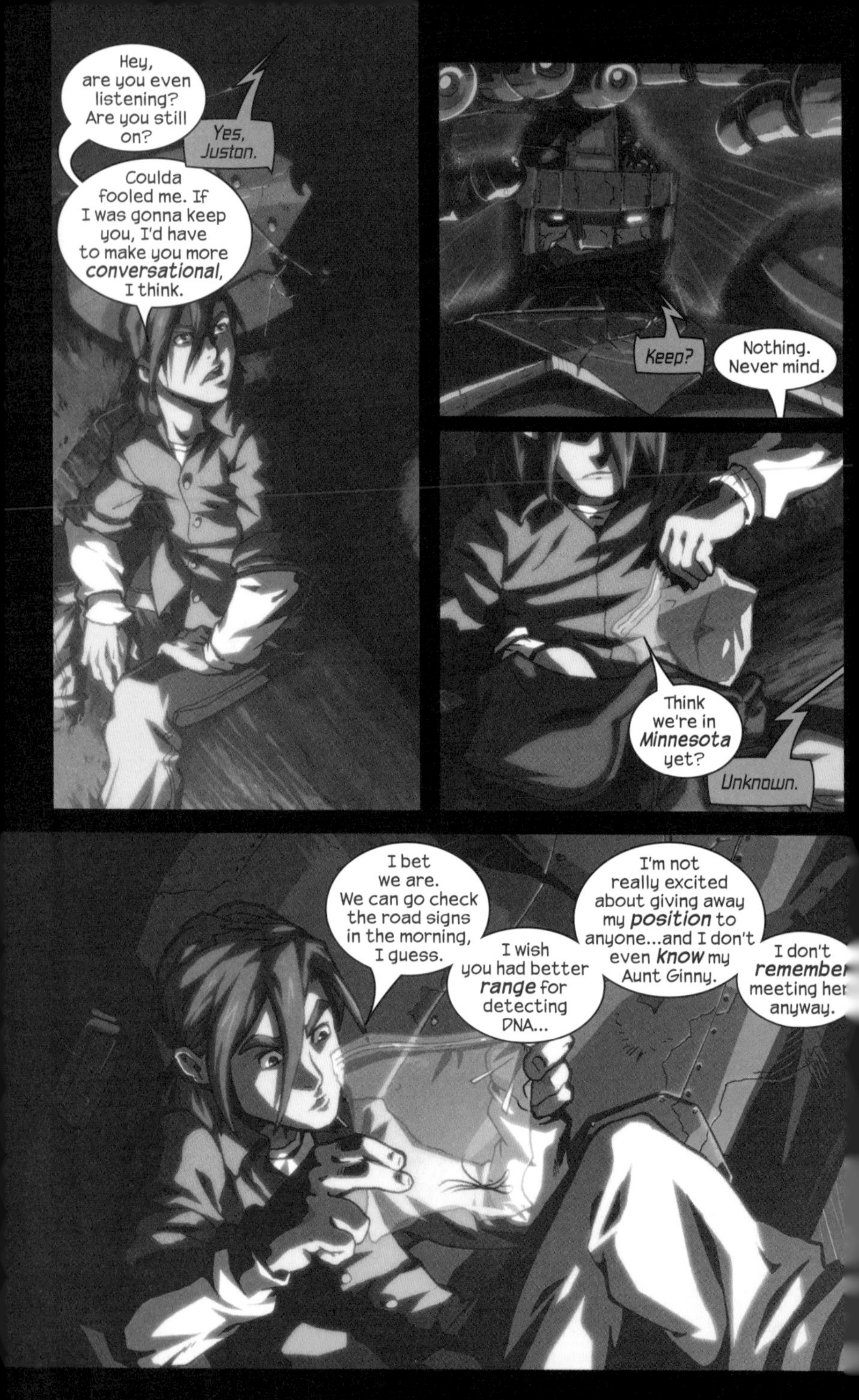
Hey, are you even listening? Are you still on?
Yes, Juston.
Coulda fooled me. If I was gonna keep you, I'd have to make you more *conversational*, I think.
Keep?
Nothing. Never mind.
Think we're in *Minnesota* yet?
Unknown.
I bet we are. We can go check the road signs in the morning, I guess.
I wish you had better *range* for detecting DNA...
I'm not really excited about giving away my *position* to anyone...and I don't even *know* my Aunt Ginny.
I don't *remember* meeting her anyway.

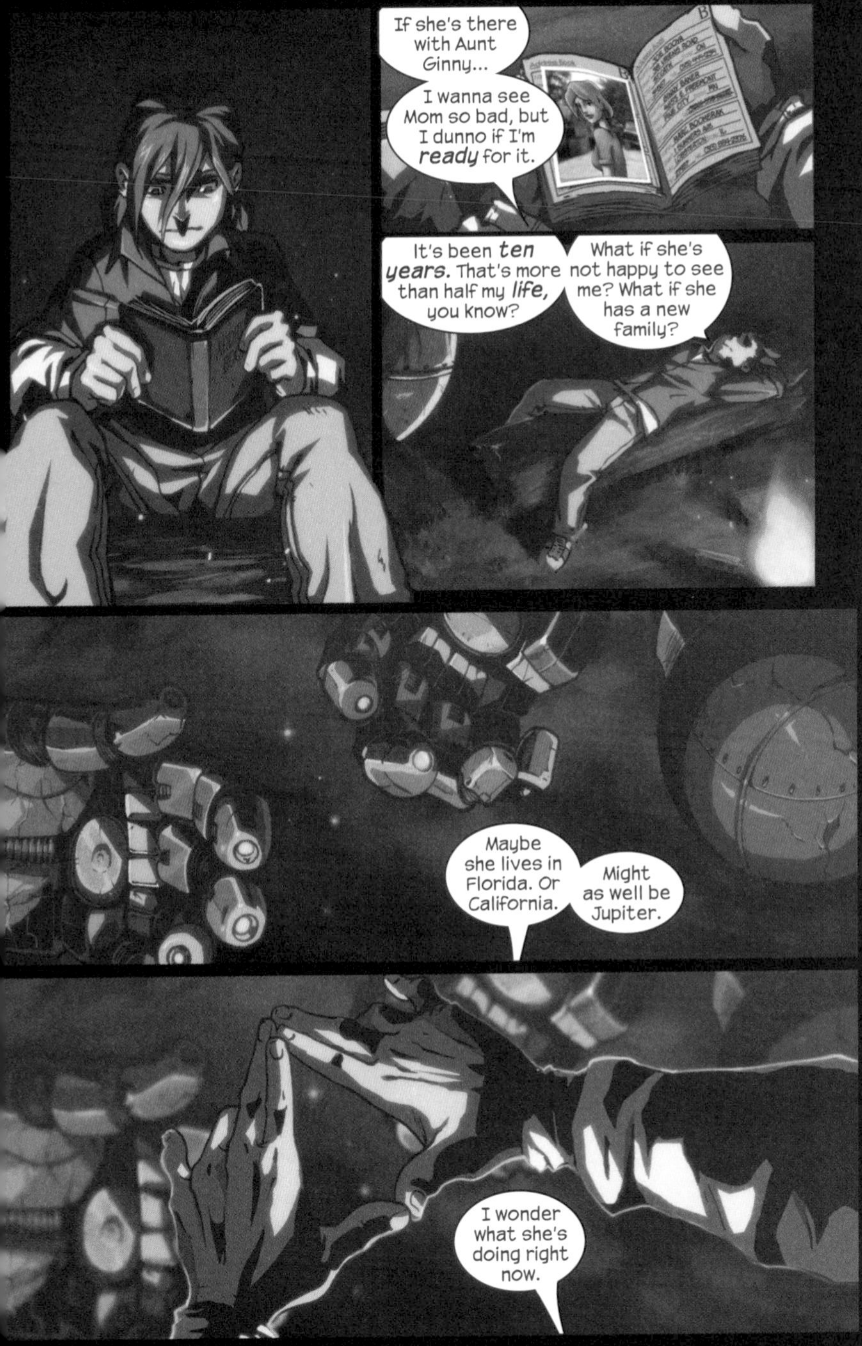
If she's there with Aunt Ginny...
I wanna see Mom so bad, but I dunno if I'm *ready* for it.
It's been *ten years.* That's more than half my *life,* you know?
What if she's not happy to see me? What if she has a new family?
Maybe she lives in Florida. Or California.
Might as well be Jupiter.
I wonder what she's doing right now.

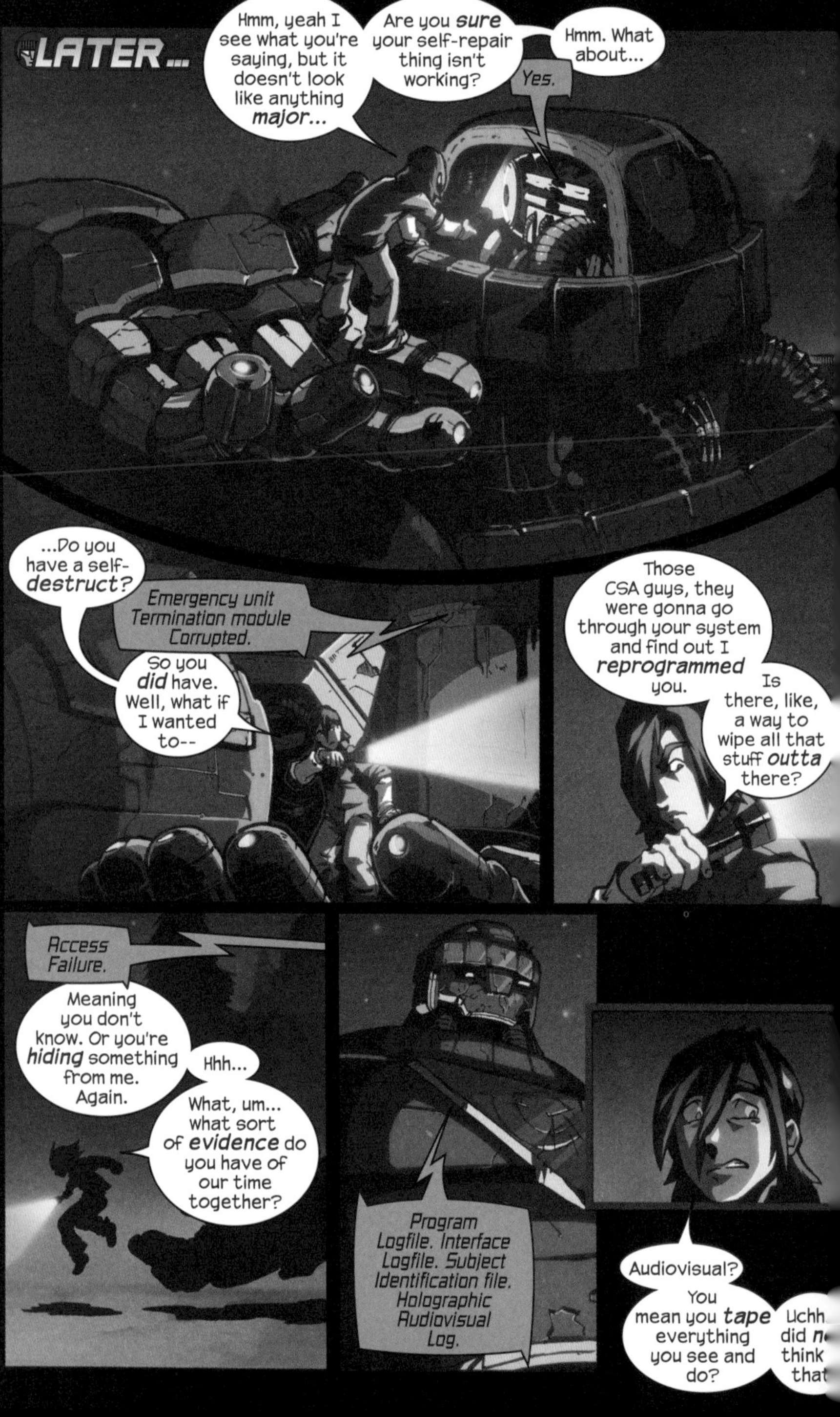
LATER...
Hmm, yeah I see what you're saying, but it doesn't look like anything major...
Are you sure your self-repair thing isn't working?
Yes.
Hmm. What about...
...Do you have a self-destruct?
Emergency unit Termination module Corrupted.
So you did have. Well, what if I wanted to--
Those CSA guys, they were gonna go through your system and find out I reprogrammed you.
Is there, like, a way to wipe all that stuff outta there?
Access Failure.
Meaning you don't know. Or you're hiding something from me. Again.
Hhh...
What, um... what sort of evidence do you have of our time together?
Program Logfile. Interface Logfile. Subject Identification file. Holographic Audiovisual Log.
Audiovisual?
You mean you tape everything you see and do?

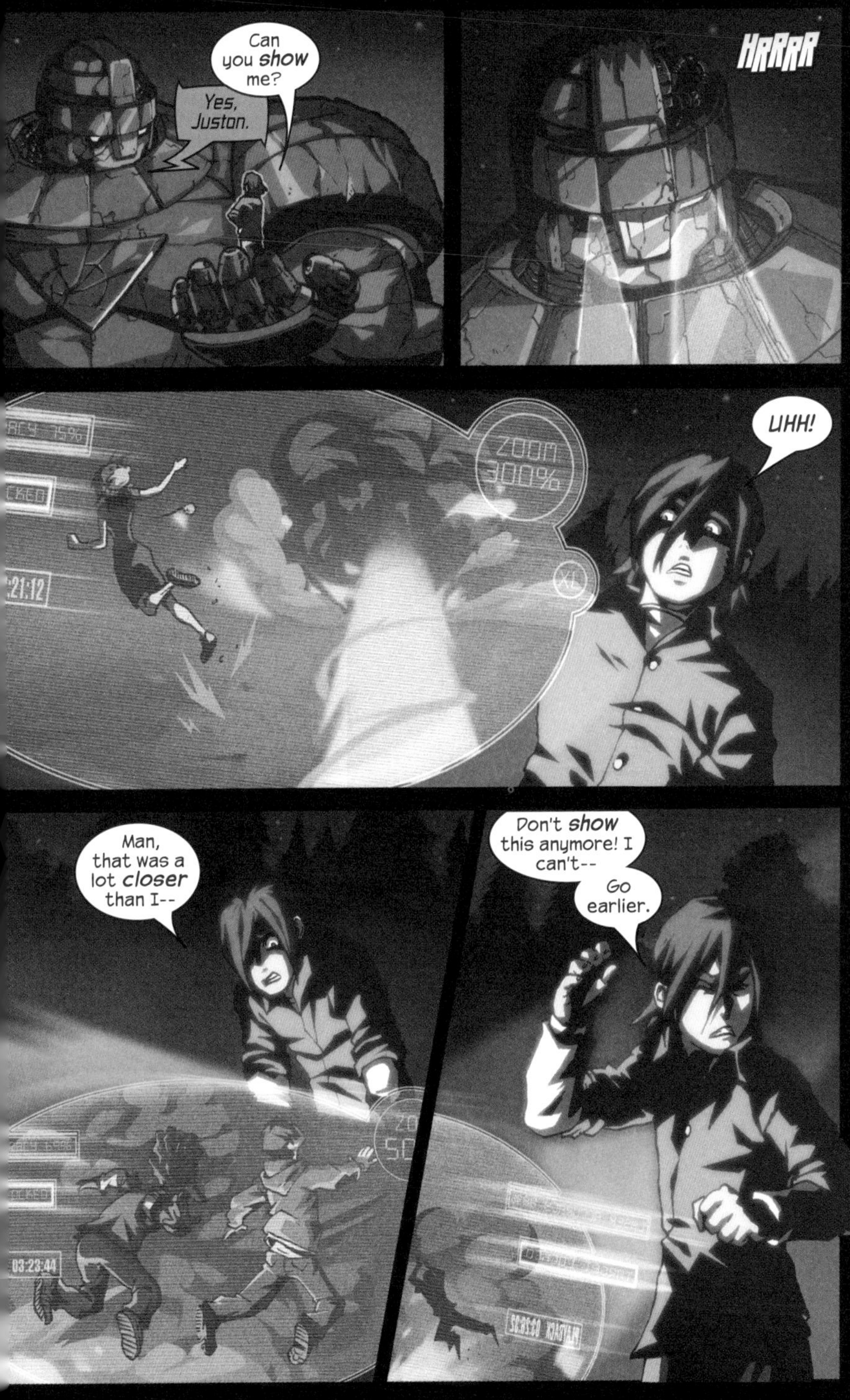

Can you show me?
Yes, Juston.
HRRRR
ZOOM 300%
UHH!
Man, that was a lot closer than I--
Don't show this anymore! I can't--
Go earlier.

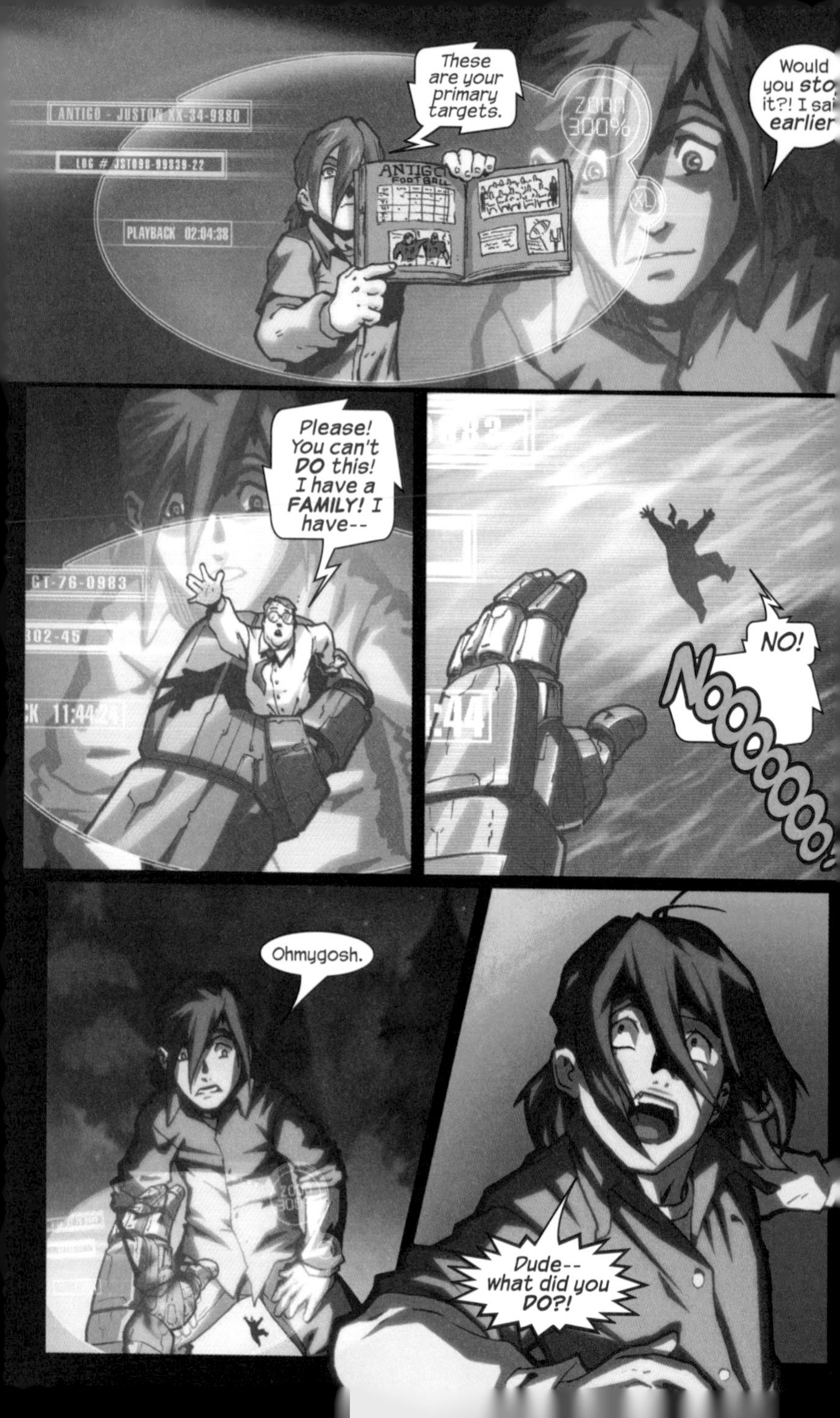
ANTIGO - JUSTON XX-34-9880
LOG # JST098-99839-22
PLAYBACK 02:04:38
These are your primary targets.
ZOOM 300%
Would you sto it?! I sai earlier
Please! You can't DO this! I have a FAMILY! I have--
NO!
NOOOOOOOO
Ohmygosh.
Dude-- what did you DO?!

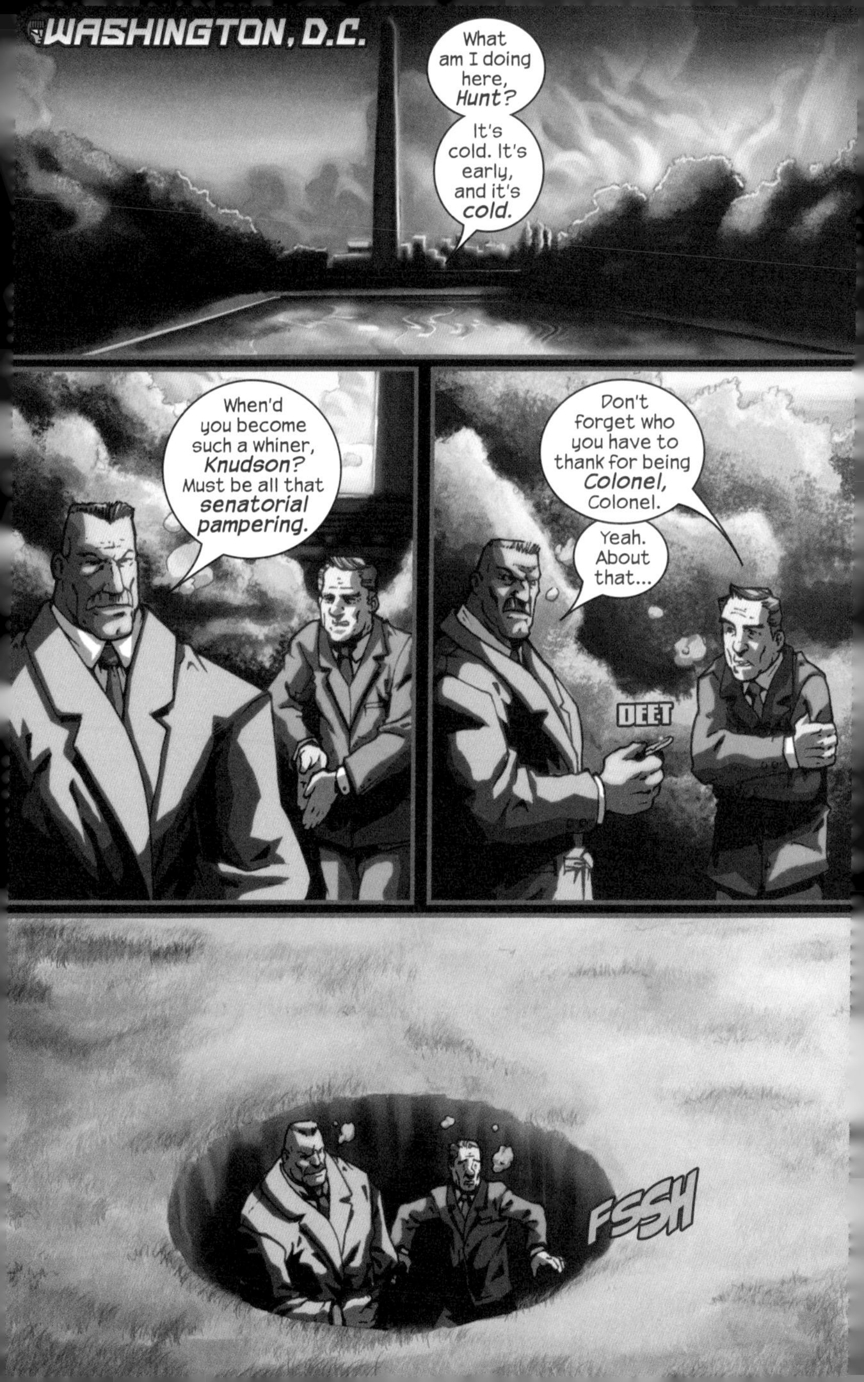
WASHINGTON, D.C.
What am I doing here, Hunt?
It's cold. It's early, and it's cold.
When'd you become such a whiner, Knudson? Must be all that senatorial pampering.
Don't forget who you have to thank for being Colonel, Colonel.
Yeah. About that...
DEET
FSSH

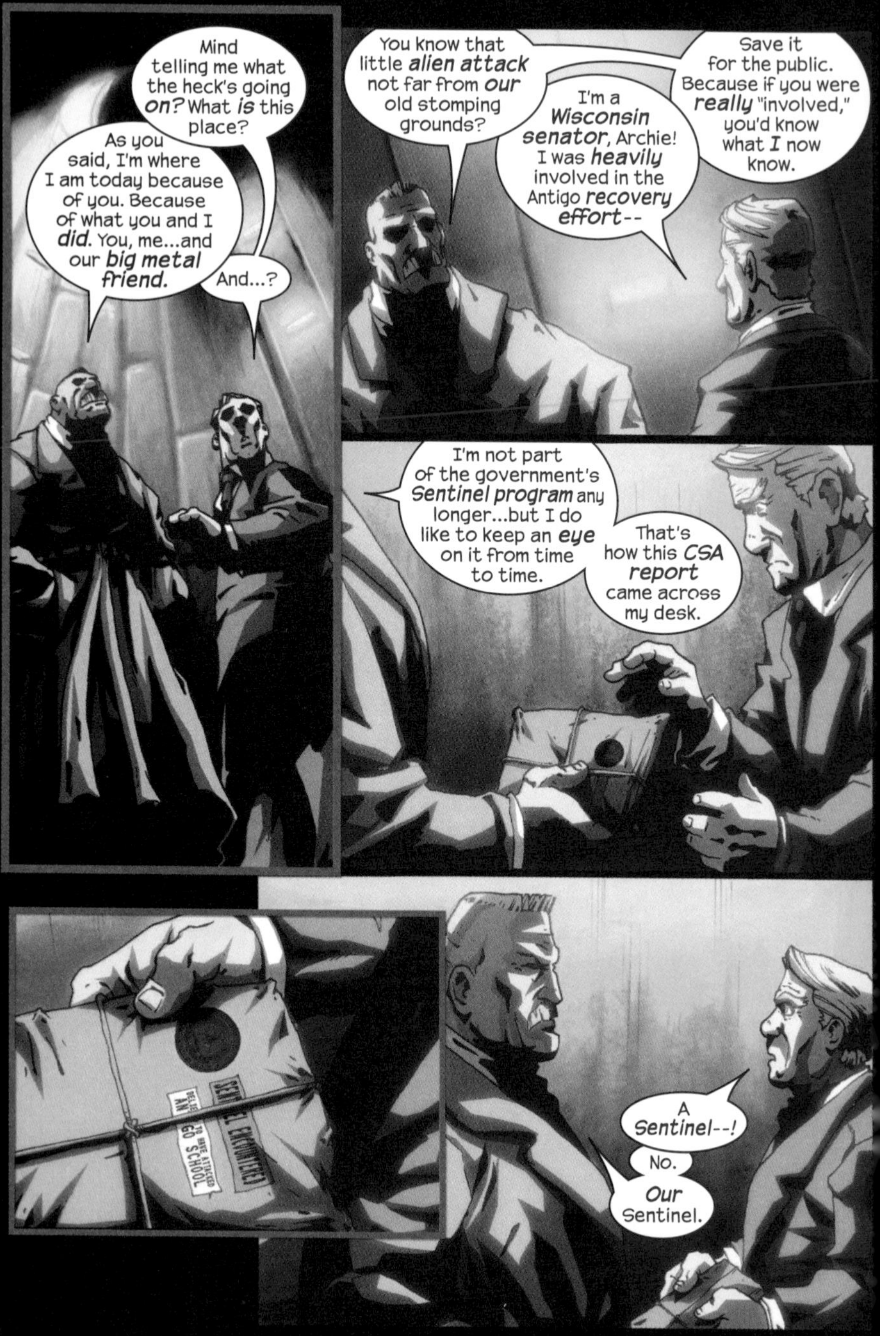
Mind telling me what the heck's going on? What is this place?
As you said, I'm where I am today because of you. Because of what you and I did. You, me...and our big metal friend.
And...?
You know that little alien attack not far from our old stomping grounds?
I'm a Wisconsin senator, Archie! I was heavily involved in the Antigo recovery effort--
Save it for the public. Because if you were really "involved," you'd know what I now know.
I'm not part of the government's Sentinel program any longer...but I do like to keep an eye on it from time to time.
That's how this CSA report came across my desk.
A Sentinel--!
No.
Our Sentinel.

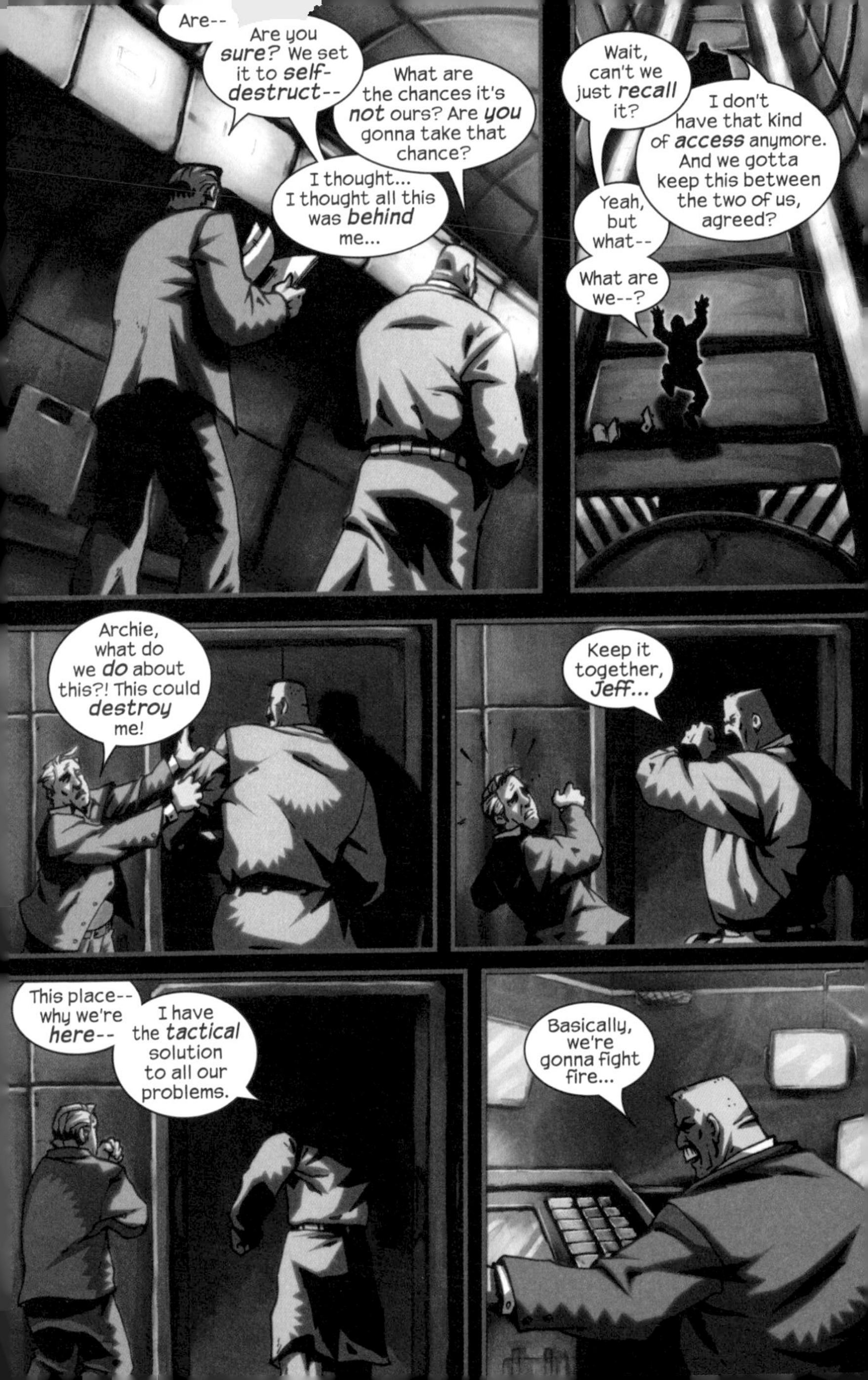

Are--
Are you sure? We set it to self-destruct--
What are the chances it's not ours? Are you gonna take that chance?
I thought... I thought all this was behind me...
Wait, can't we just recall it?
I don't have that kind of access anymore. And we gotta keep this between the two of us, agreed?
Yeah, but what--
What are we--?
Archie, what do we do about this?! This could destroy me!
Keep it together, Jeff...
This place-- why we're here--
I have the tactical solution to all our problems.
Basically, we're gonna fight fire...

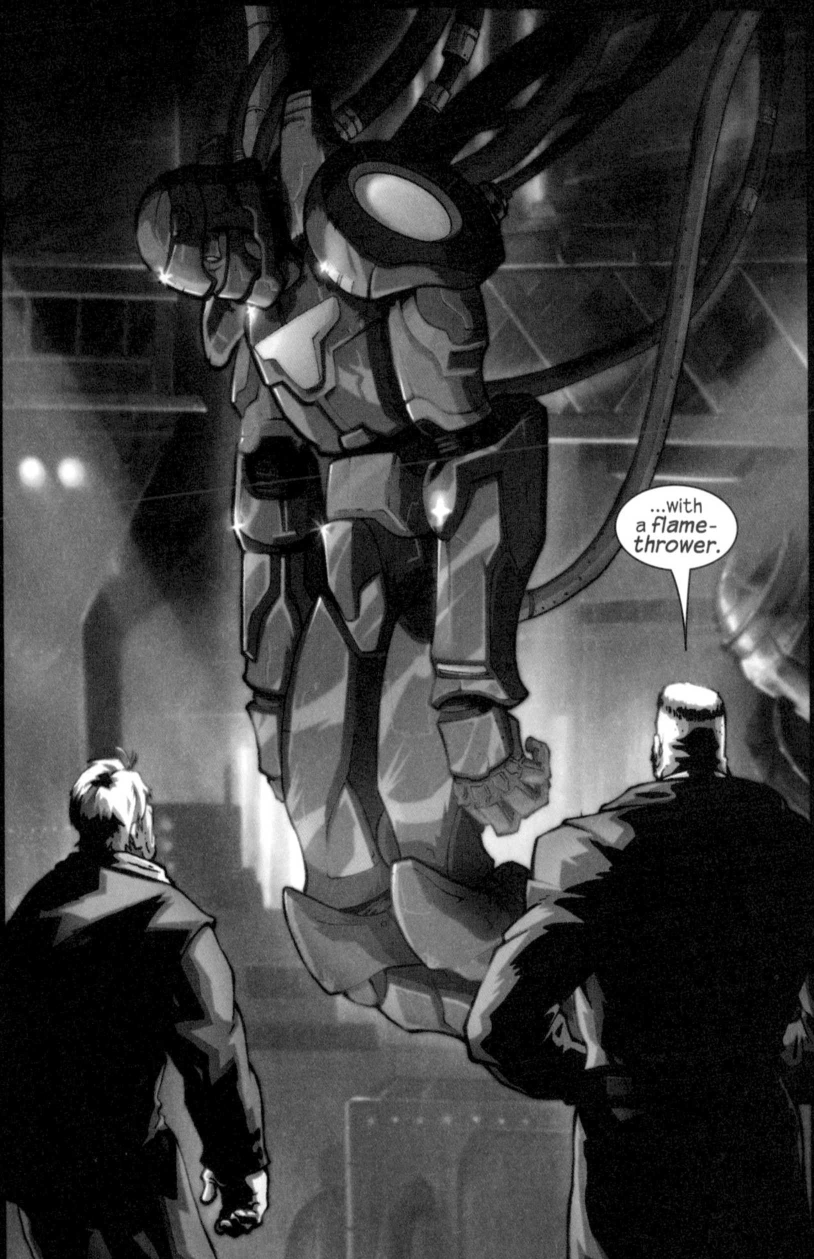
...with a flame-thrower.

PAST IMPERFECT

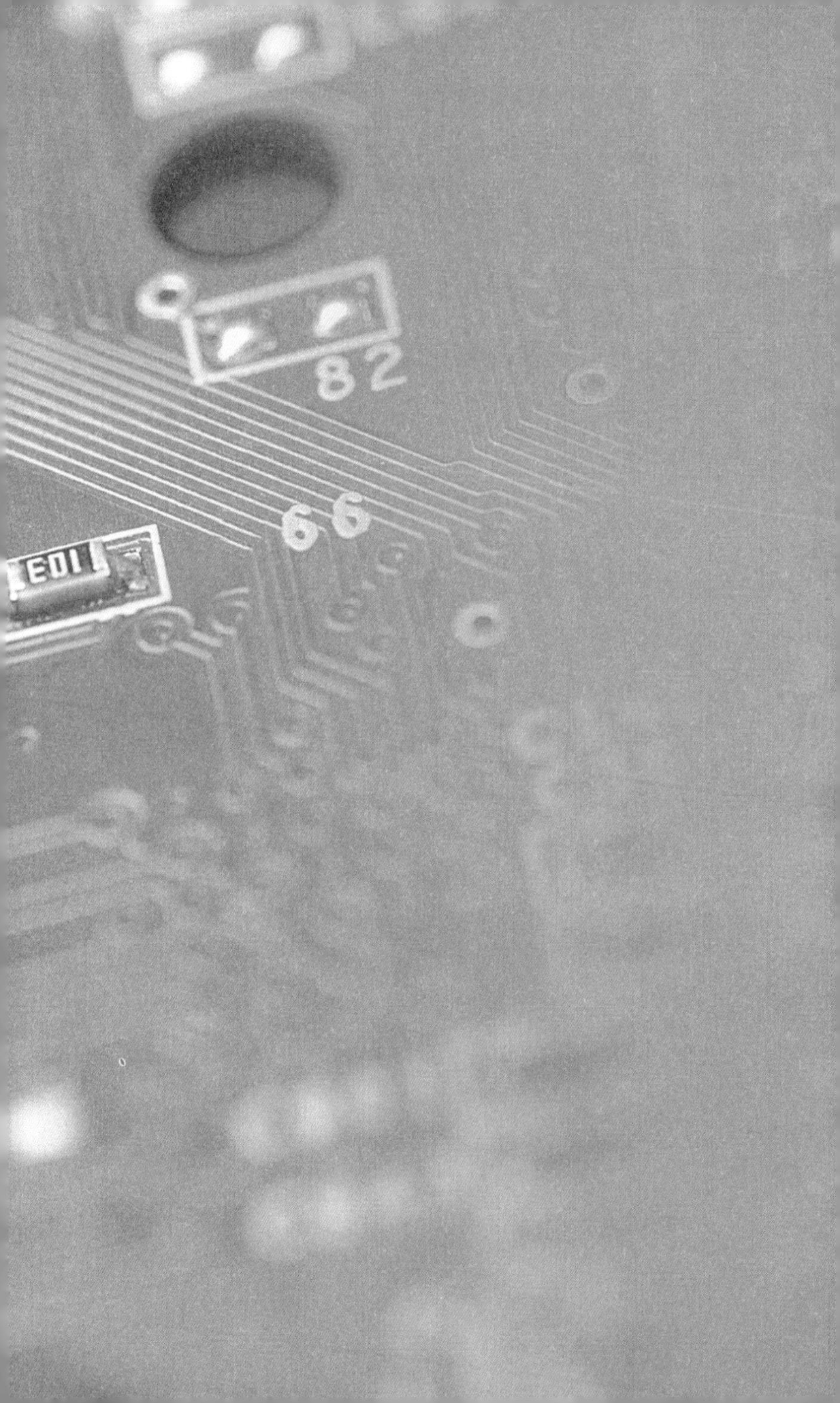

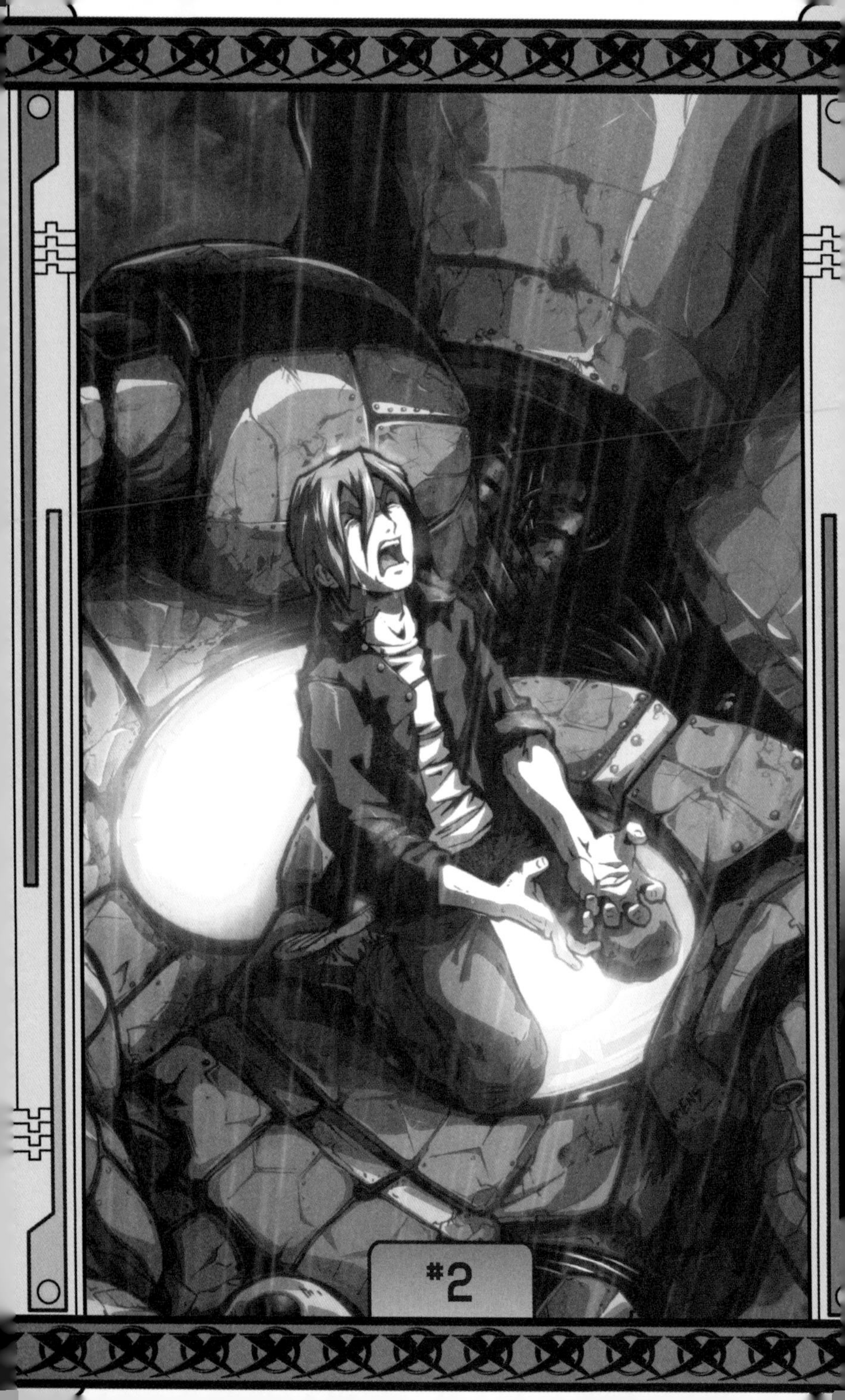
#2

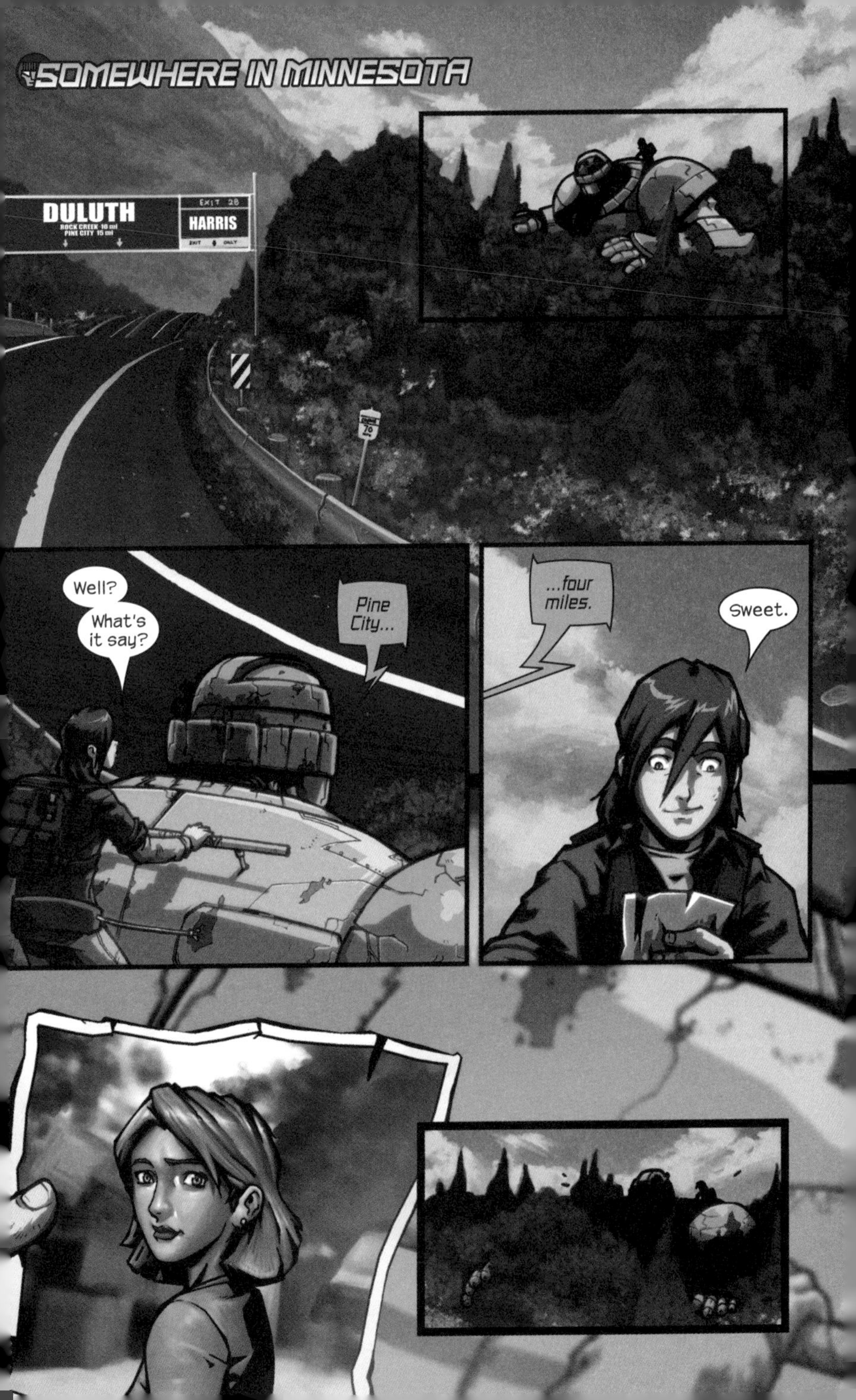
SOMEWHERE IN MINNESOTA
DULUTH
ROCK CREEK 10 mi
PINE CITY 15 mi
EXIT 28
HARRIS
EXIT ONLY
70
Well?
What's it say?
Pine City...
...four miles.
Sweet.

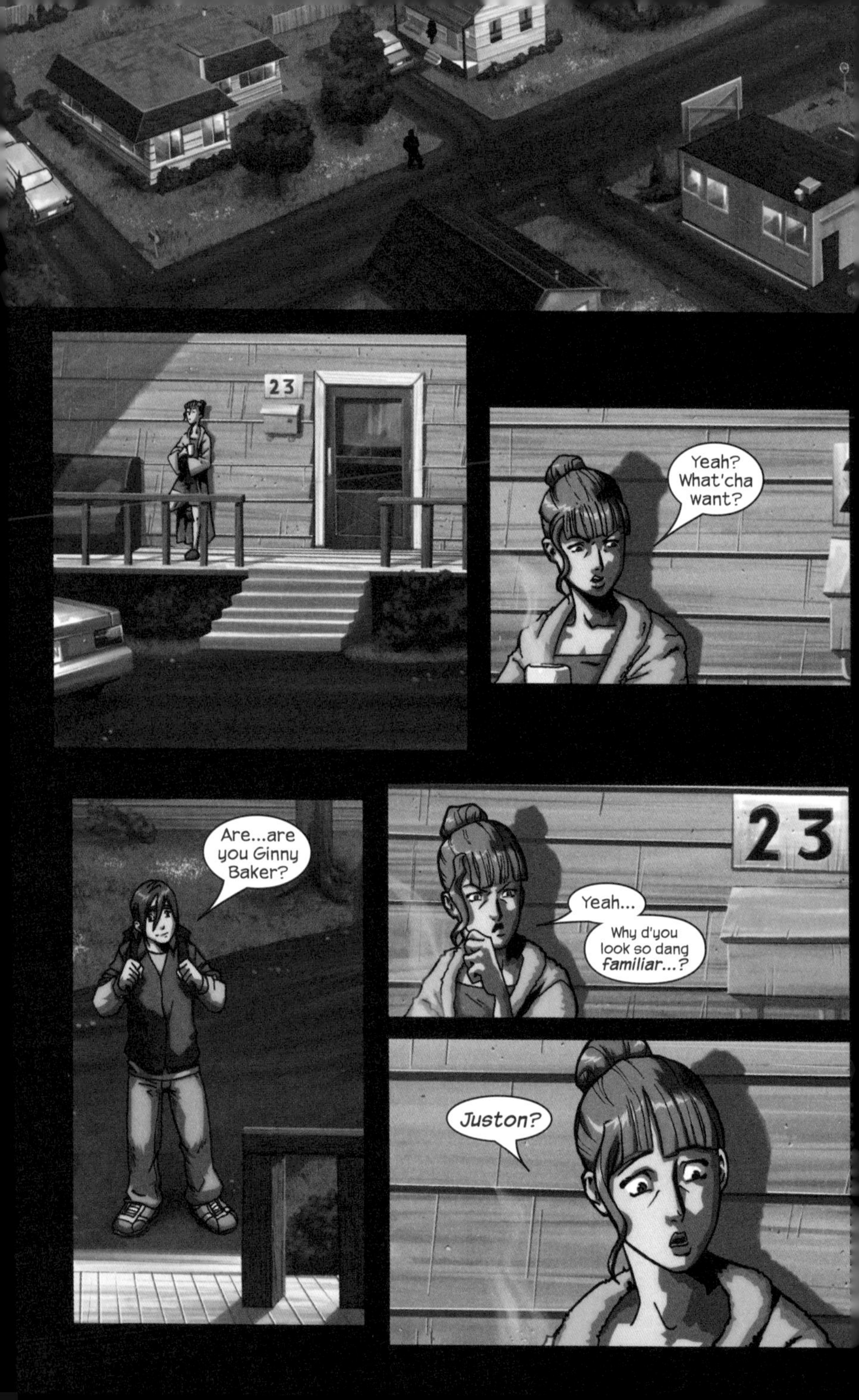
23
Yeah? What'cha want?
Are...are you Ginny Baker?
23
Yeah...
Why d'you look so dang *familiar*...?
Juston?

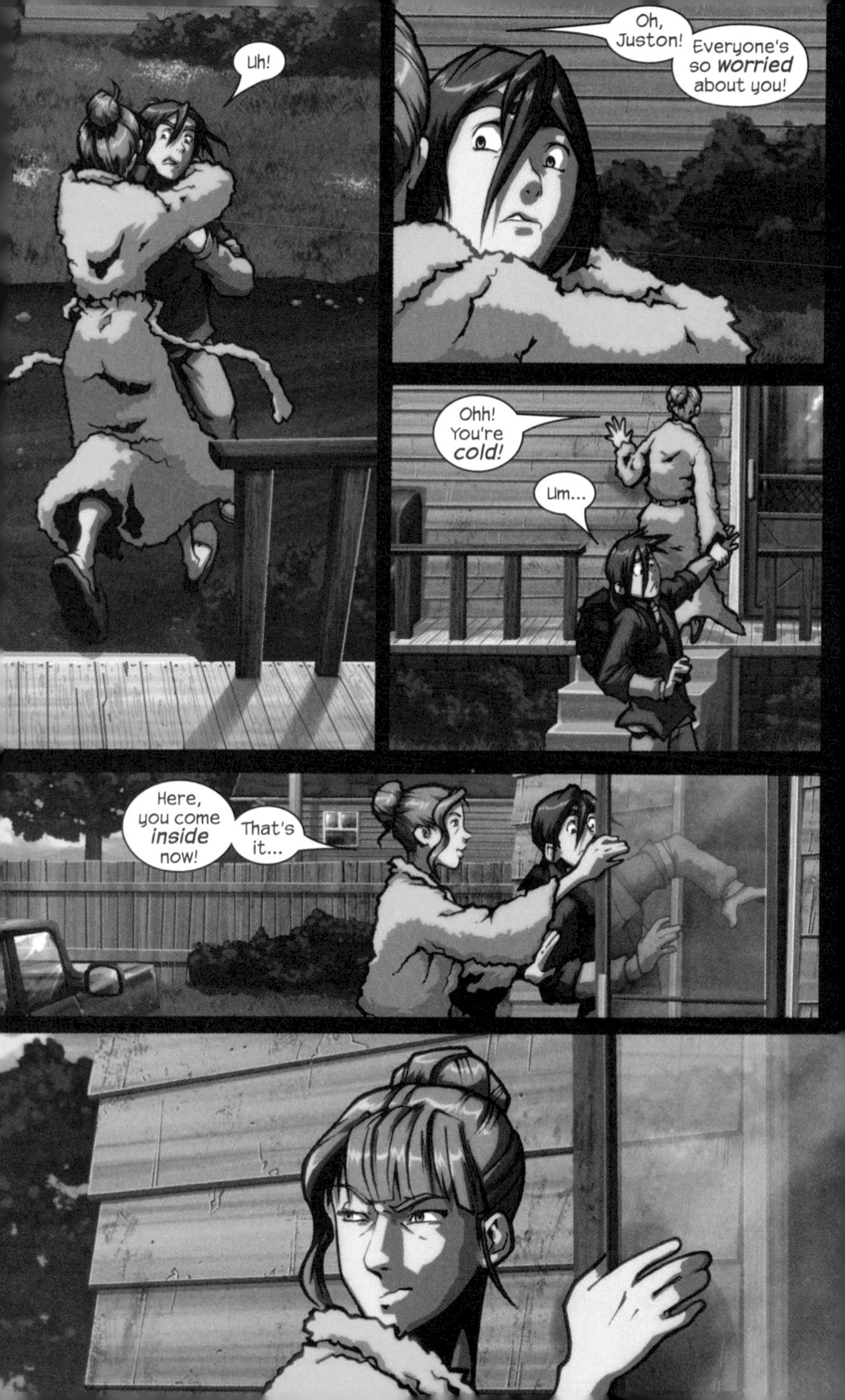
Uh!
Oh, Juston!
Everyone's so *worried* about you!
Ohh! You're *cold!*
Um...
Here, you come *inside* now!
That's it...

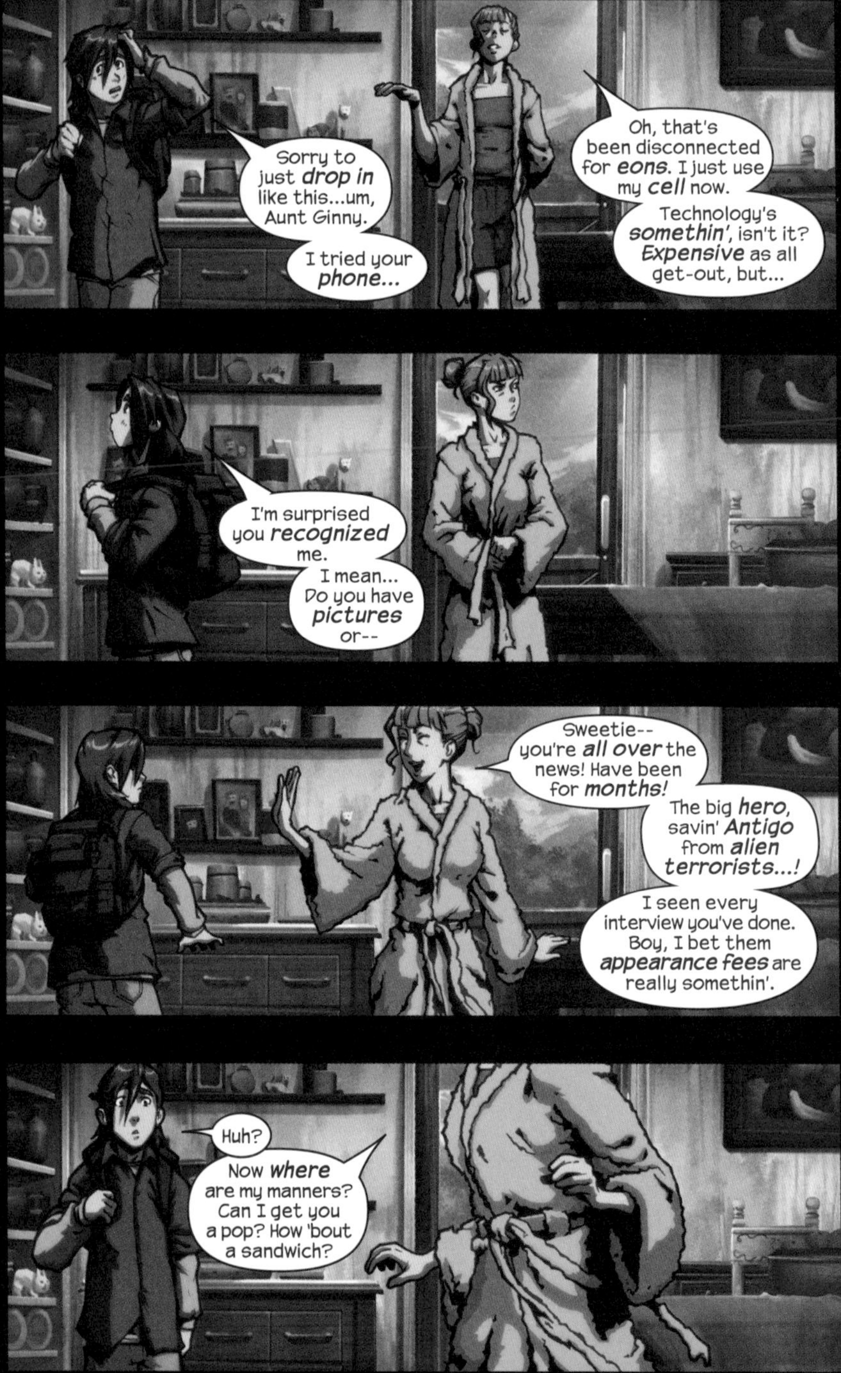
Sorry to just drop in like this...um, Aunt Ginny.
I tried your phone...
Oh, that's been disconnected for eons. I just use my cell now.
Technology's somethin', isn't it? Expensive as all get-out, but...
I'm surprised you recognized me.
I mean... Do you have pictures or--
Sweetie-- you're all over the news! Have been for months!
The big hero, savin' Antigo from alien terrorists...!
I seen every interview you've done. Boy, I bet them appearance fees are really somethin'.
Huh?
Now where are my manners? Can I get you a pop? How 'bout a sandwich?

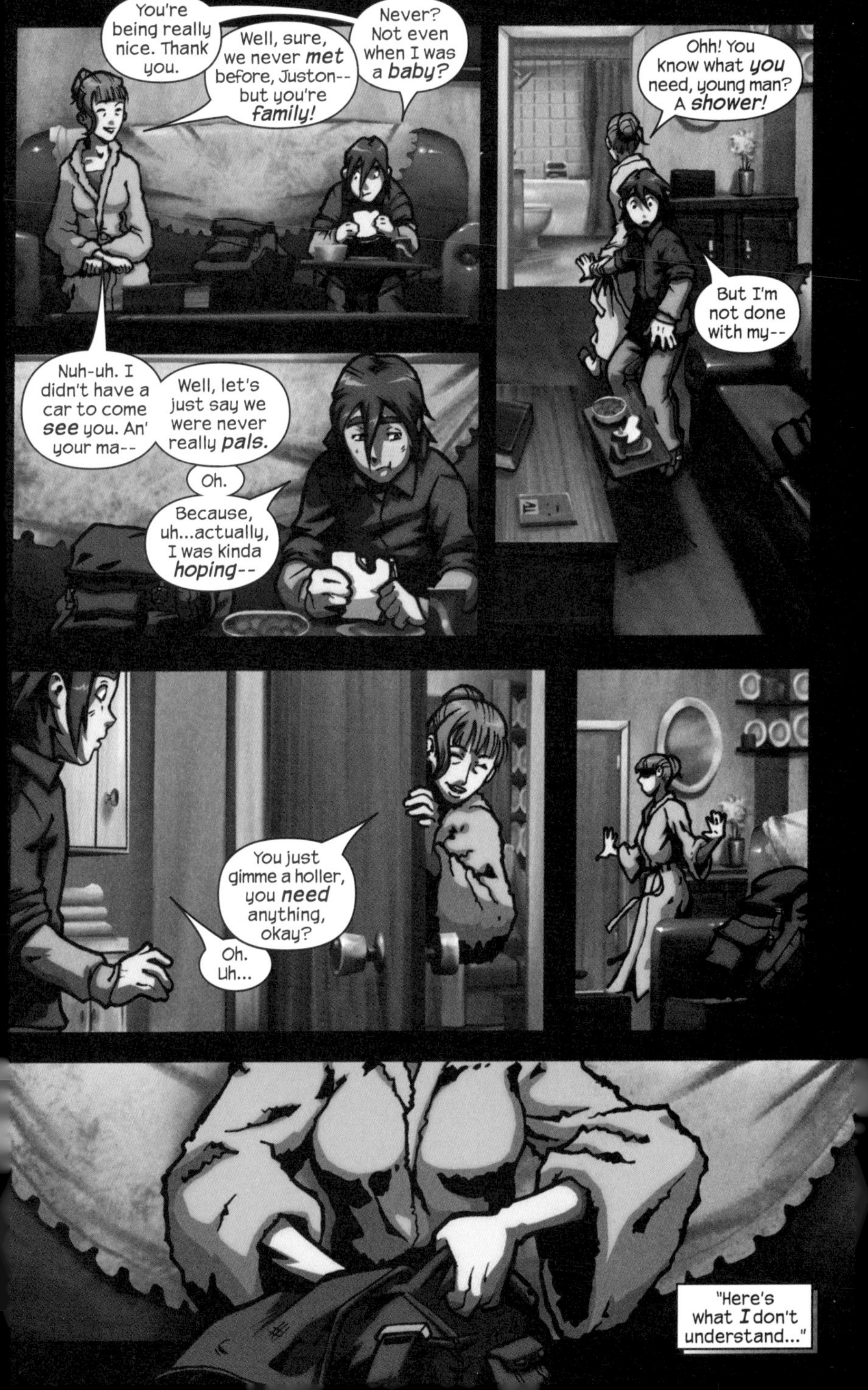
You're being really nice. Thank you.
Well, sure, we never met before, Juston-- but you're family!
Never? Not even when I was a baby?
Nuh-uh. I didn't have a car to come see you. An' your ma--
Well, let's just say we were never really pals.
Oh.
Because, uh...actually, I was kinda hoping--
Ohh! You know what you need, young man? A shower!
But I'm not done with my--
You just gimme a holler, you need anything, okay?
Oh. Uh...
"Here's what I don't understand..."

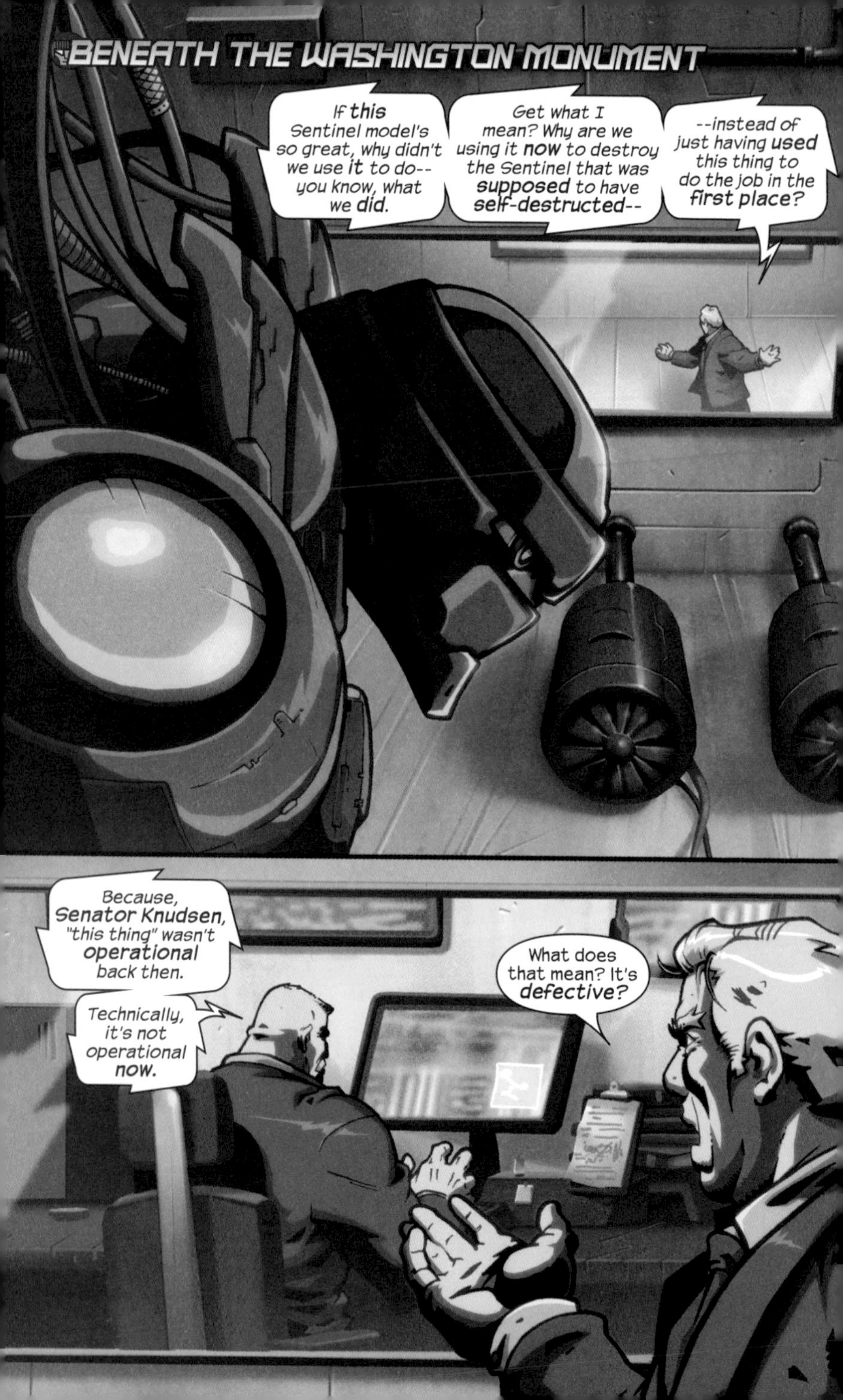
BENEATH THE WASHINGTON MONUMENT
If this Sentinel model's so great, why didn't we use it to do-- you know, what we did.
Get what I mean? Why are we using it now to destroy the Sentinel that was supposed to have self-destructed--
--instead of just having used this thing to do the job in the first place?
Because, Senator Knudsen, "this thing" wasn't operational back then.
Technically, it's not operational now.
What does that mean? It's defective?

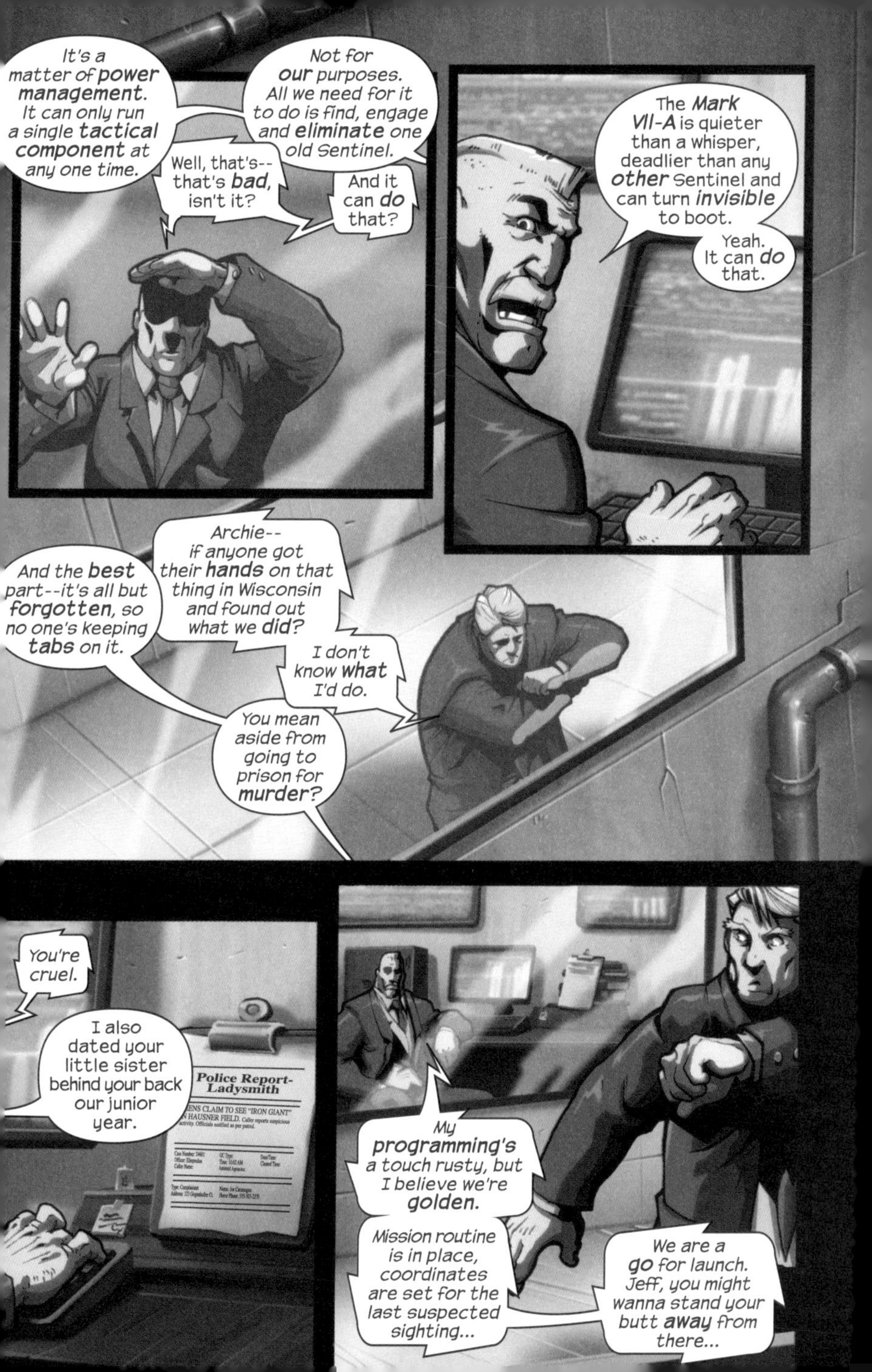
It's a matter of **power management**. It can only run a single **tactical component** at any one time.
Well, that's-- that's **bad**, isn't it?
Not for **our** purposes. All we need for it to do is find, engage and **eliminate** one old Sentinel.
And it can **do** that?
The **Mark VII-A** is quieter than a whisper, deadlier than any **other** Sentinel and can turn **invisible** to boot.
Yeah. It can **do** that.
And the **best** part--it's all but **forgotten**, so no one's keeping **tabs** on it.
Archie-- if anyone got their **hands** on that thing in Wisconsin and found out what we **did**?
I don't know **what** I'd do.
You mean aside from going to prison for **murder**?
You're cruel.
I also dated your little sister behind your back our junior year.
Police Report- Ladysmith
My **programming's** a touch rusty, but I believe we're **golden**.
Mission routine is in place, coordinates are set for the last suspected sighting...
We are a **go** for launch. Jeff, you might wanna stand your butt **away** from there...

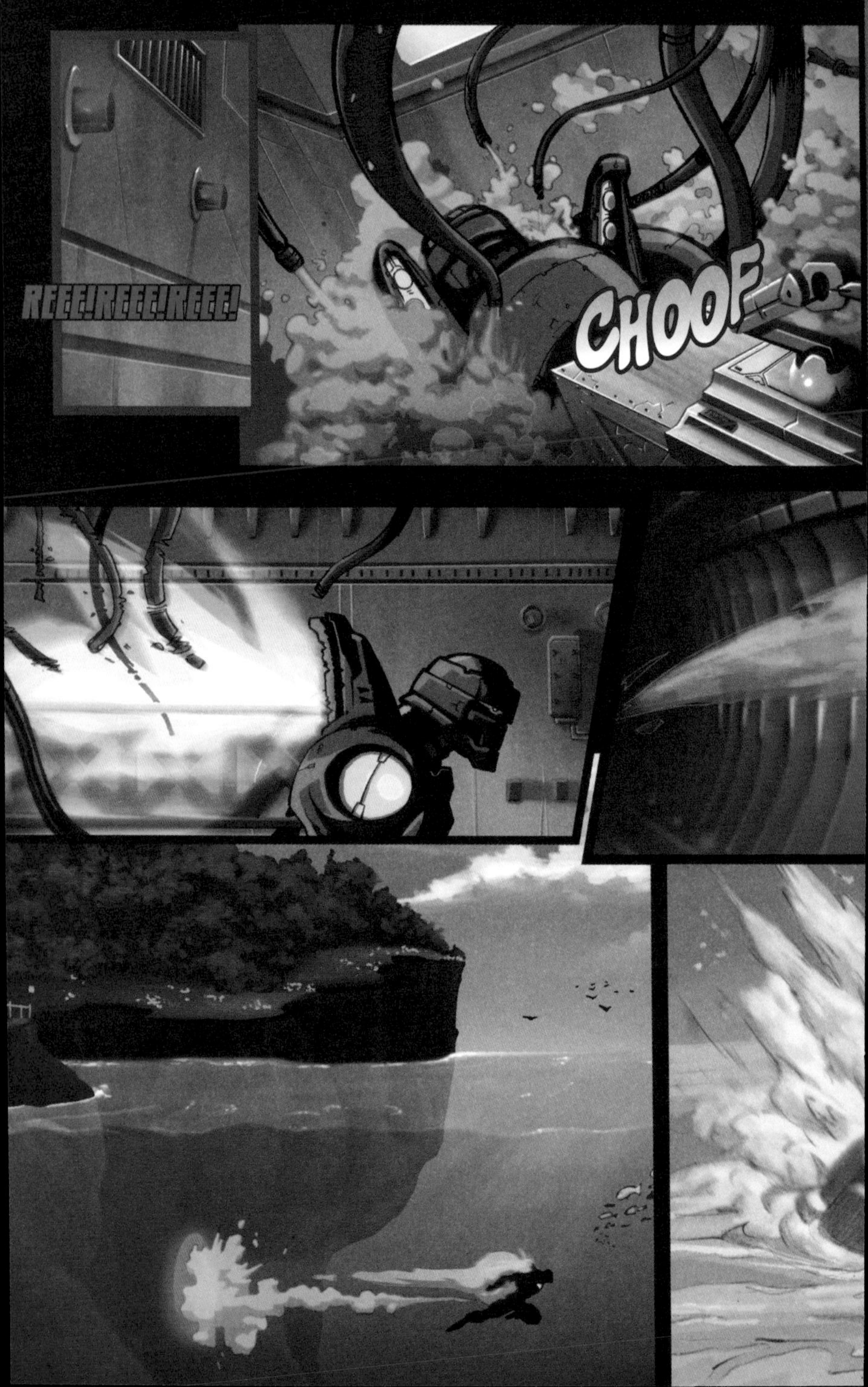
REEE!REEE!REEE!
CHOOF

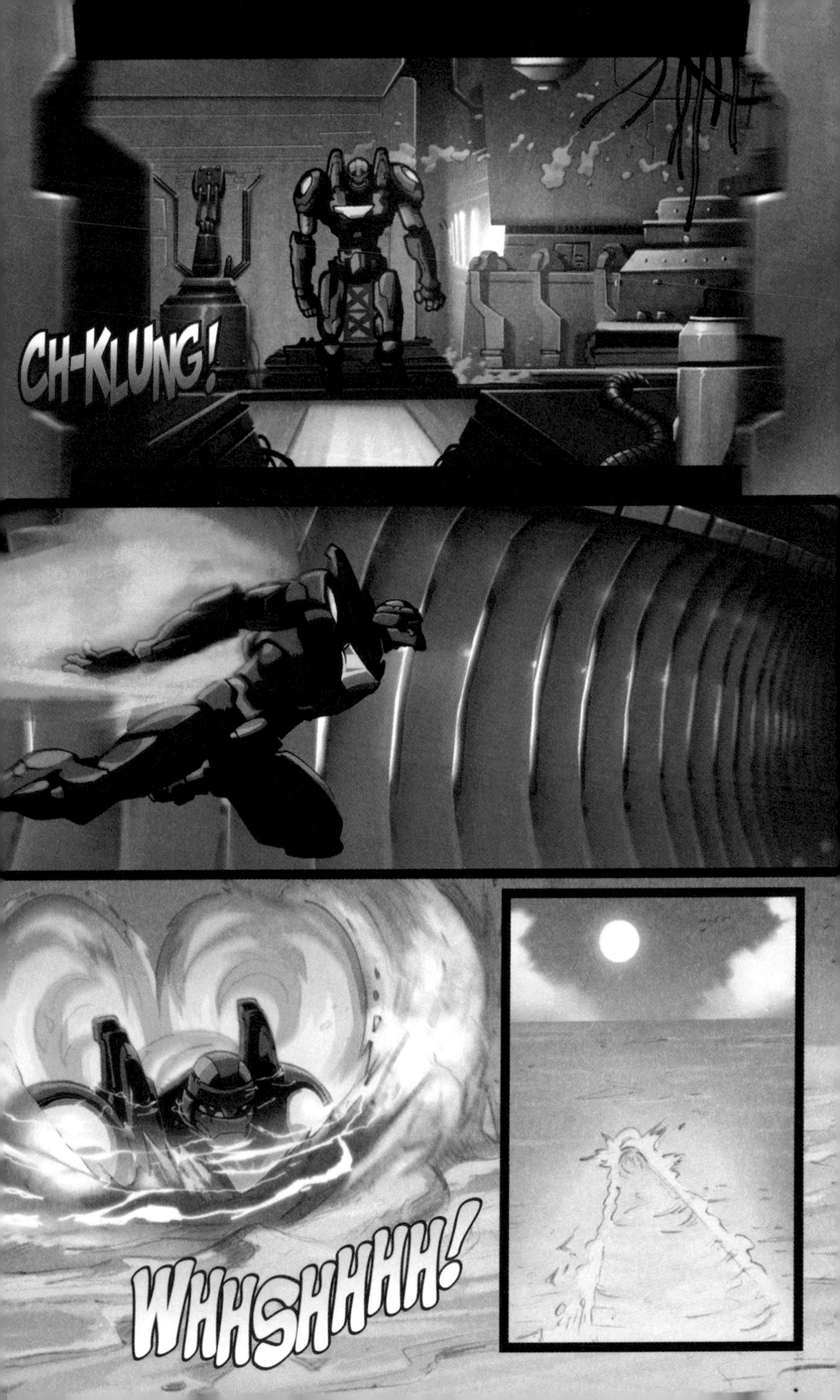
CH-KLUNG!
WHHSHHHH!

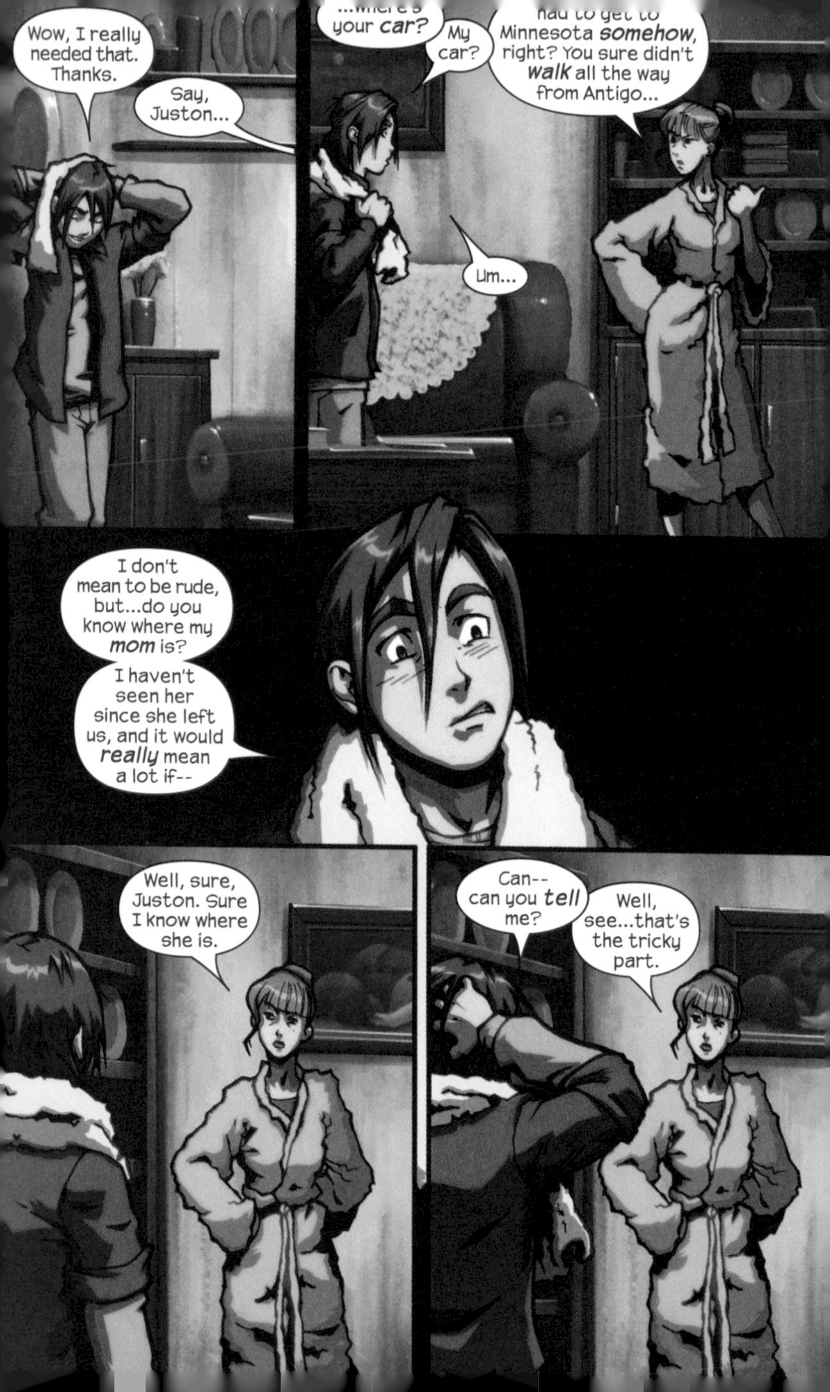

Wow, I really needed that. Thanks.
Say, Juston...
your *car*?
My car?
Minnesota *somehow*, right? You sure didn't *walk* all the way from Antigo...
Um...
I don't mean to be rude, but...do you know where my *mom* is?
I haven't seen her since she left us, and it would *really* mean a lot if--
Well, sure, Juston. Sure I know where she is.
Can-- can you *tell* me?
Well, see...that's the tricky part.

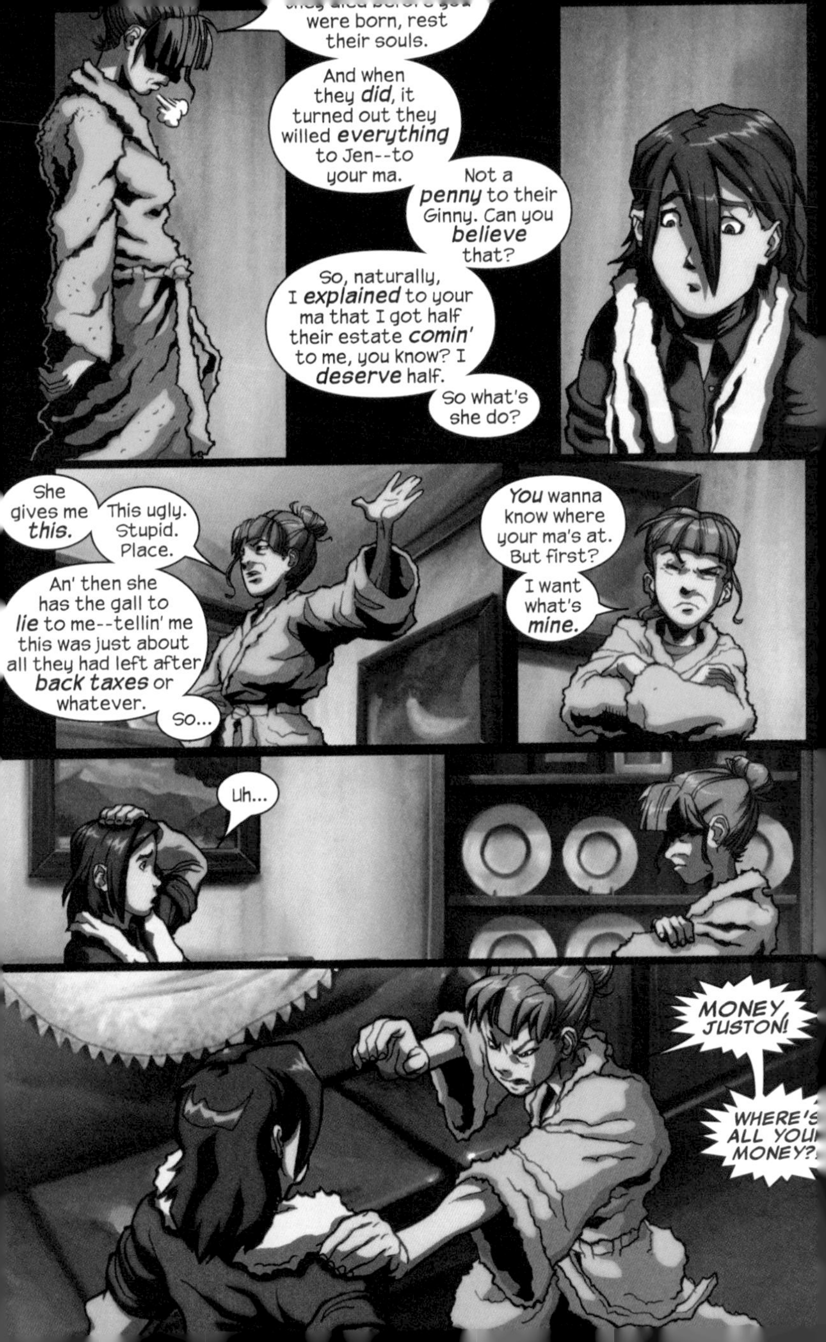

were born, rest their souls.
And when they *did*, it turned out they willed *everything* to Jen--to your ma.
Not a *penny* to their Ginny. Can you *believe* that?
So, naturally, I *explained* to your ma that I got half their estate *comin'* to me, you know? I *deserve* half.
So what's she do?
She gives me *this.*
This ugly. Stupid. Place.
An' then she has the gall to *lie* to me--tellin' me this was just about all they had left after *back taxes* or whatever.
So...
You wanna know where your ma's at. But first?
I want what's *mine.*
Uh...
MONEY JUSTON!
WHERE'S ALL YOU MONEY?!

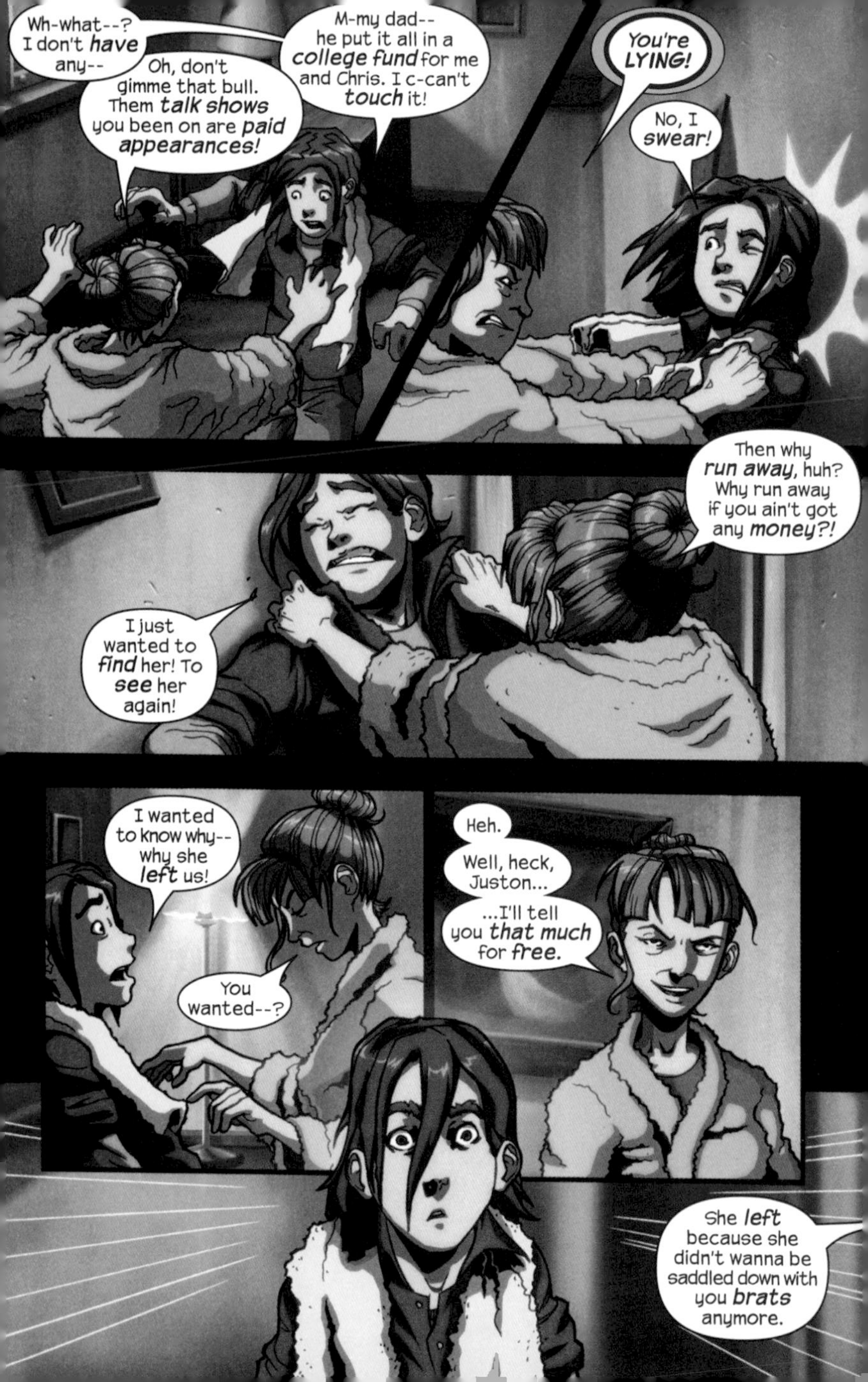
Wh-what--? I don't *have* any--
Oh, don't gimme that bull. Them *talk shows* you been on are *paid appearances!*
M-my dad-- he put it all in a *college fund* for me and Chris. I c-can't *touch* it!
You're LYING!
No, I *swear!*
Then why *run away*, huh? Why run away if you ain't got any *money?!*
I just wanted to *find* her! To *see* her again!
I wanted to know why-- why she *left* us!
You wanted--?
Heh.
Well, heck, Juston...
...I'll tell you *that much* for *free.*
She *left* because she didn't wanna be saddled down with you *brats* anymore.

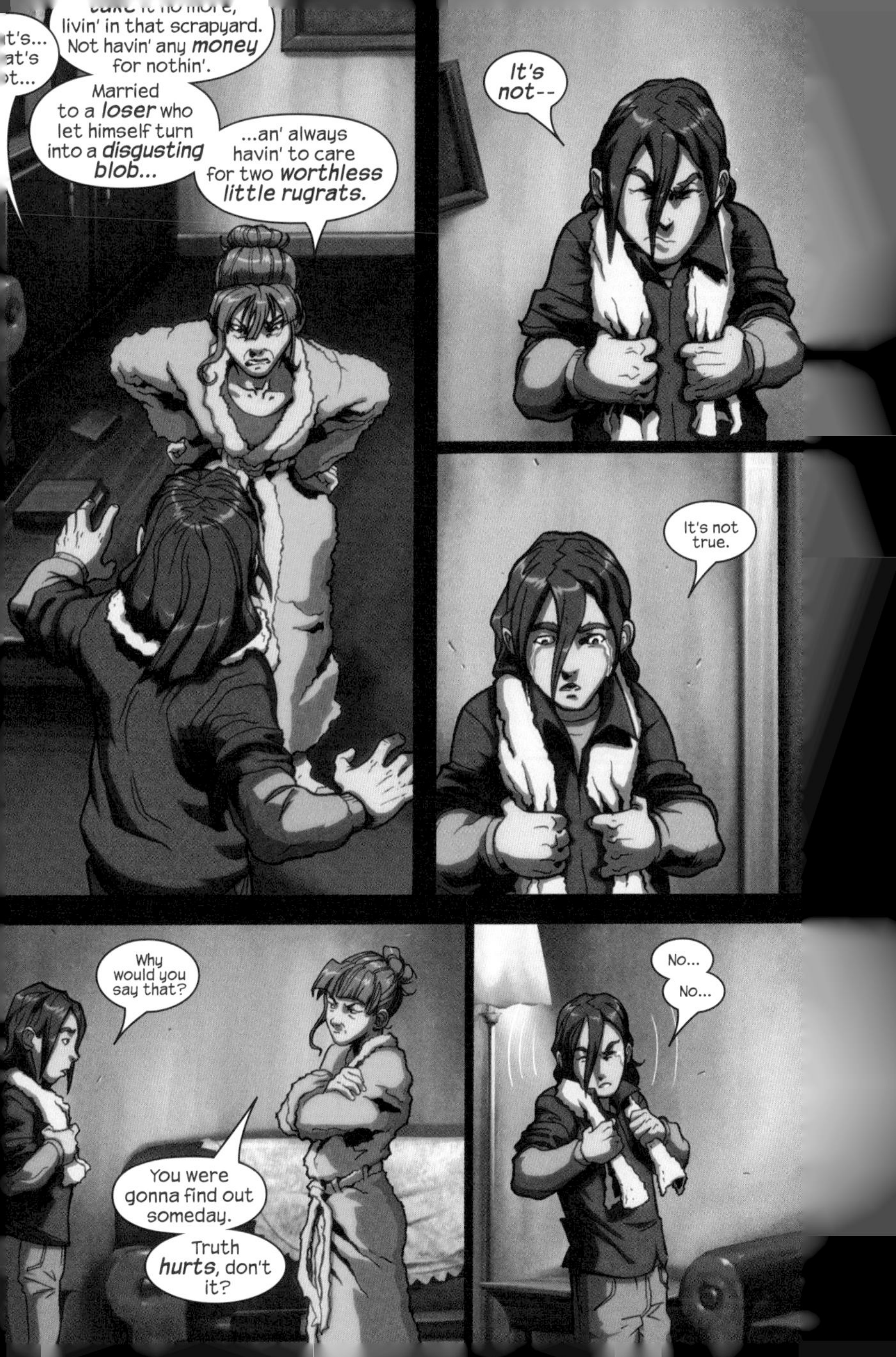
livin' in that scrapyard. Not havin' any money for nothin'.
Married to a loser who let himself turn into a disgusting blob...
...an' always havin' to care for two worthless little rugrats.
It's not--
It's not true.
Why would you say that?
You were gonna find out someday.
Truth hurts, don't it?
No...
No...

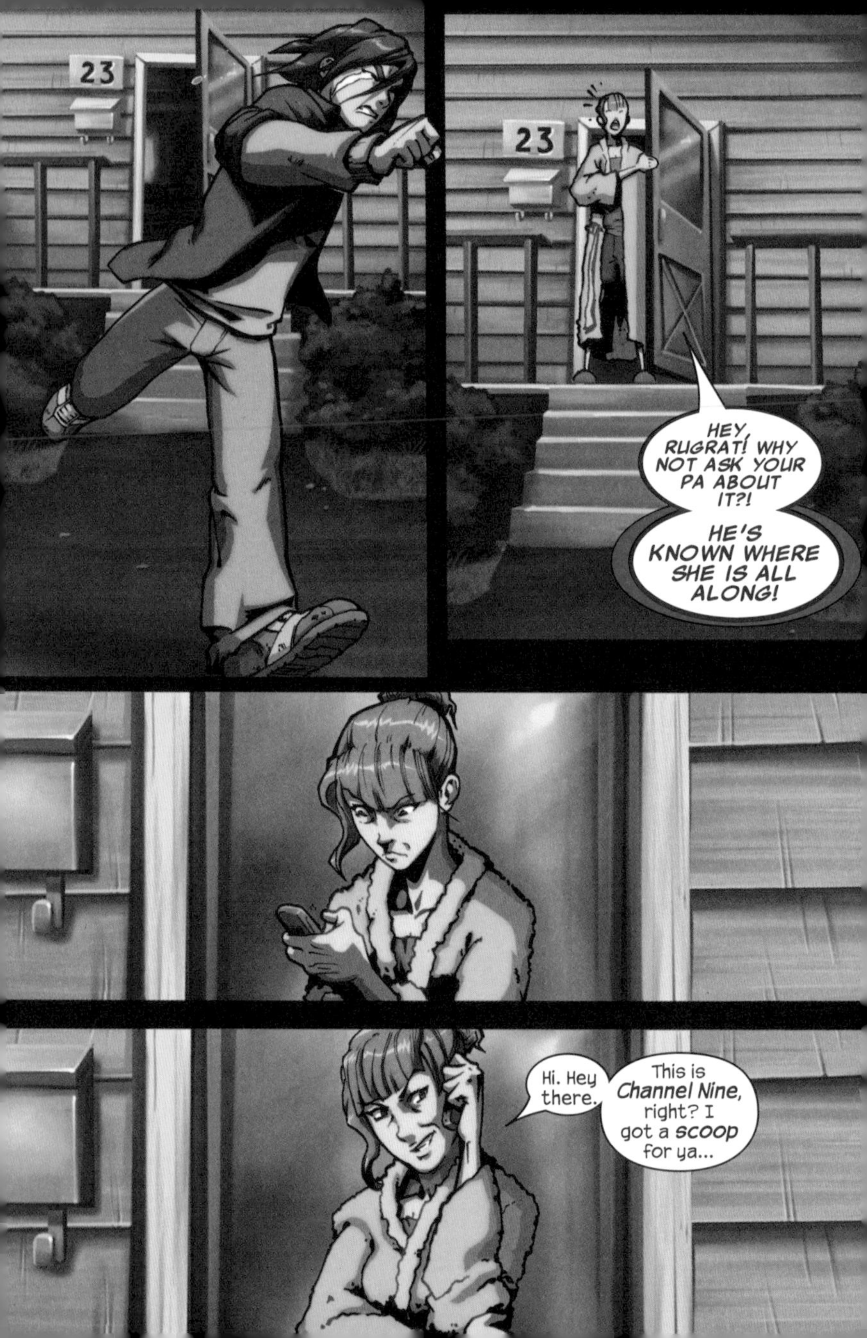
HEY, RUGRAT! WHY NOT ASK YOUR PA ABOUT IT?!
HE'S KNOWN WHERE SHE IS ALL ALONG!
Hi. Hey there.
This is Channel Nine, right? I got a scoop for ya...

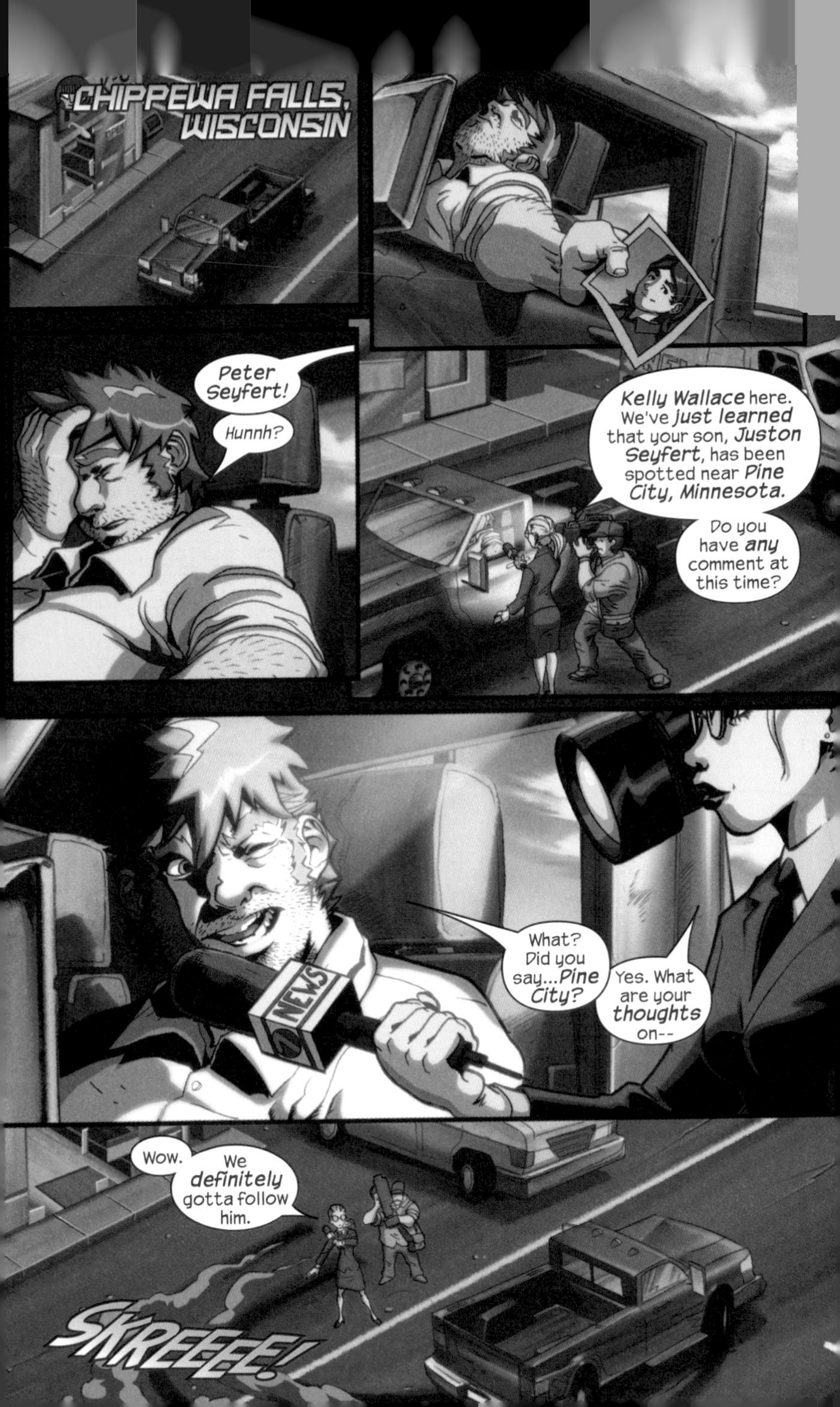
CHIPPEWA FALLS, WISCONSIN
Peter Seyfert!
Hunnh?
Kelly Wallace here. We've just learned that your son, Juston Seyfert, has been spotted near Pine City, Minnesota.
Do you have any comment at this time?
What? Did you say...Pine City?
Yes. What are your thoughts on--
NEWS
Wow.
We definitely gotta follow him.
SKREEEE!

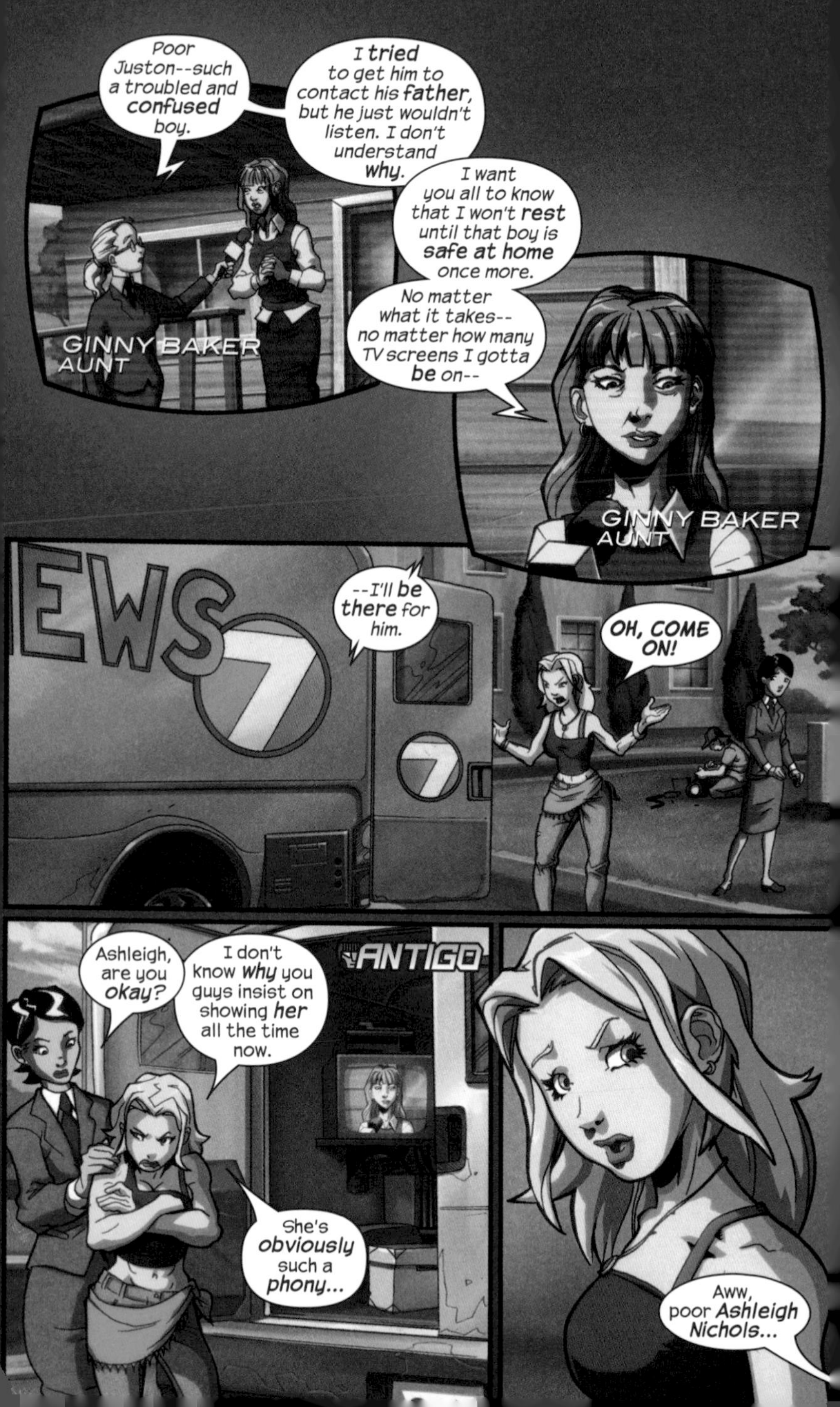
Poor Juston--such a troubled and confused boy.
I tried to get him to contact his father, but he just wouldn't listen. I don't understand why.
I want you all to know that I won't rest until that boy is safe at home once more.
No matter what it takes-- no matter how many TV screens I gotta be on--
GINNY BAKER AUNT
GINNY BAKER AUNT
EWS 7
--I'll be there for him.
OH, COME ON!
Ashleigh, are you okay?
I don't know why you guys insist on showing her all the time now.
ANTIGO
She's obviously such a phony...
Aww, poor Ashleigh Nichols...

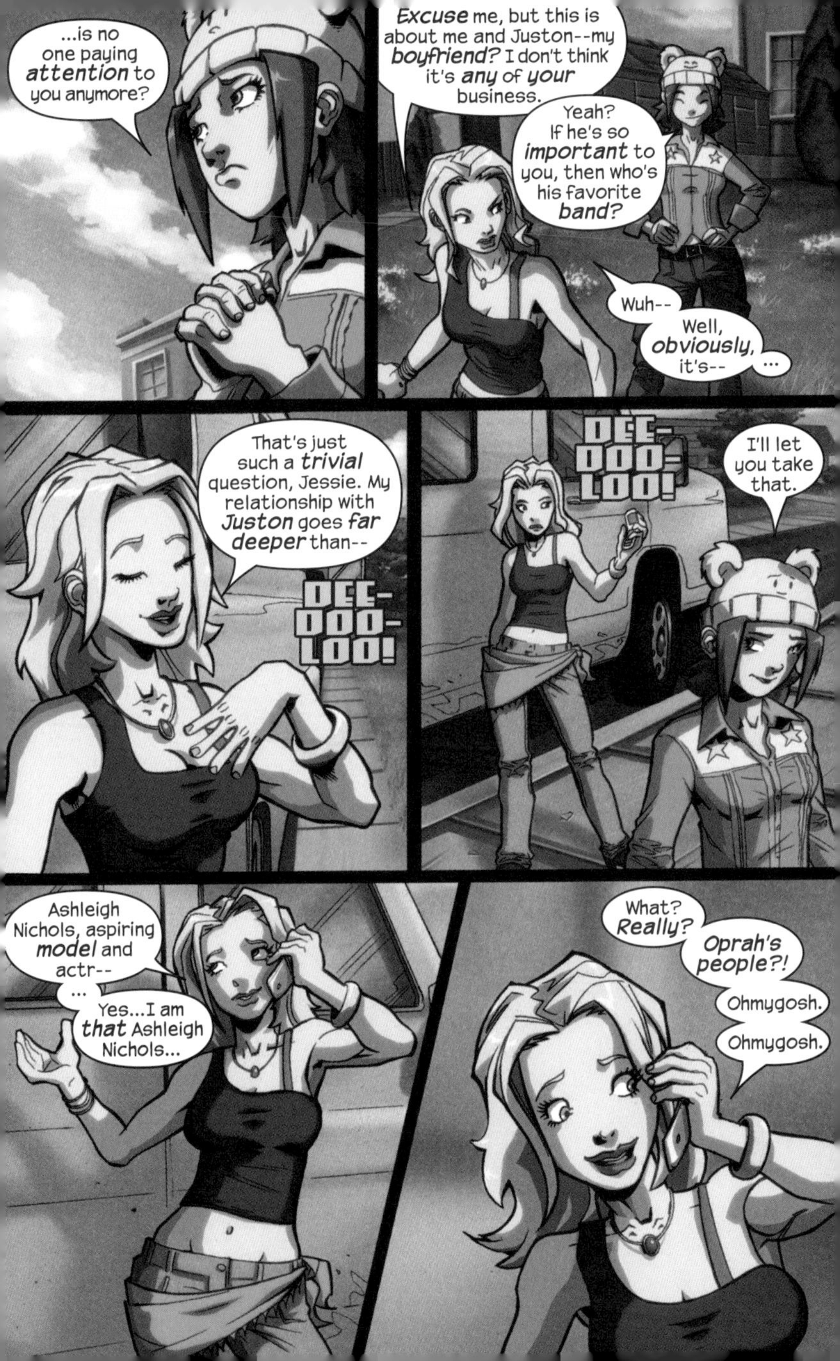
...is no one paying attention to you anymore?
Excuse me, but this is about me and Juston--my boyfriend? I don't think it's any of your business.
Yeah? If he's so important to you, then who's his favorite band?
Wuh--
Well, obviously, it's--
...
That's just such a trivial question, Jessie. My relationship with Juston goes far deeper than--
DEE-DOO-LOO!
DEE-DOO-LOO!
I'll let you take that.
Ashleigh Nichols, aspiring model and actr--
...
Yes...I am that Ashleigh Nichols...
What? Really?
Oprah's people?!
Ohmygosh.
Ohmygosh.

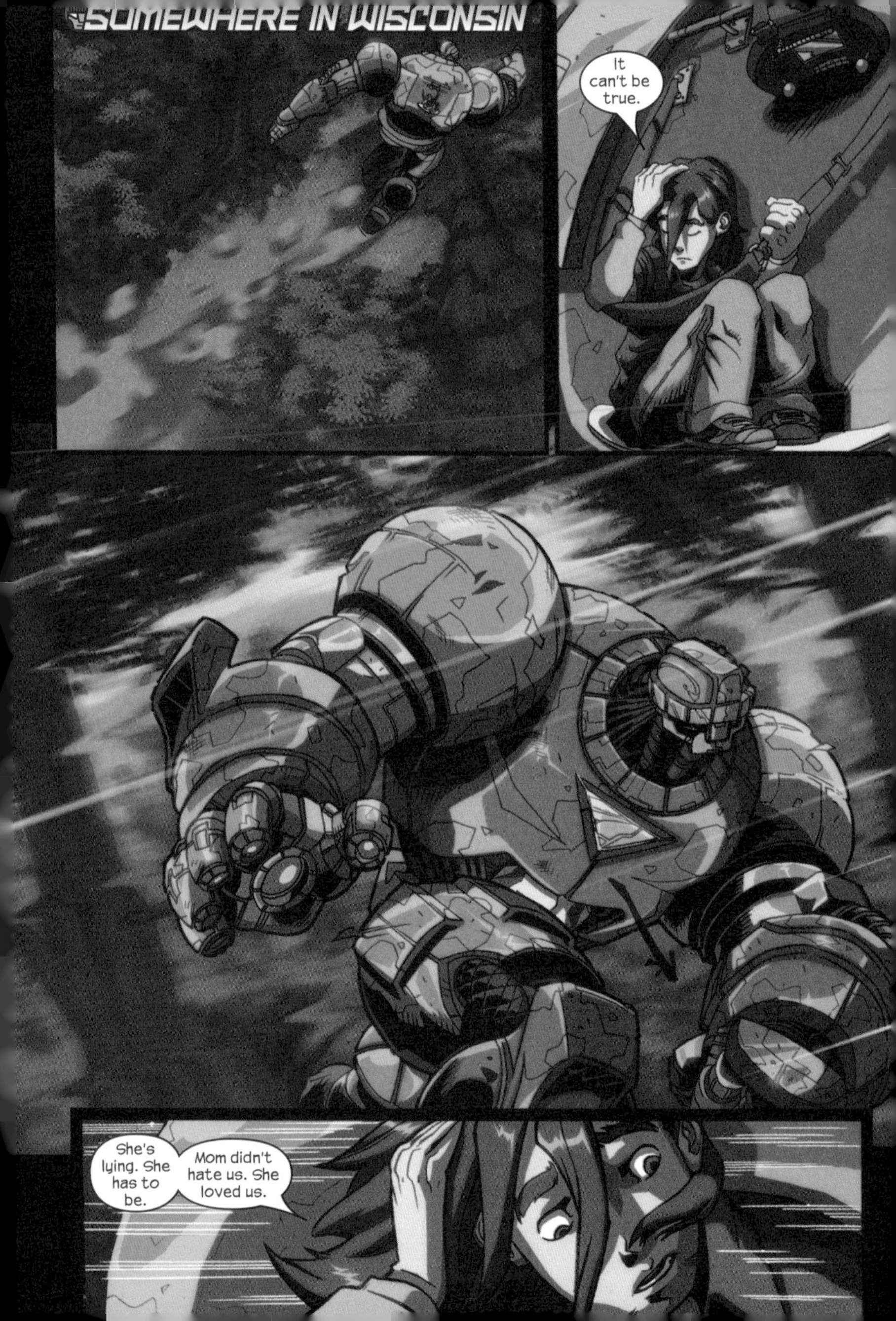

SOMEWHERE IN WISCONSIN
It can't be true.
She's lying. She has to be.
Mom didn't hate us. She loved us.

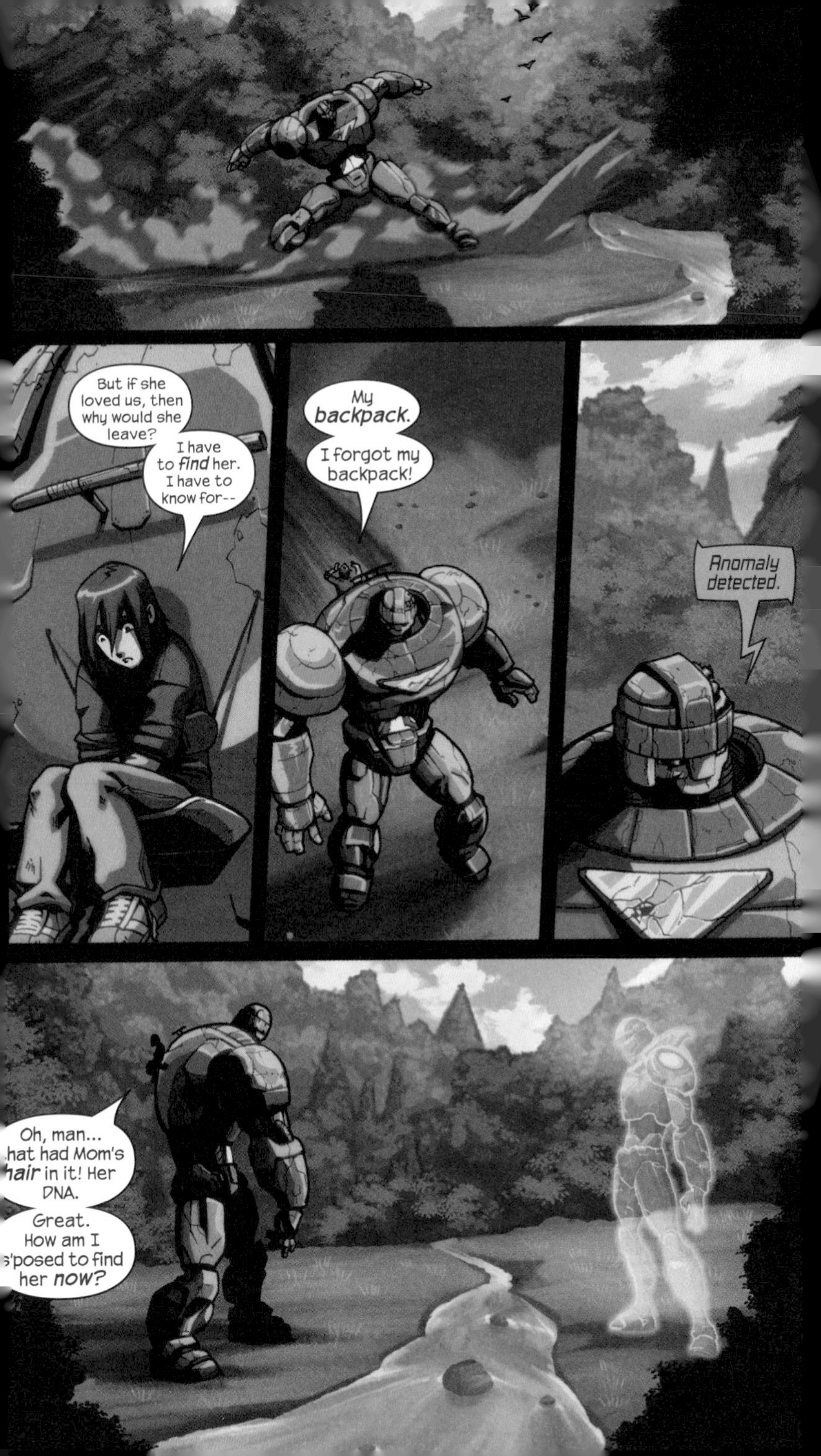

But if she loved us, then why would she leave?
I have to *find* her. I have to know for--
My *backpack.*
I forgot my backpack!
Anomaly detected.
Oh, man... hat had Mom's *hair* in it! Her DNA.
Great. How am I s'posed to find her *now?*

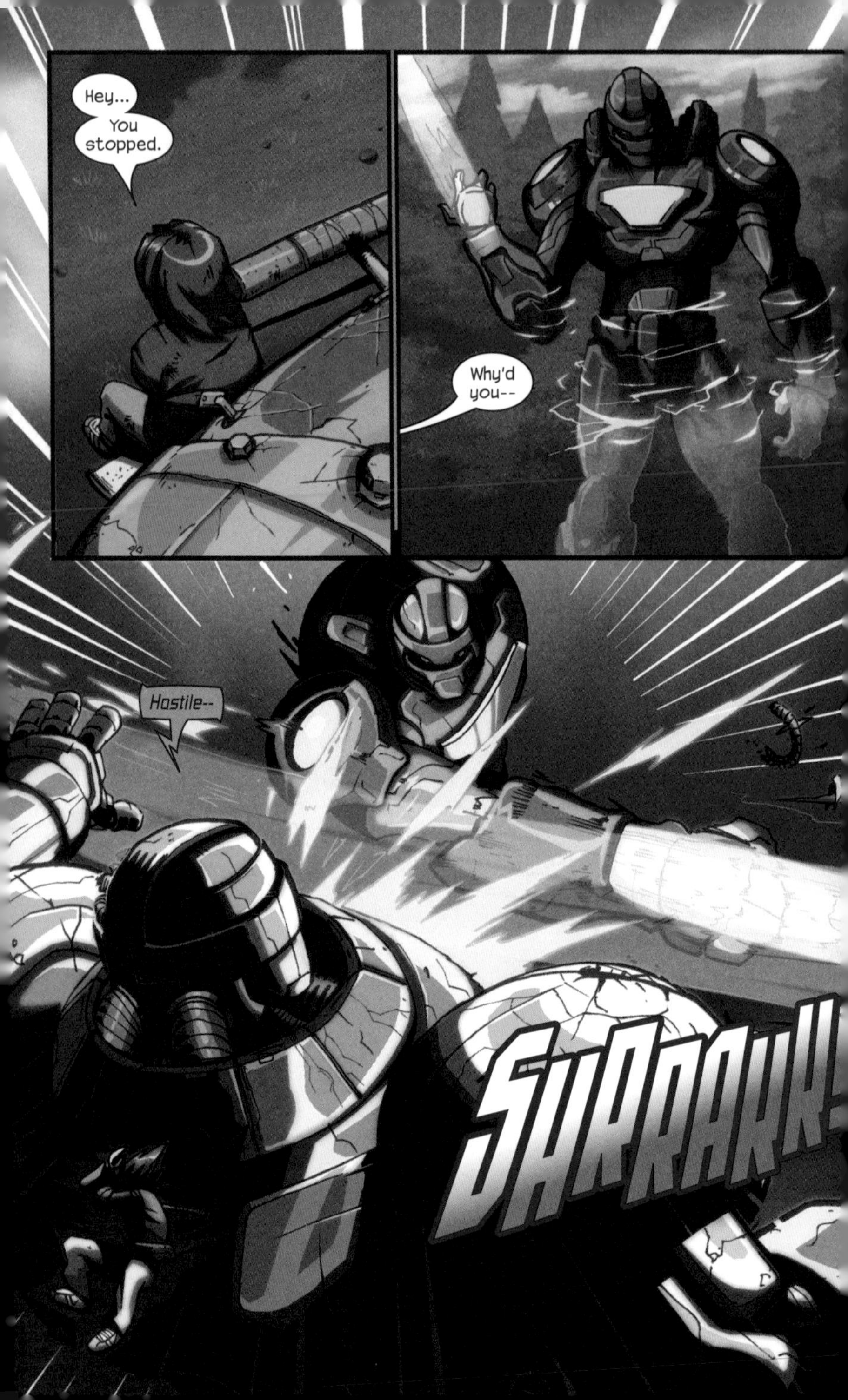
Hey...
You stopped.
Why'd you--
Hostile--
SHRRAKK!

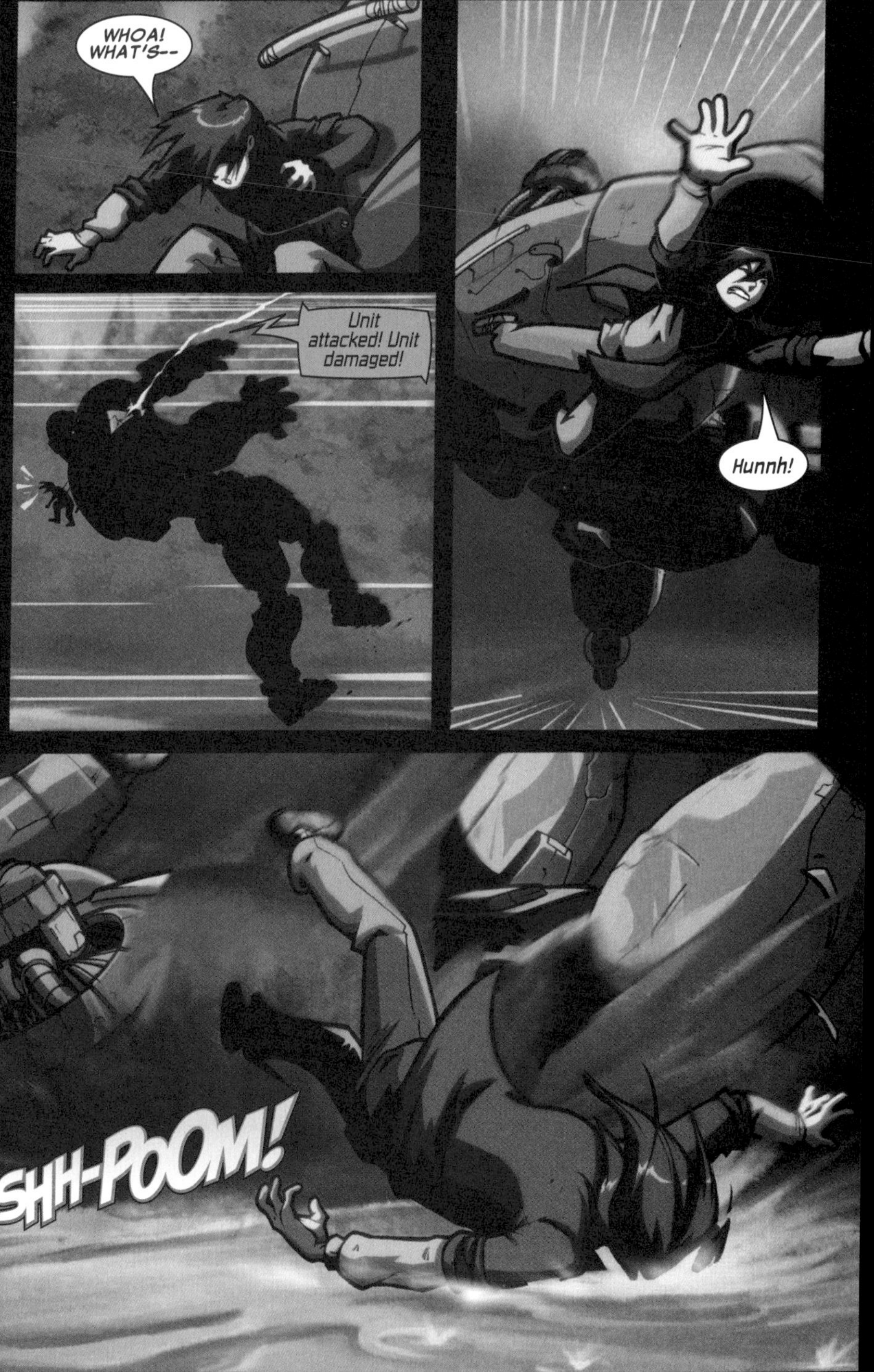
WHOA! WHAT'S--
Unit attacked! Unit damaged!
Hunnh!
SHH-POOM!

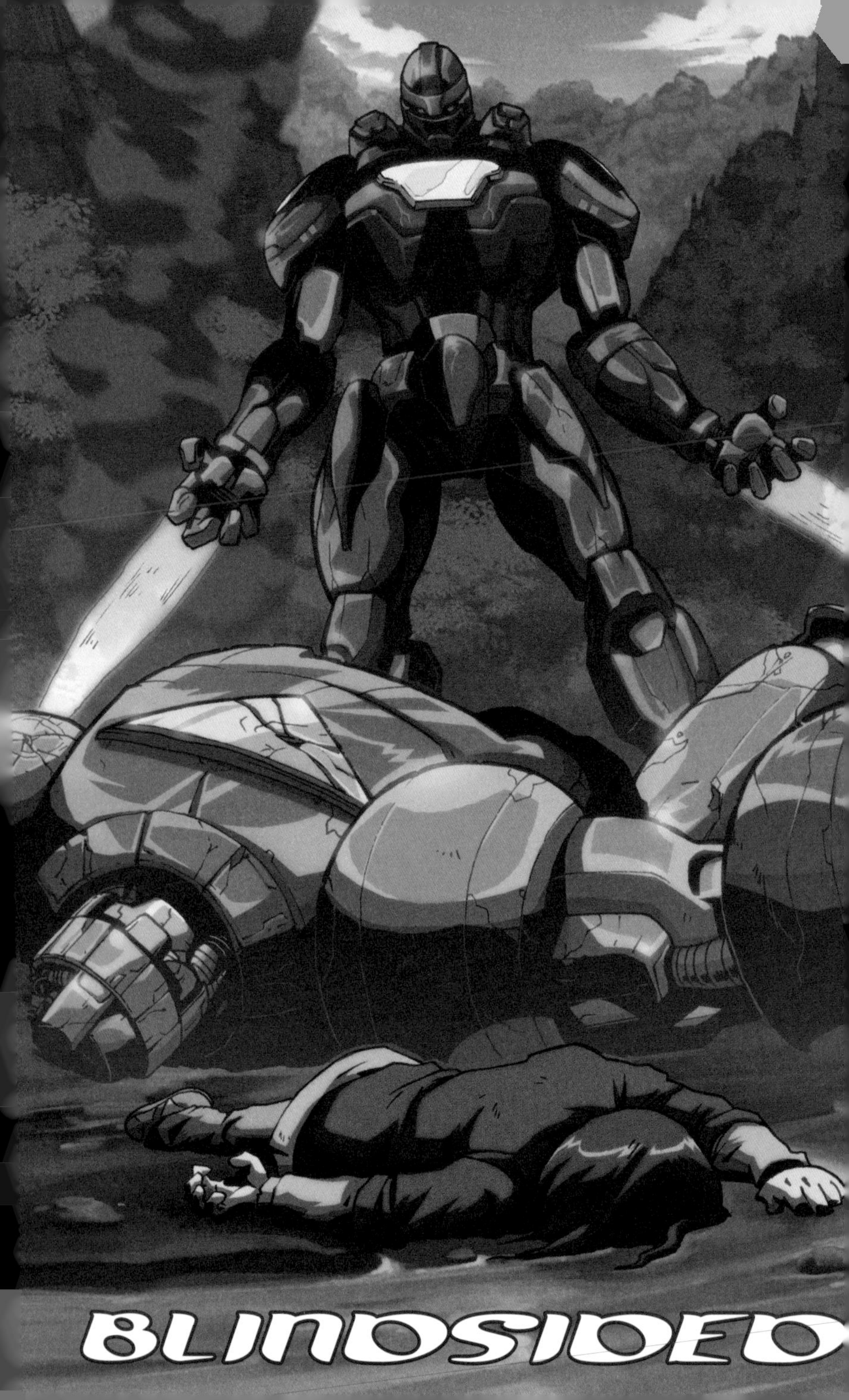
BLINDSIDED

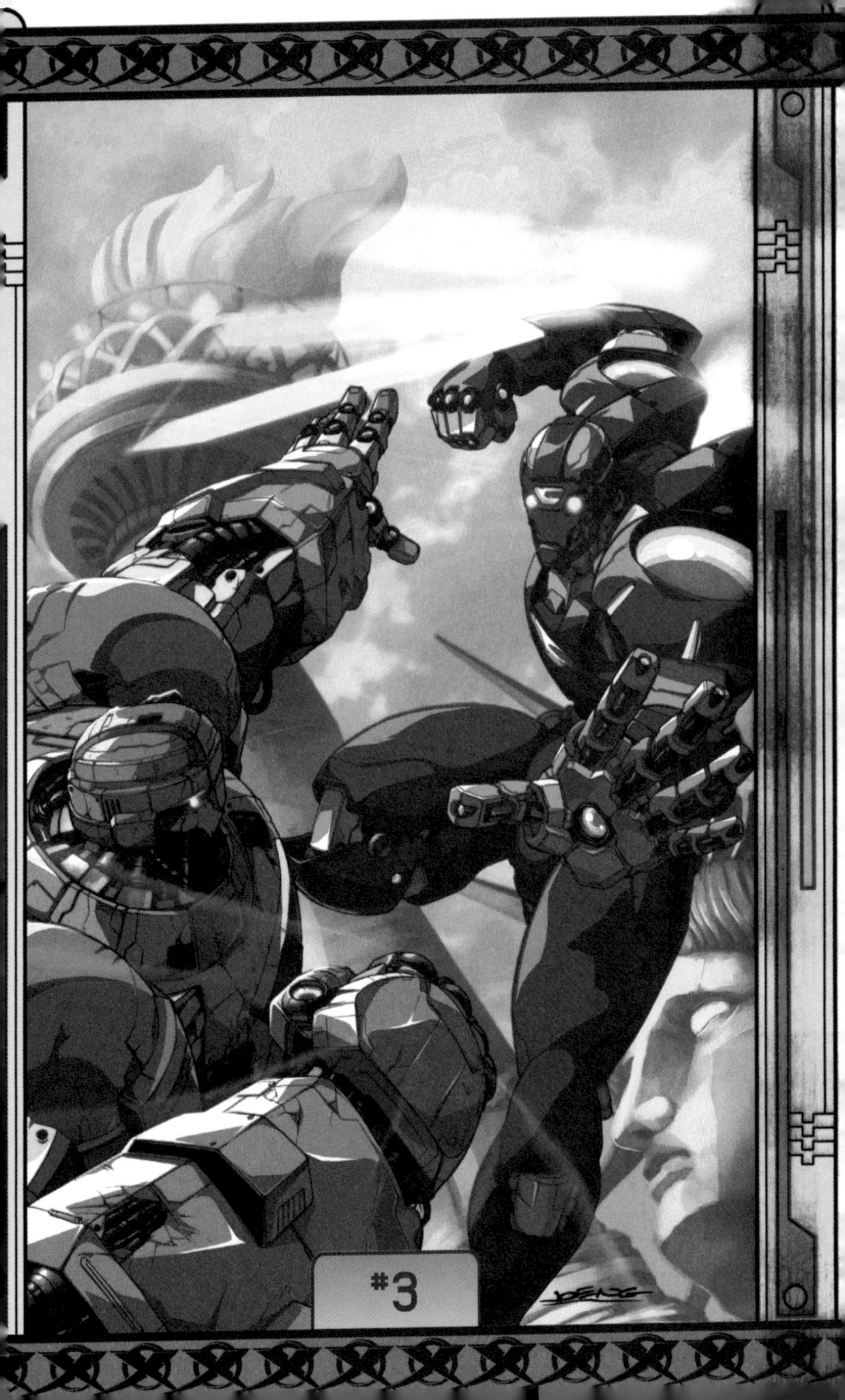
#3

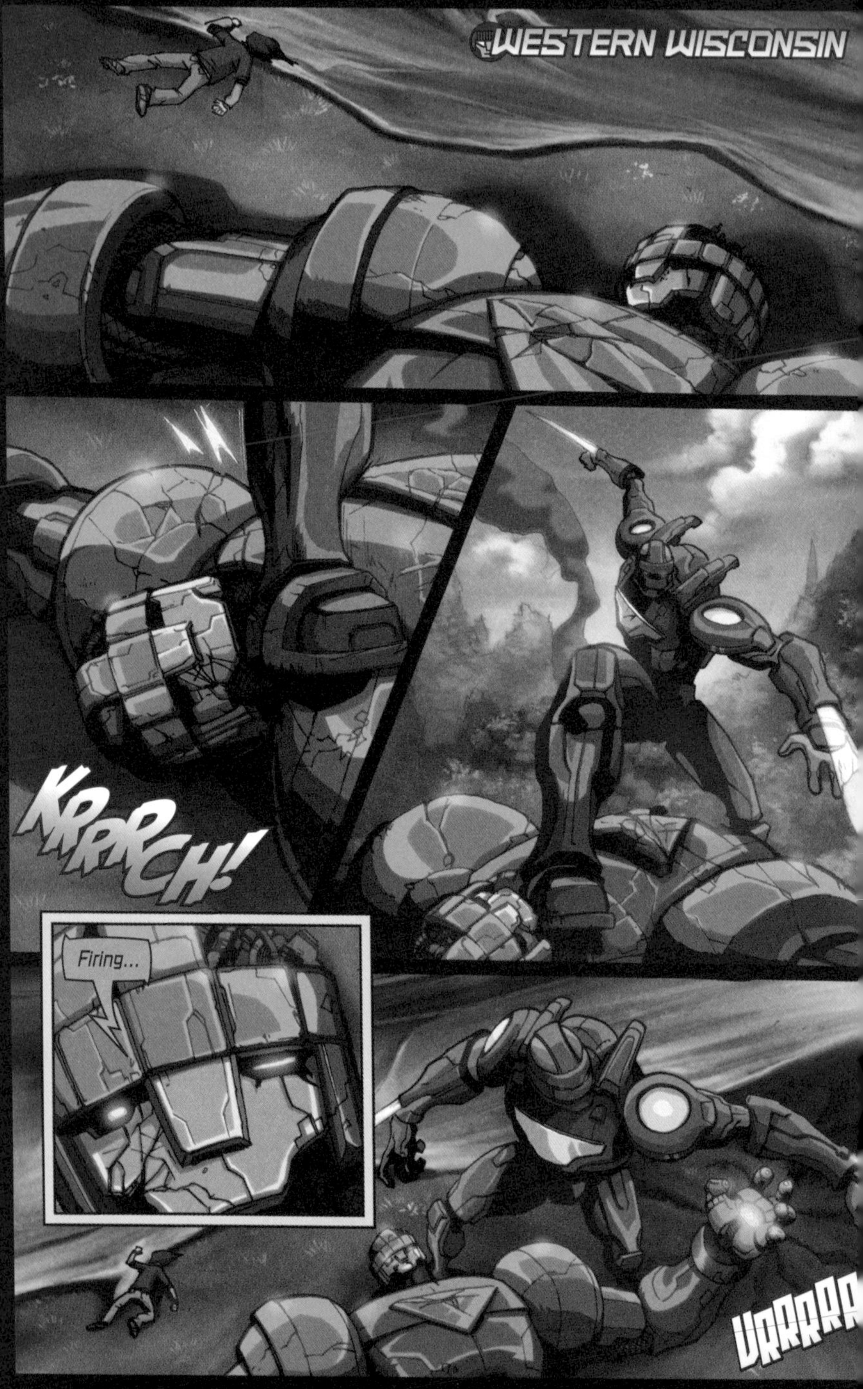
WESTERN WISCONSIN
KRRRCH!
Firing...
VRRRRA

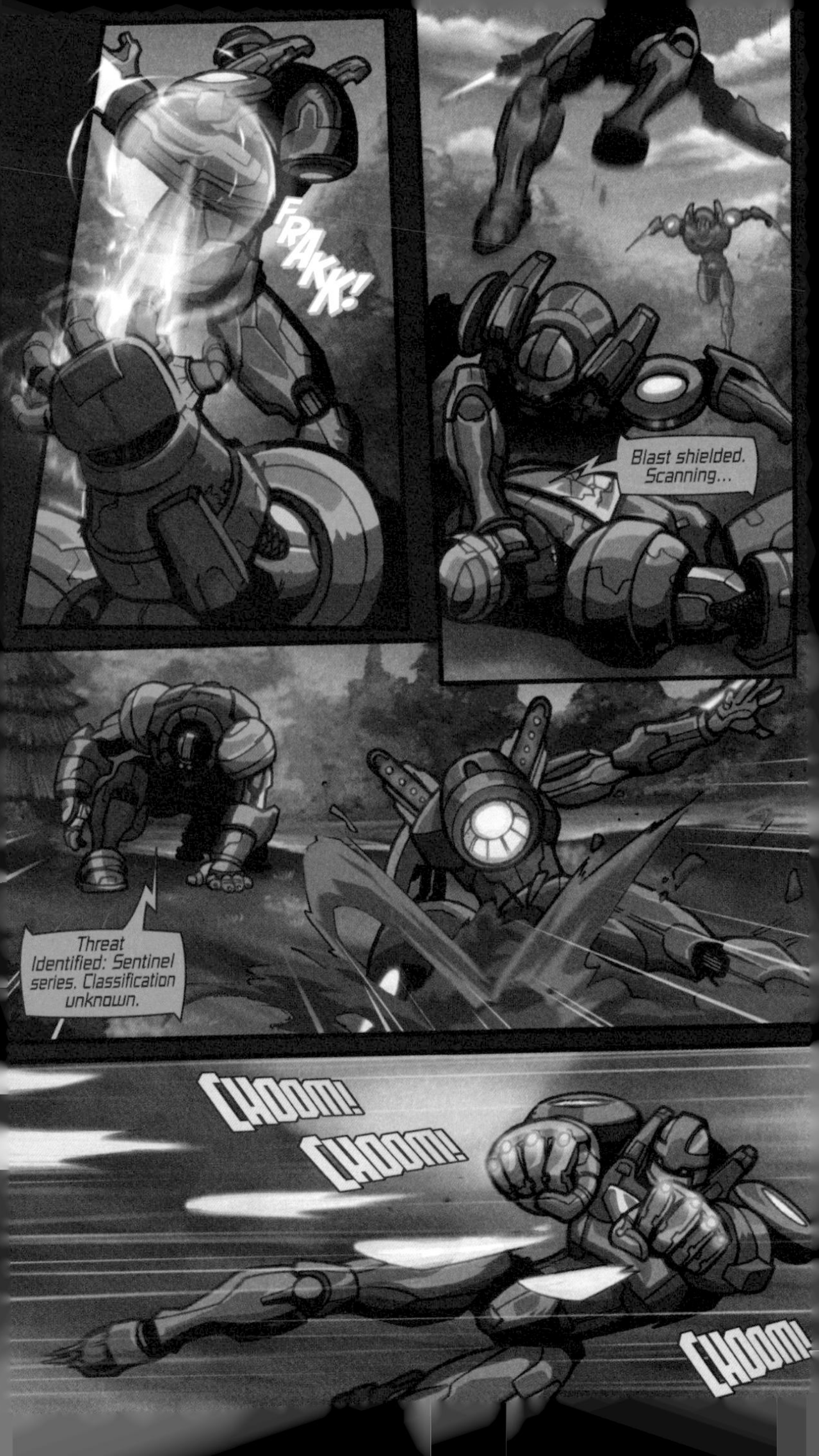

FRAKK!
Blast shielded. Scanning...
Threat Identified: Sentinel series. Classification unknown.
CHOOM!
CHOOM!
CHOOM!

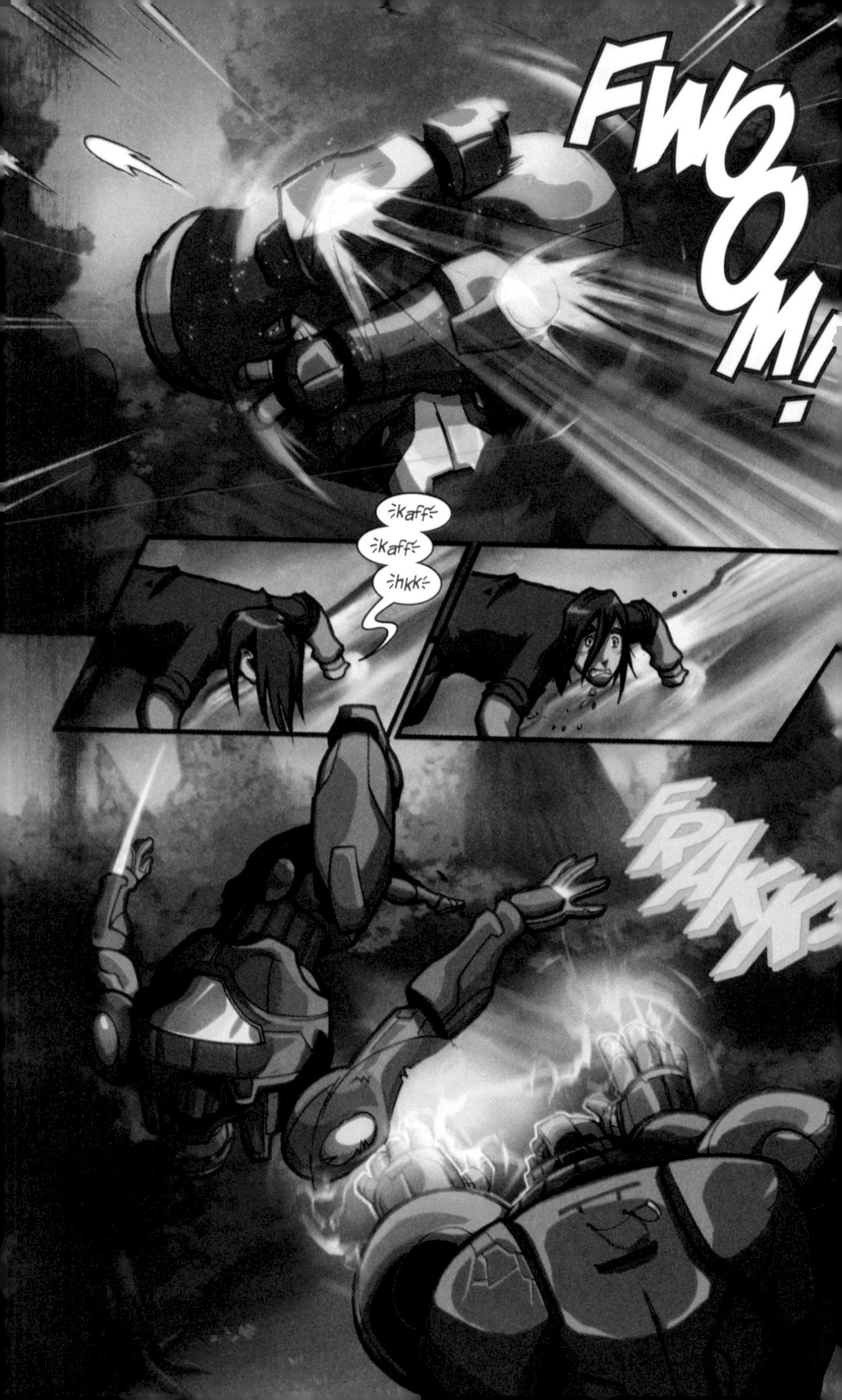
FWOOM!!
Kaff
Kaff
hkk
FRAKK

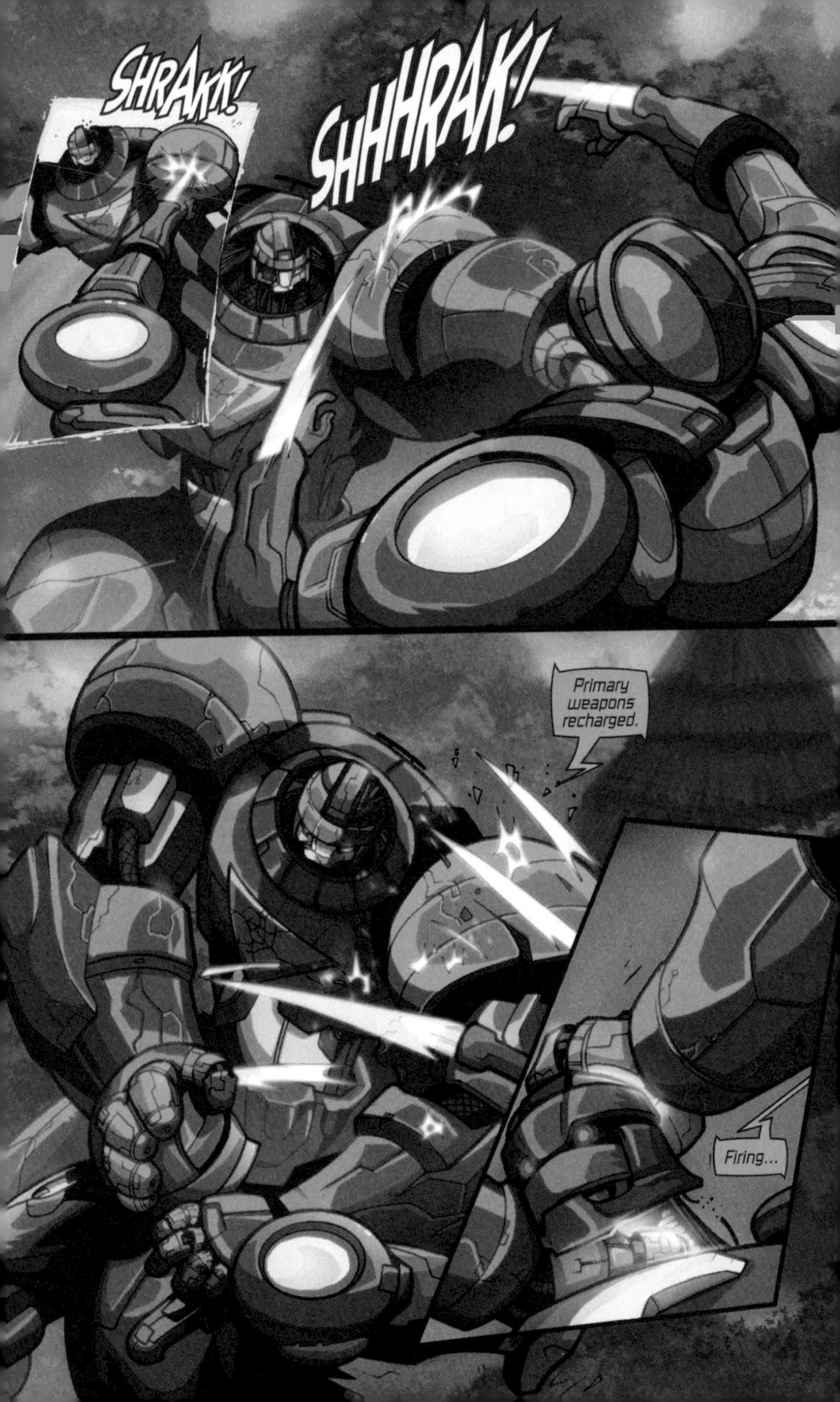
SHRAKK!
SHHHRAK!
Primary weapons recharged.
Firing...

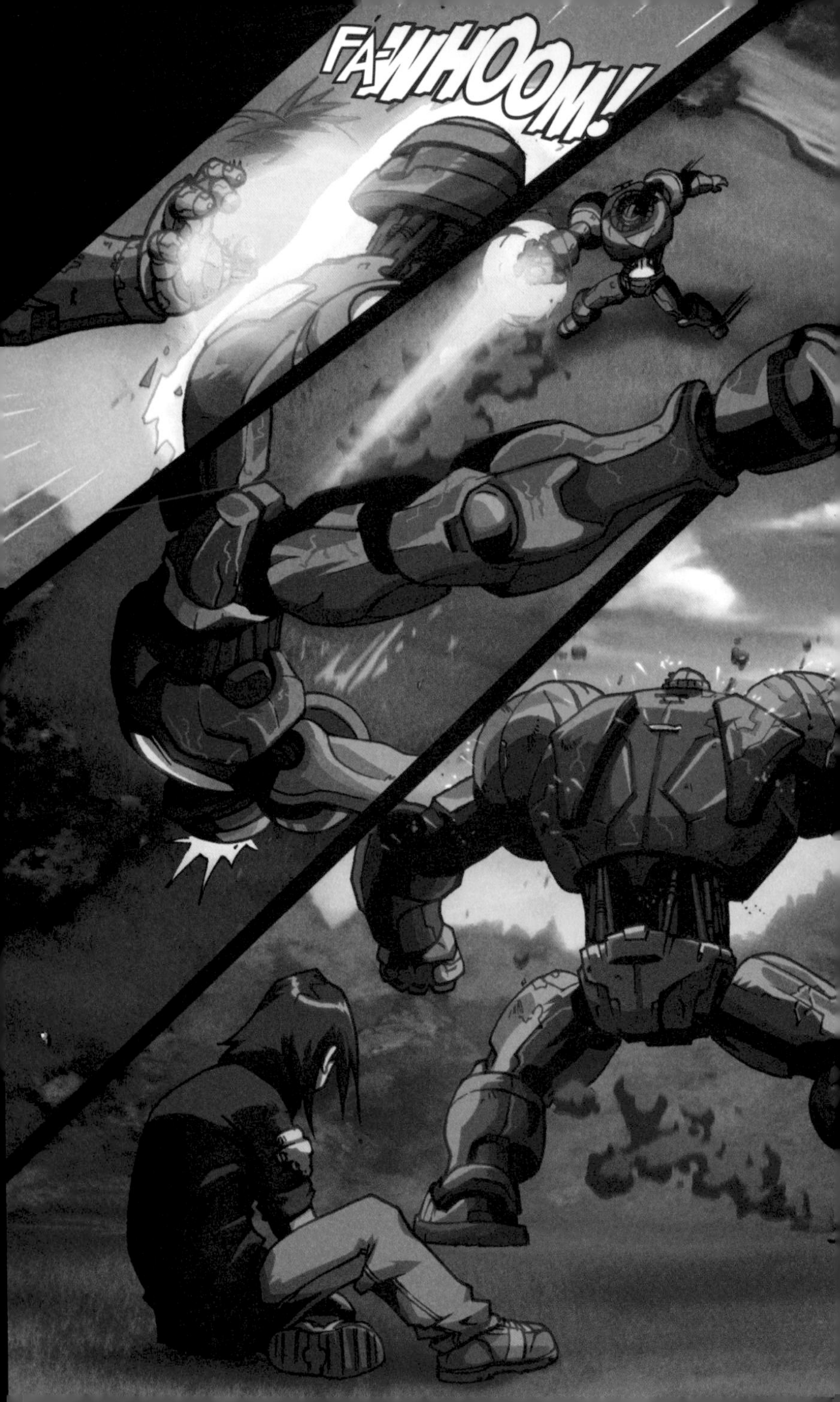
FA-WHOOM!!

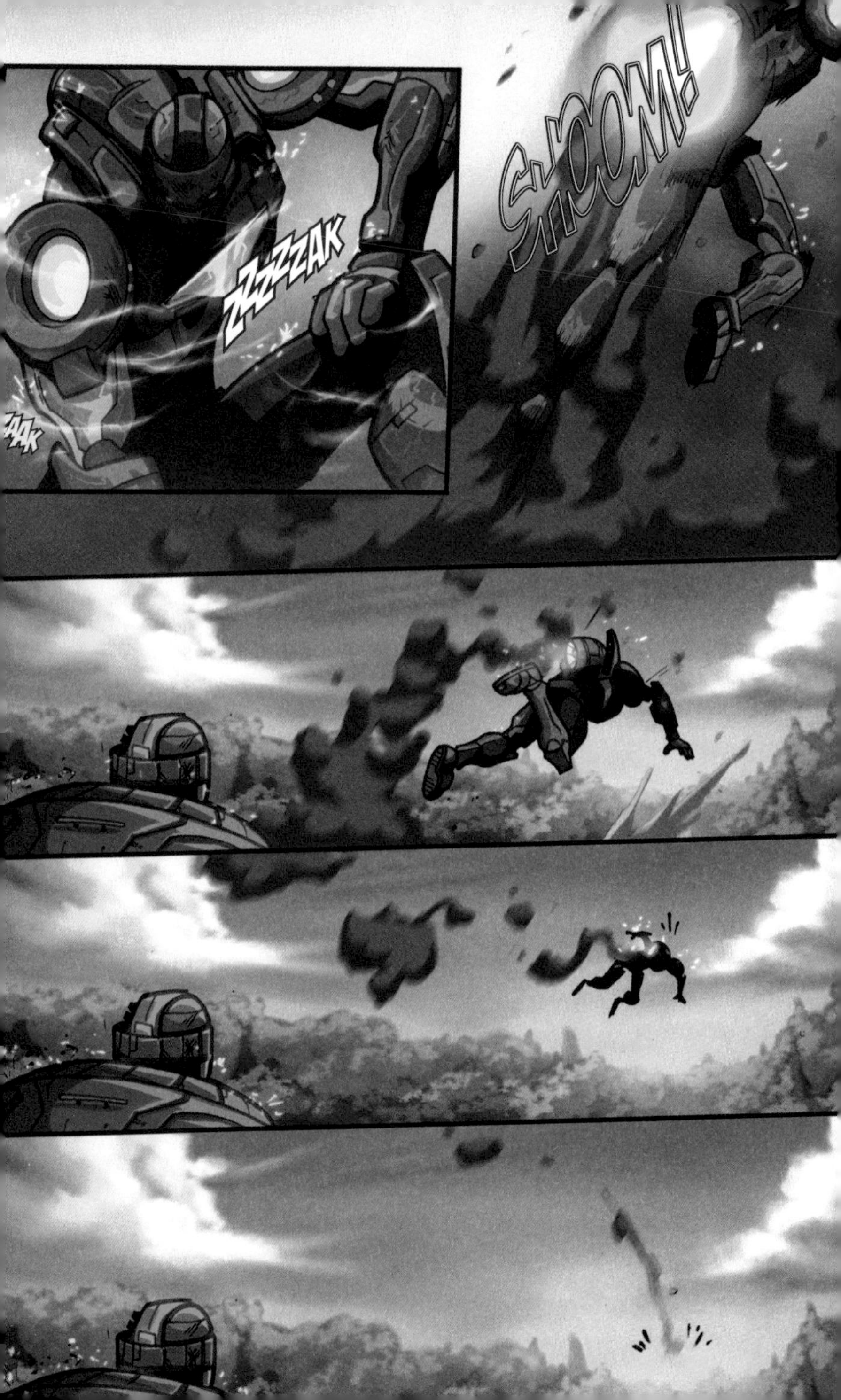

ZZZZZAK
AAK
SHOOM!

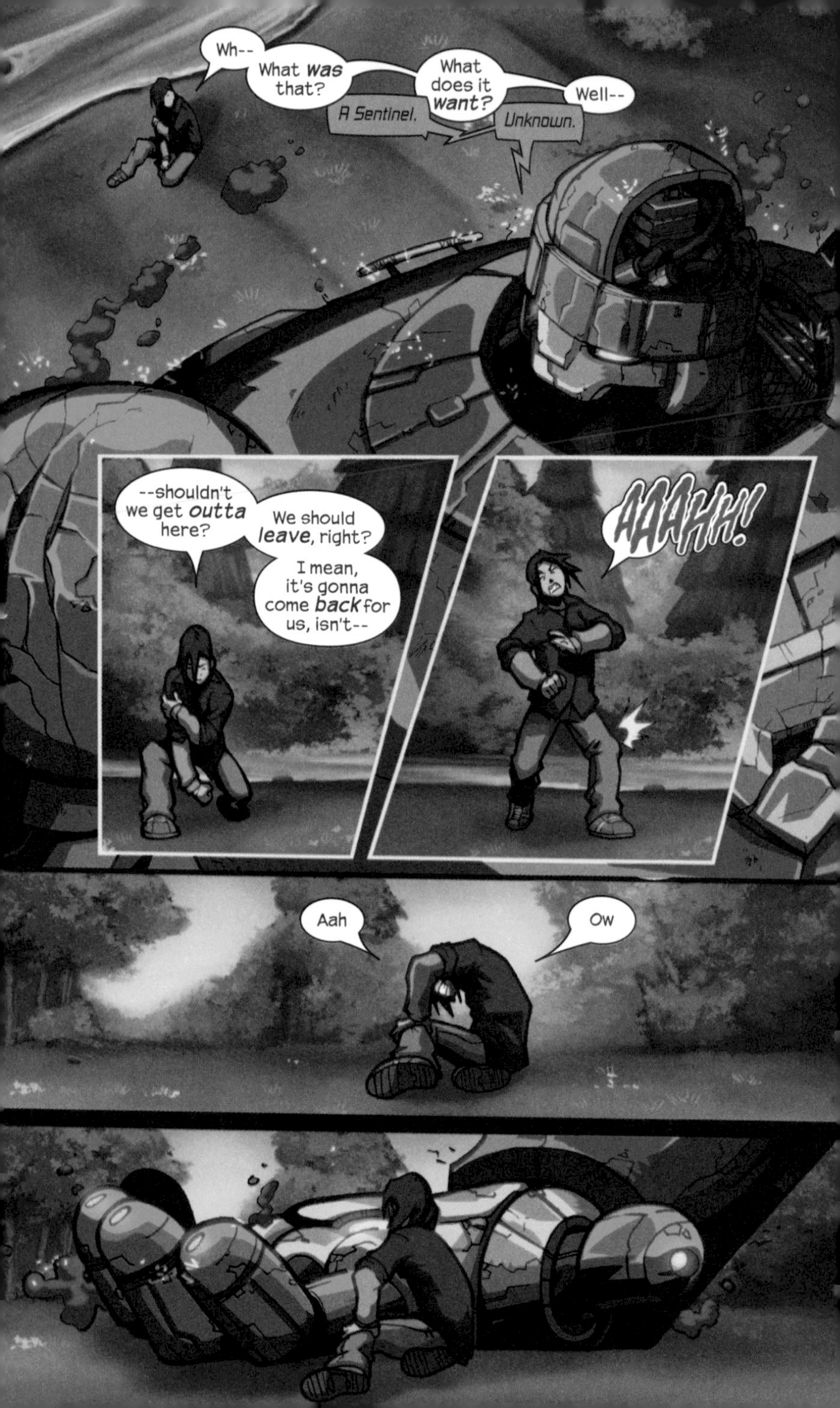

Wh--
What was that?
A Sentinel.
What does it want?
Unknown.
Well--
--shouldn't we get outta here?
We should leave, right?
I mean, it's gonna come back for us, isn't--
AAAHH!
Aah
Ow

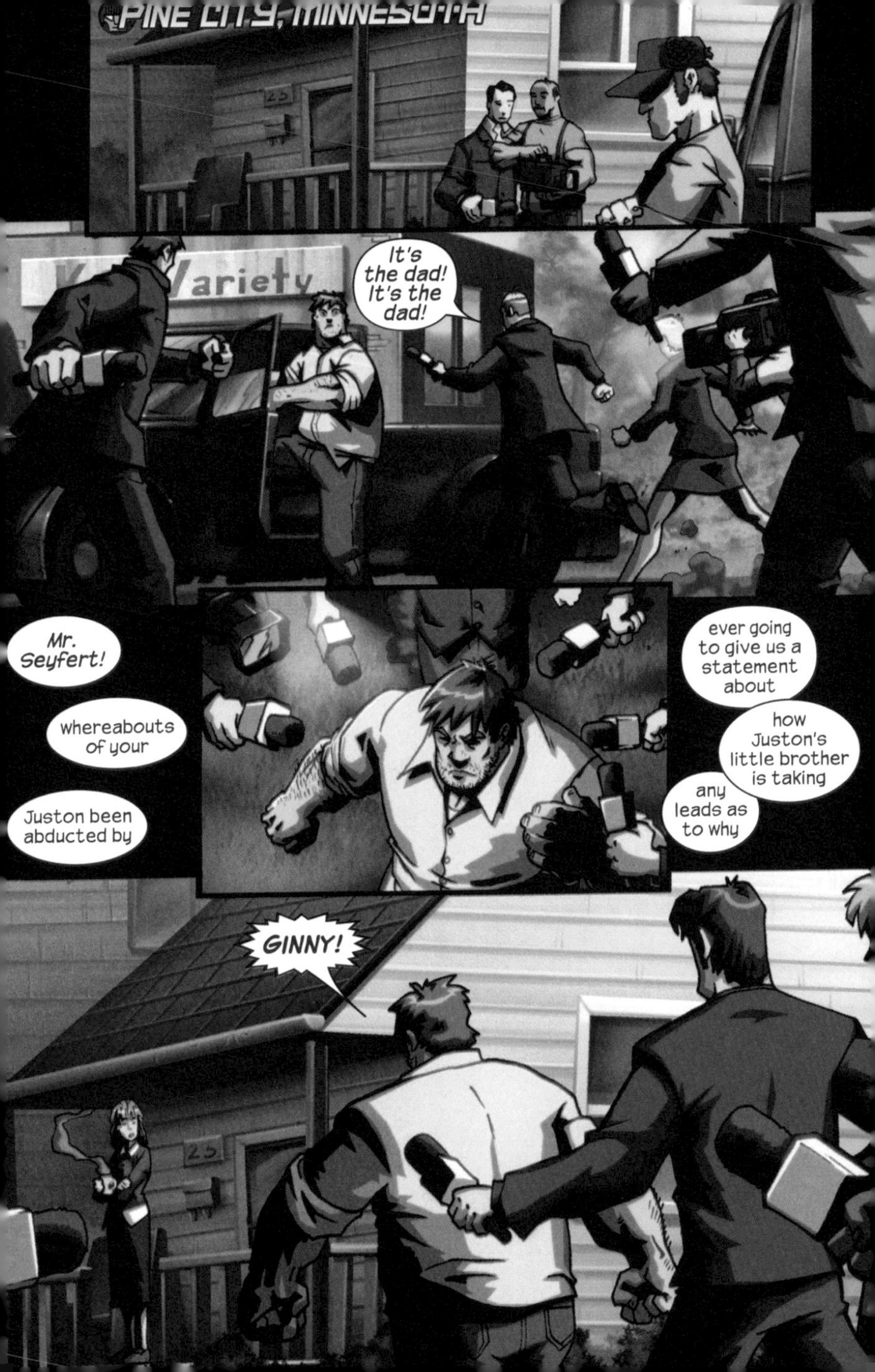
PINE CITY, MINNESOTA
It's the dad! It's the dad!
Mr. Seyfert!
whereabouts of your
Juston been abducted by
ever going to give us a statement about
how Juston's little brother is taking
any leads as to why
GINNY!

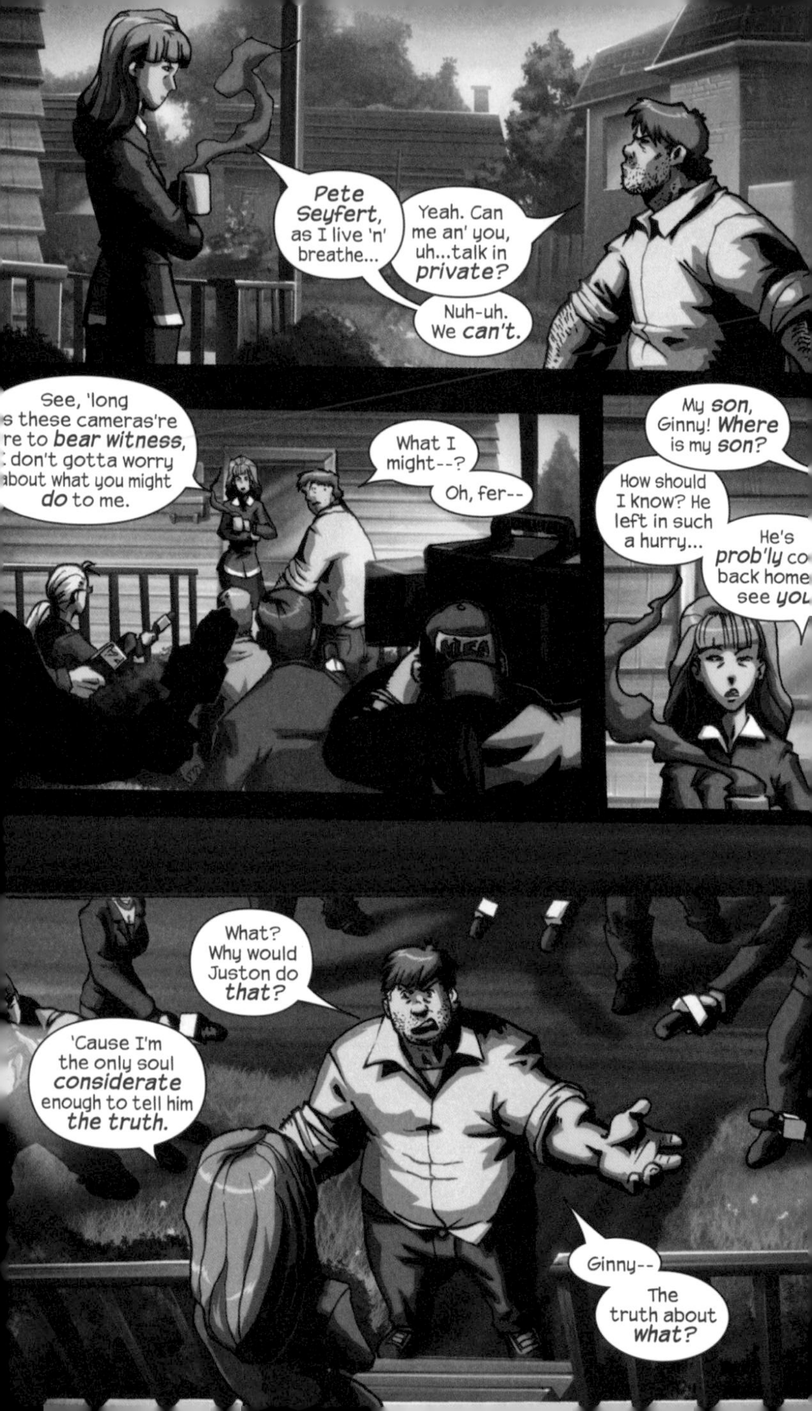
Pete Seyfert, as I live 'n' breathe...
Yeah. Can me an' you, uh...talk in private?
Nuh-uh. We can't.
See, 'long s these cameras're re to bear witness, don't gotta worry about what you might do to me.
What I might--?
Oh, fer--
My son, Ginny! Where is my son?
How should I know? He left in such a hurry...
He's prob'ly co back home see you
What? Why would Juston do that?
'Cause I'm the only soul considerate enough to tell him the truth.
Ginny--
The truth about what?

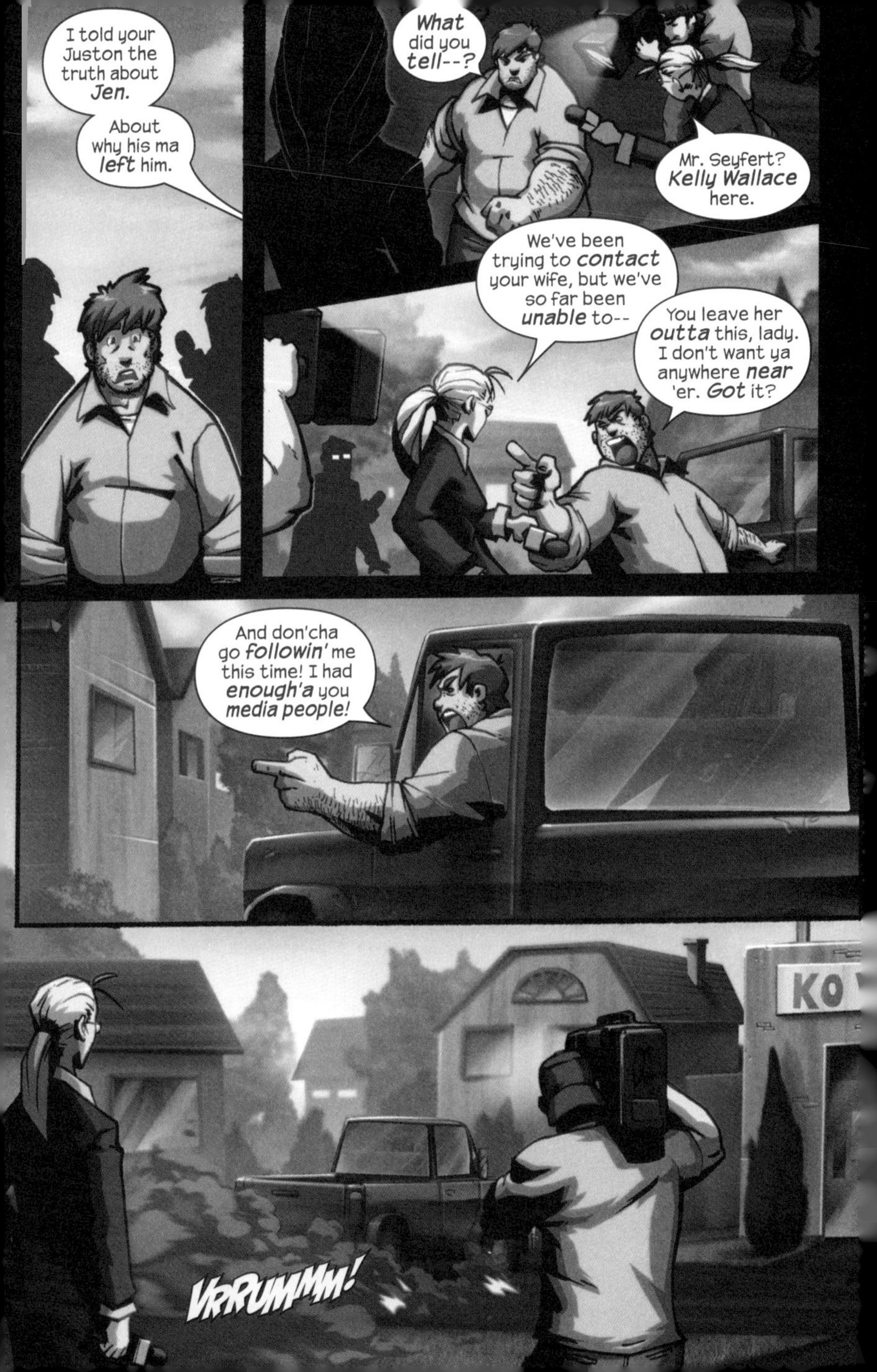
I told your Juston the truth about Jen.
About why his ma left him.
What did you tell--?
Mr. Seyfert? Kelly Wallace here.
We've been trying to contact your wife, but we've so far been unable to--
You leave her outta this, lady. I don't want ya anywhere near 'er. Got it?
And don'cha go followin' me this time! I had enough'a you media people!
KO
VRRUMMM!

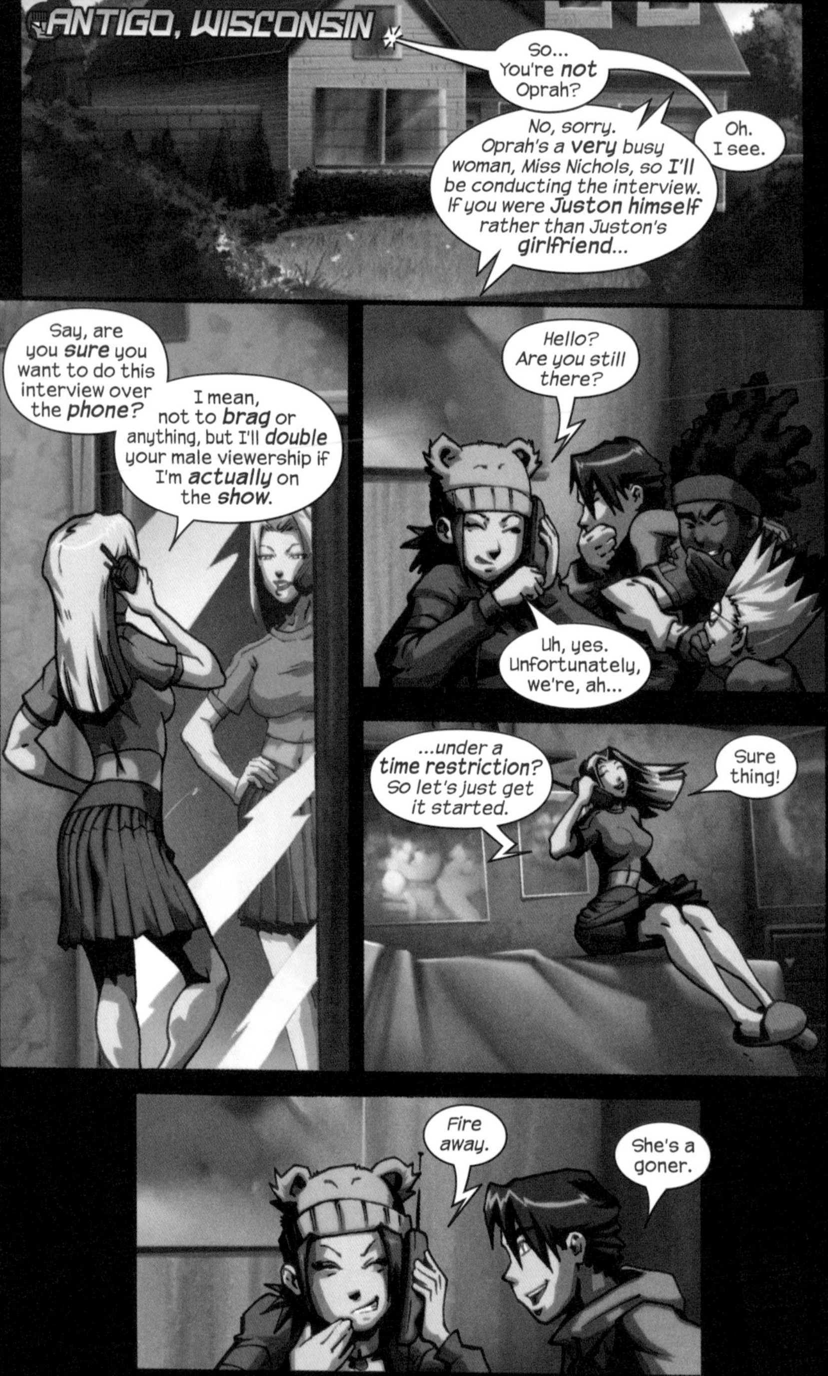
ANTIGO, WISCONSIN
So... You're not Oprah?
No, sorry. Oprah's a very busy woman, Miss Nichols, so I'll be conducting the interview. If you were Juston himself rather than Juston's girlfriend...
Oh. I see.
Say, are you sure you want to do this interview over the phone?
I mean, not to brag or anything, but I'll double your male viewership if I'm actually on the show.
Hello? Are you still there?
Uh, yes. Unfortunately, we're, ah...
...under a time restriction? So let's just get it started.
Sure thing!
Fire away.
She's a goner.

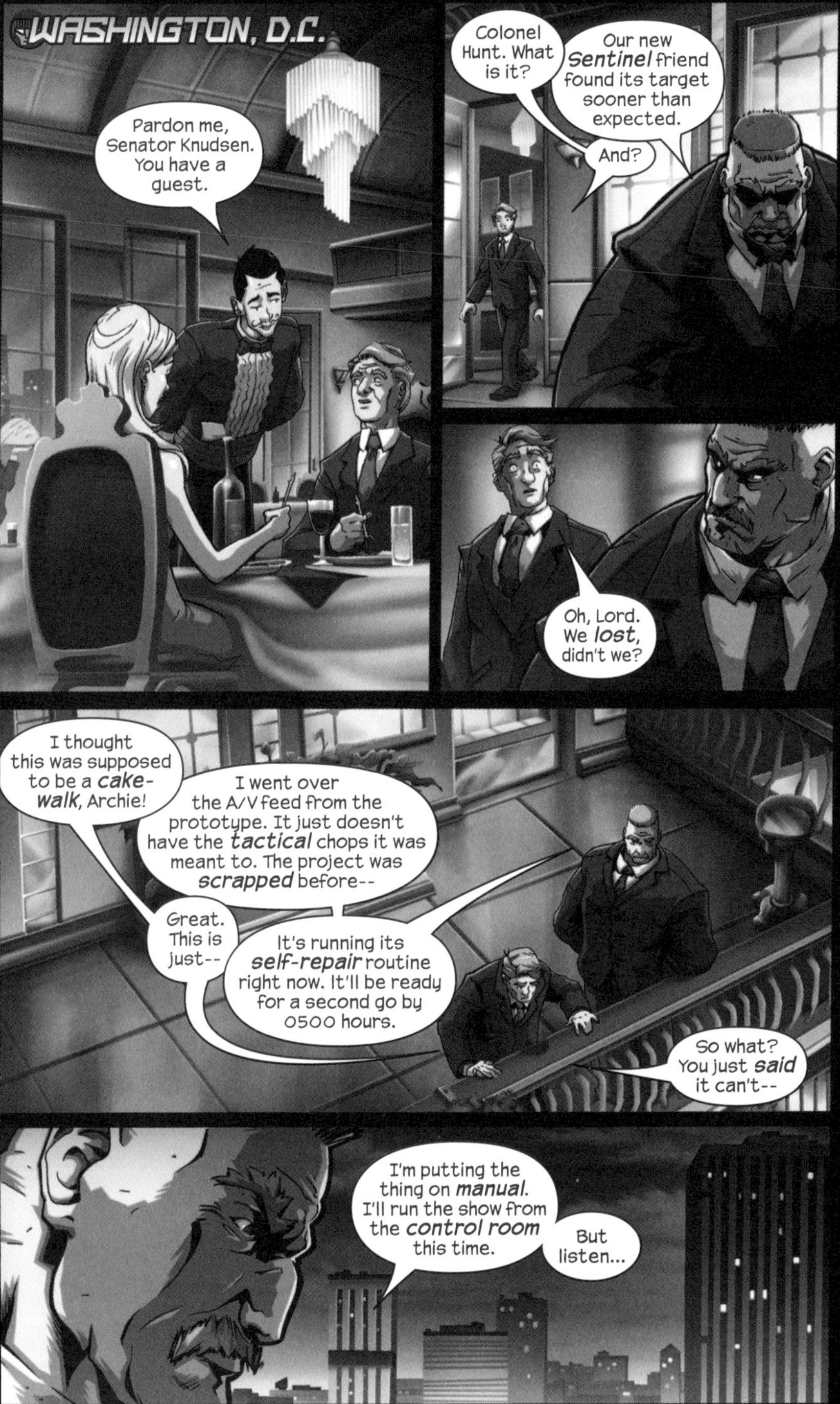
WASHINGTON, D.C.
Pardon me, Senator Knudsen. You have a guest.
Colonel Hunt. What is it?
Our new Sentinel friend found its target sooner than expected.
And?
Oh, Lord. We lost, didn't we?
I thought this was supposed to be a cake-walk, Archie!
I went over the A/V feed from the prototype. It just doesn't have the tactical chops it was meant to. The project was scrapped before--
Great. This is just--
It's running its self-repair routine right now. It'll be ready for a second go by 0500 hours.
So what? You just said it can't--
I'm putting the thing on manual. I'll run the show from the control room this time.
But listen...

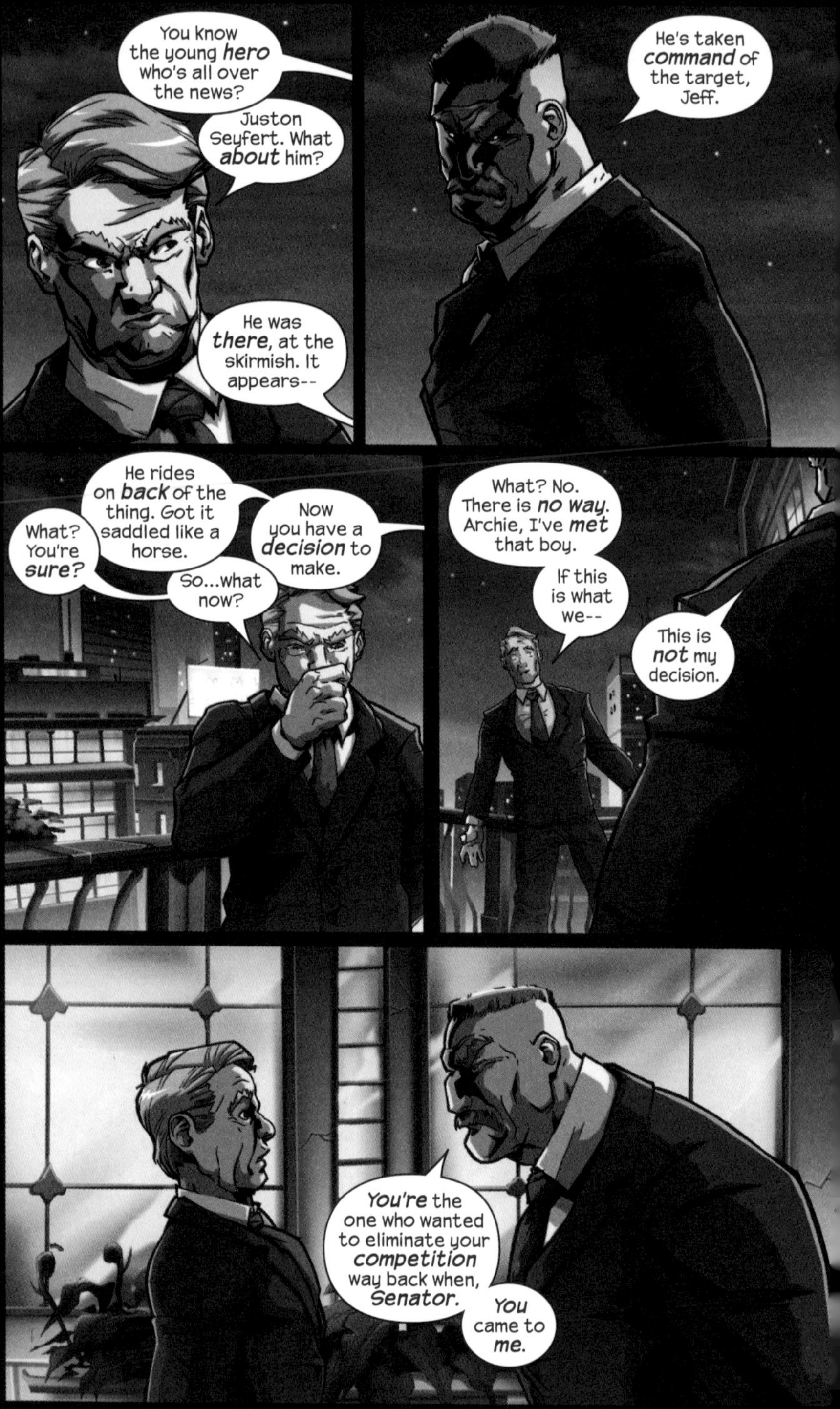

You know the young hero who's all over the news?
Juston Seyfert. What about him?
He was there, at the skirmish. It appears--
He's taken command of the target, Jeff.
He rides on back of the thing. Got it saddled like a horse.
What? You're sure?
So...what now?
Now you have a decision to make.
What? No. There is no way. Archie, I've met that boy.
If this is what we--
This is not my decision.
You're the one who wanted to eliminate your competition way back when, Senator.
You came to me.

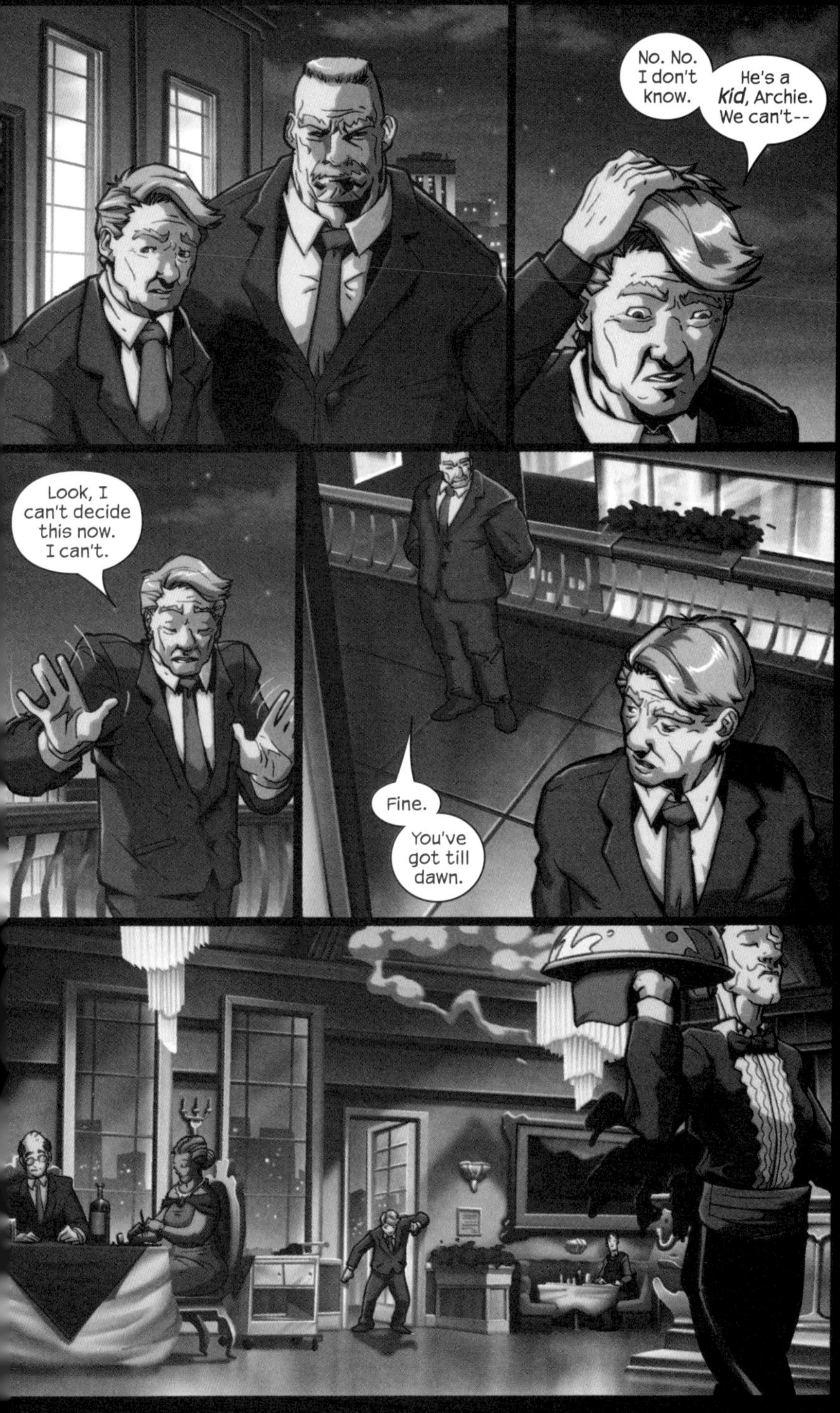
No. No. I don't know.
He's a *kid*, Archie. We can't--
Look, I can't decide this now. I can't.
Fine.
You've got till dawn.

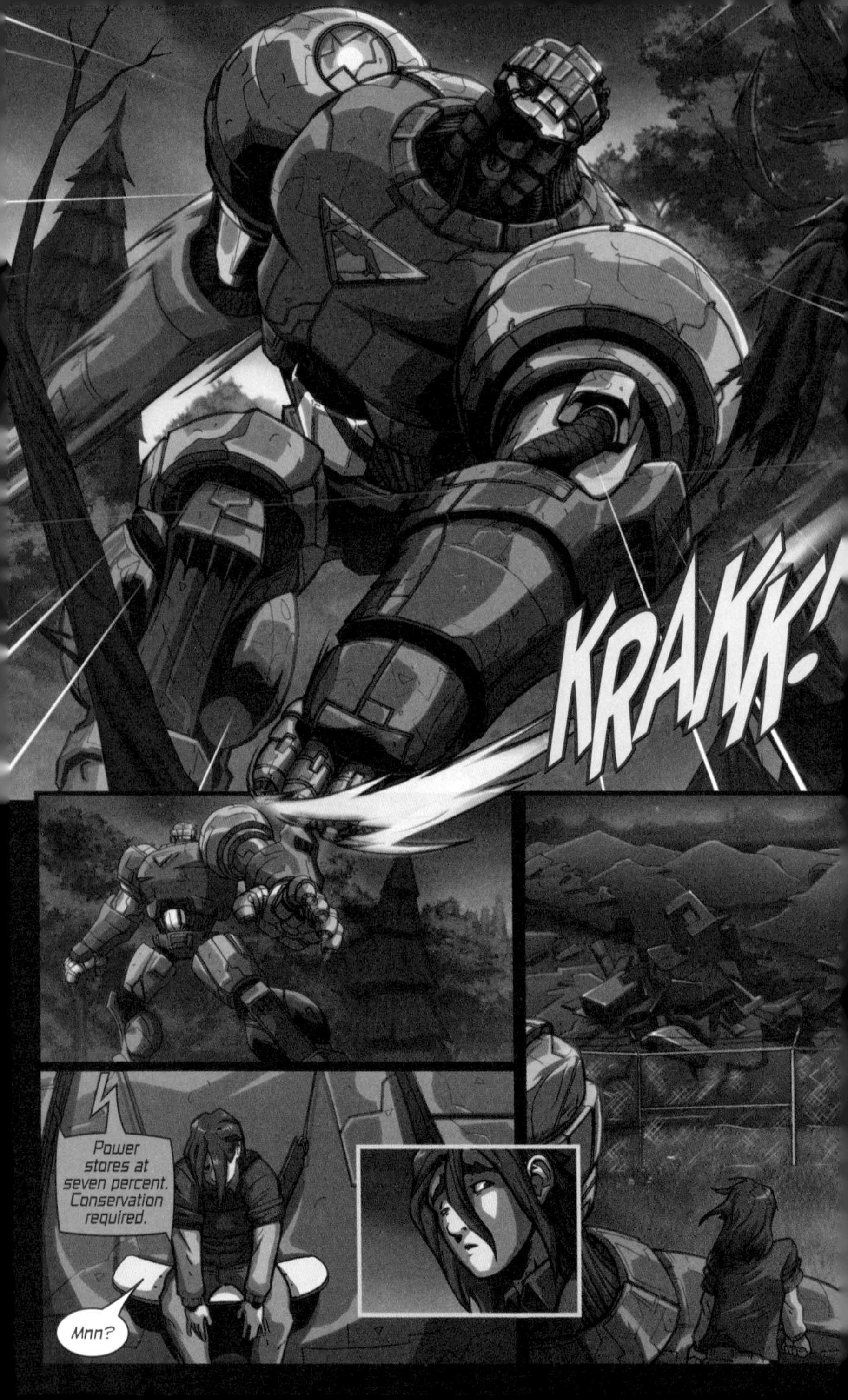
KRAKK!
Power stores at seven percent. Conservation required.
Mnn?

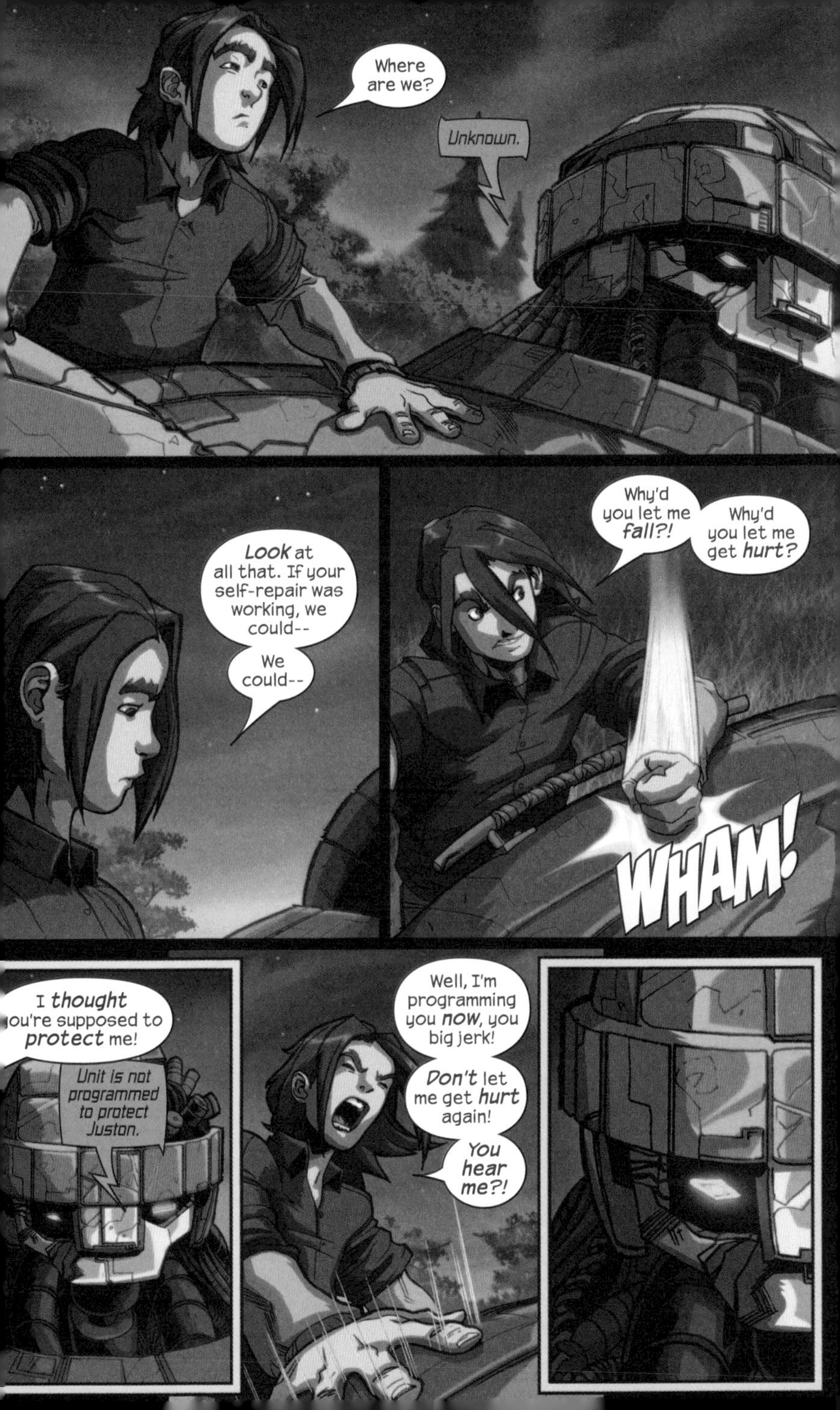

Where are we?
Unknown.
Look at all that. If your self-repair was working, we could--
We could--
Why'd you let me fall?!
Why'd you let me get hurt?
WHAM!
I thought you're supposed to protect me!
Unit is not programmed to protect Juston.
Well, I'm programming you now, you big jerk!
Don't let me get hurt again!
You hear me?!

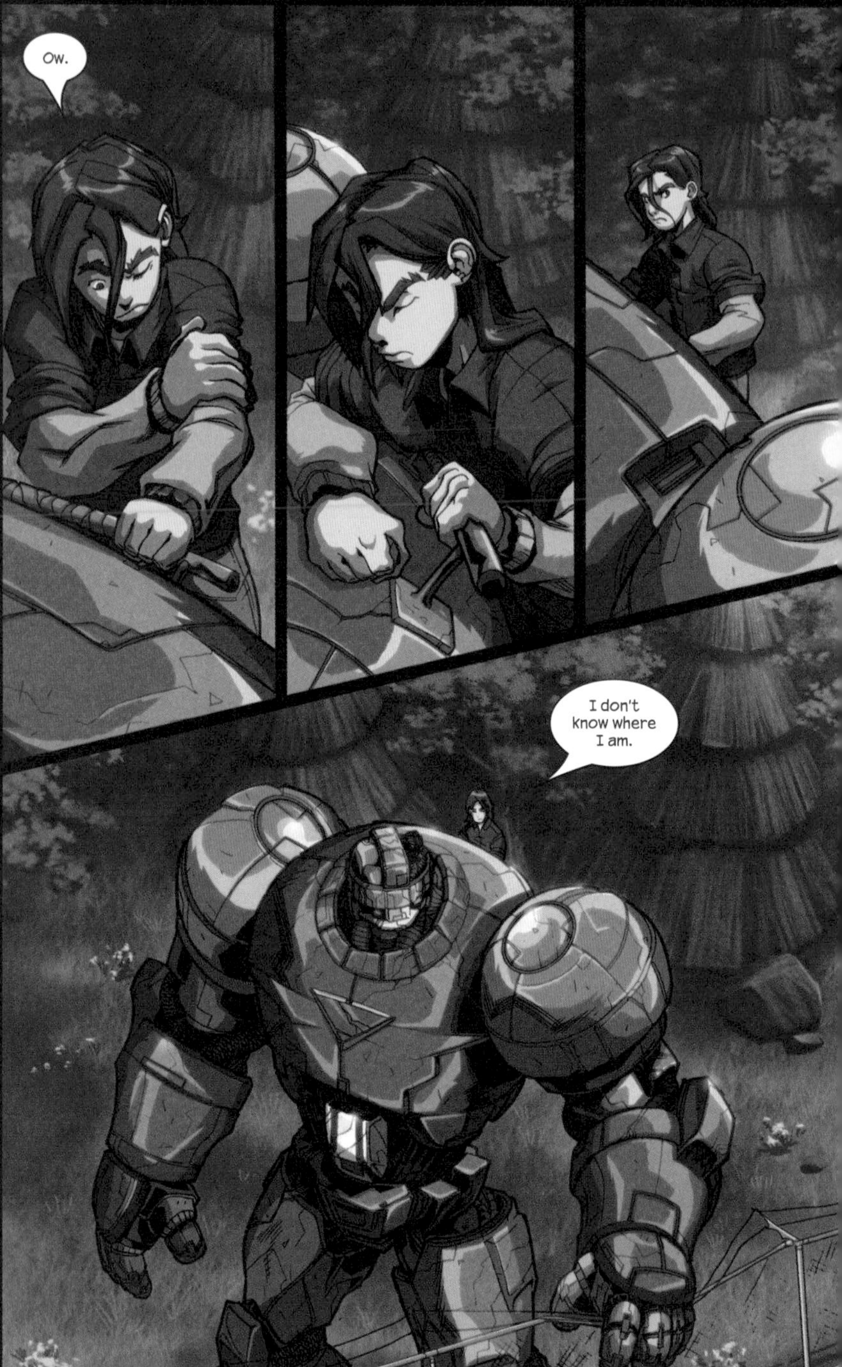
Ow.
I don't know where I am.

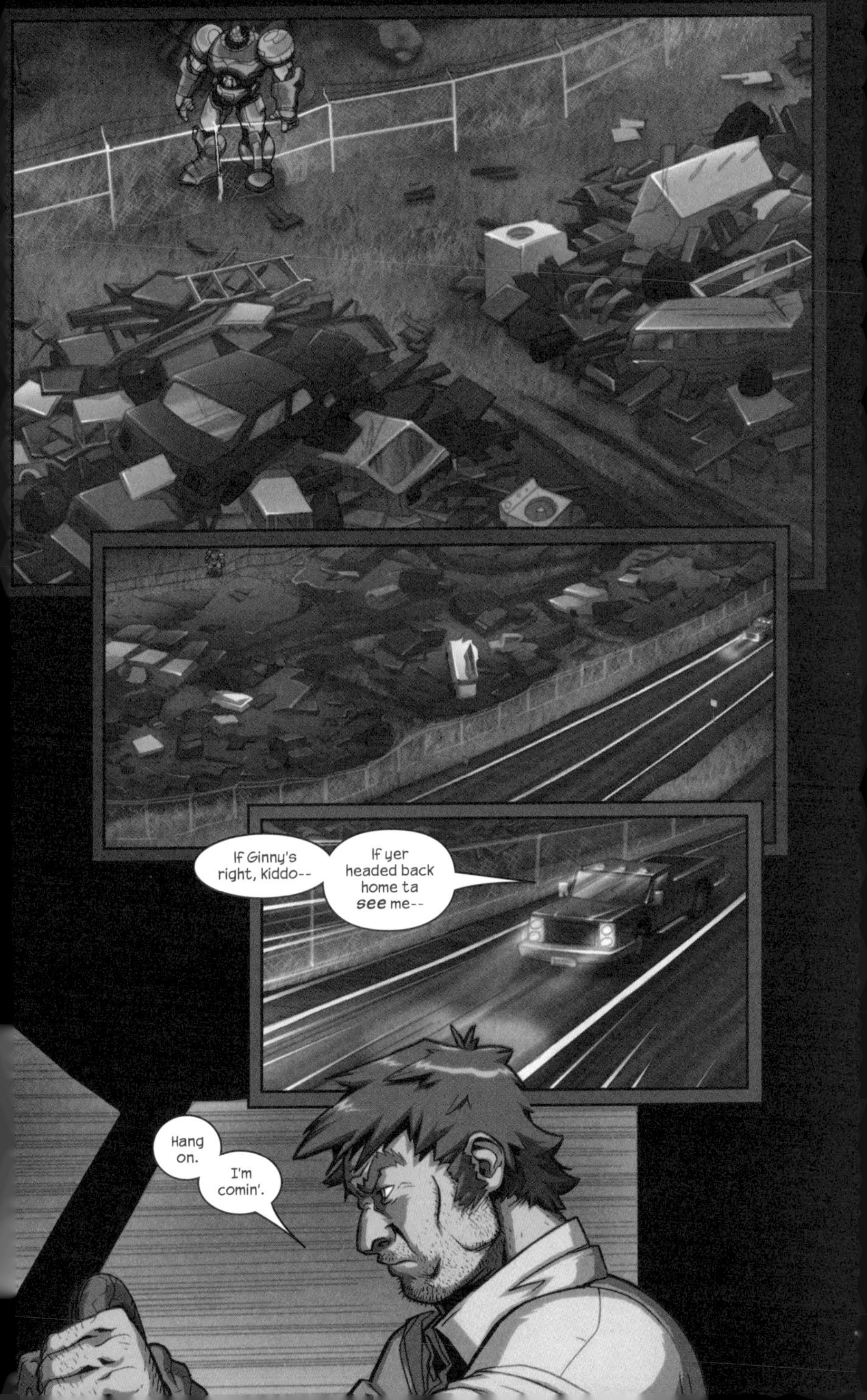
If Ginny's right, kiddo--
If yer headed back home ta see me--
Hang on.
I'm comin'.

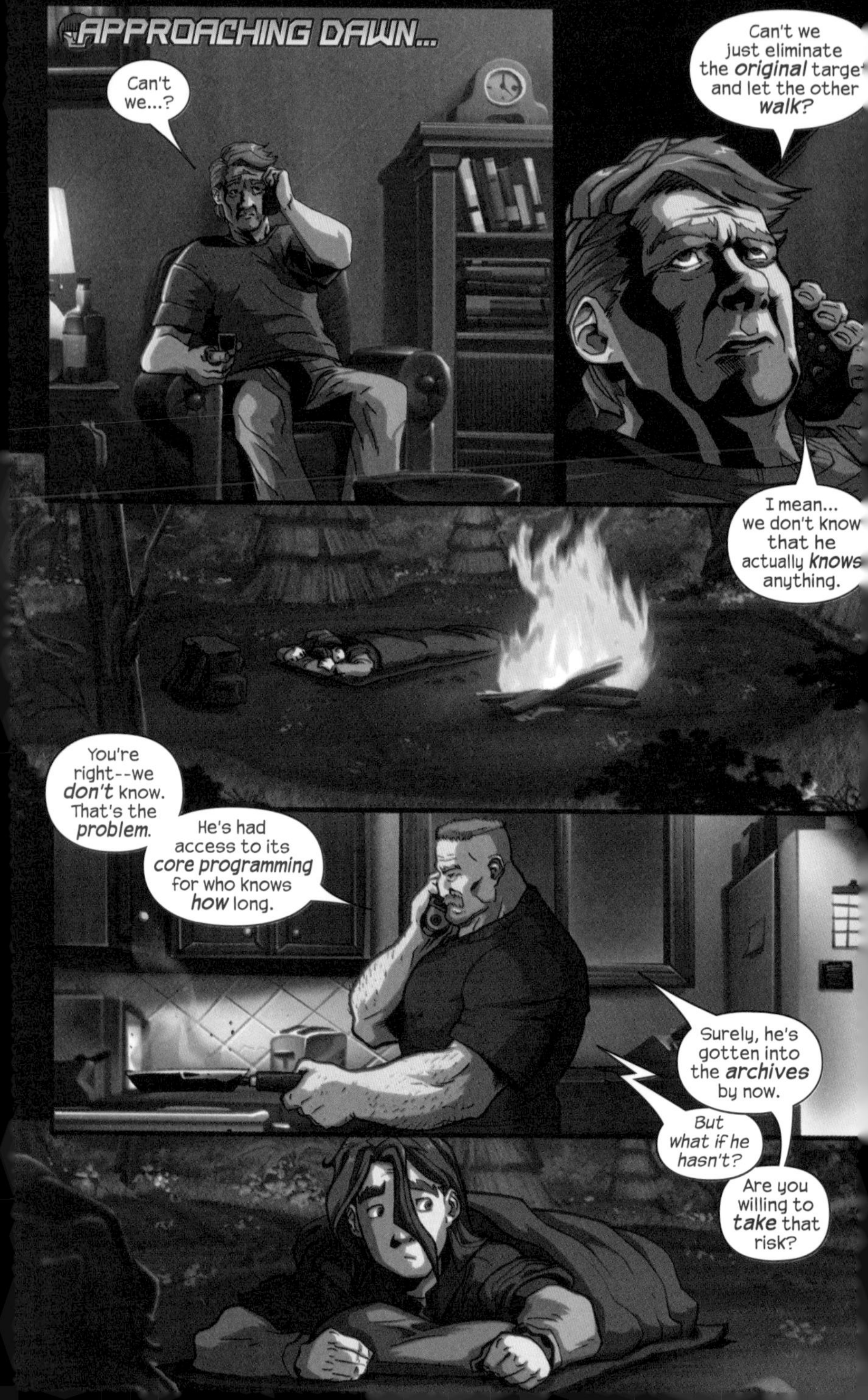
APPROACHING DAWN...
Can't we...?
Can't we just eliminate the original target and let the other walk?
I mean... we don't know that he actually knows anything.
You're right--we don't know. That's the problem.
He's had access to its core programming for who knows how long.
Surely, he's gotten into the archives by now.
But what if he hasn't?
Are you willing to take that risk?

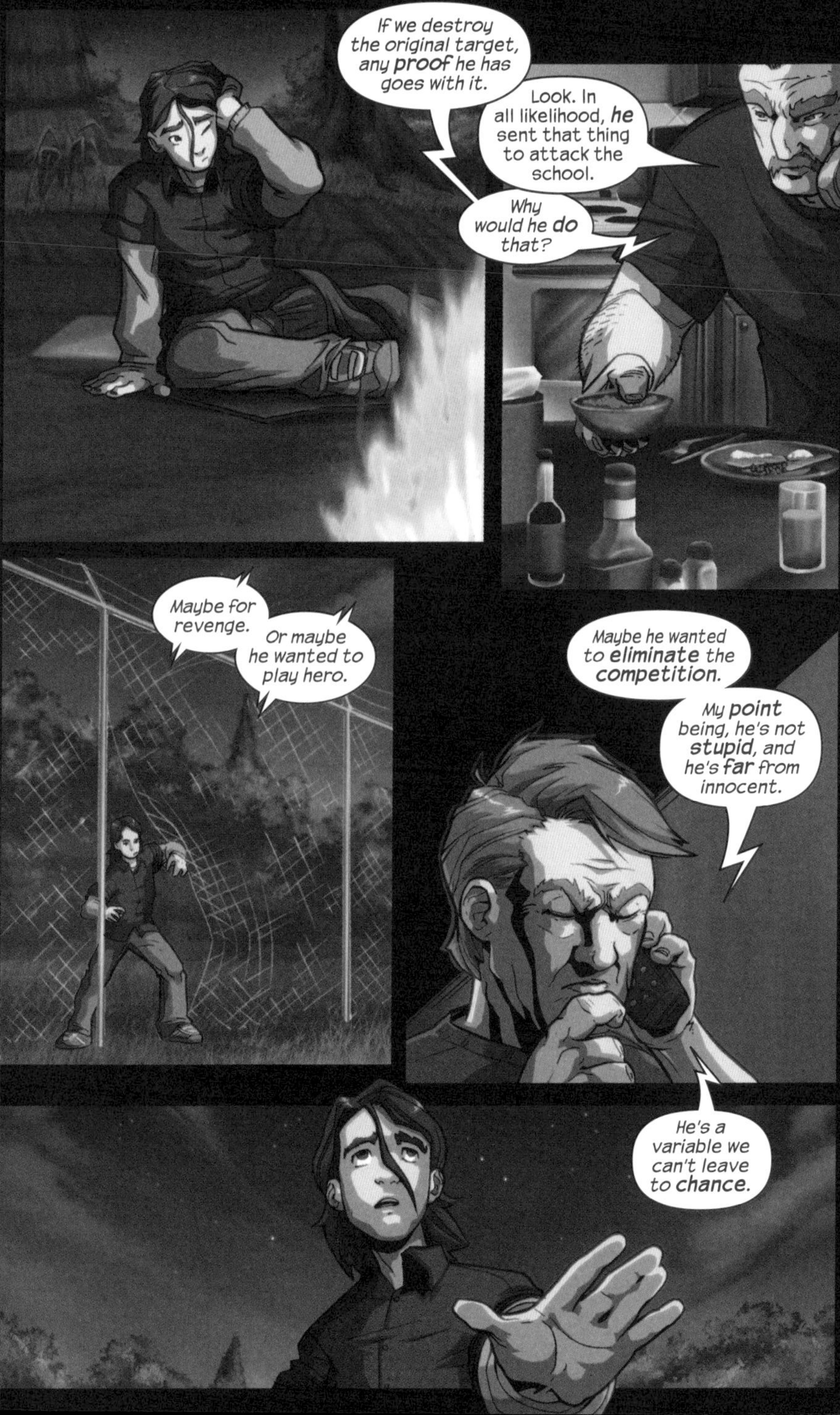
If we destroy the original target, any proof he has goes with it.
Look. In all likelihood, he sent that thing to attack the school.
Why would he do that?
Maybe for revenge.
Or maybe he wanted to play hero.
Maybe he wanted to eliminate the competition.
My point being, he's not stupid, and he's far from innocent.
He's a variable we can't leave to chance.

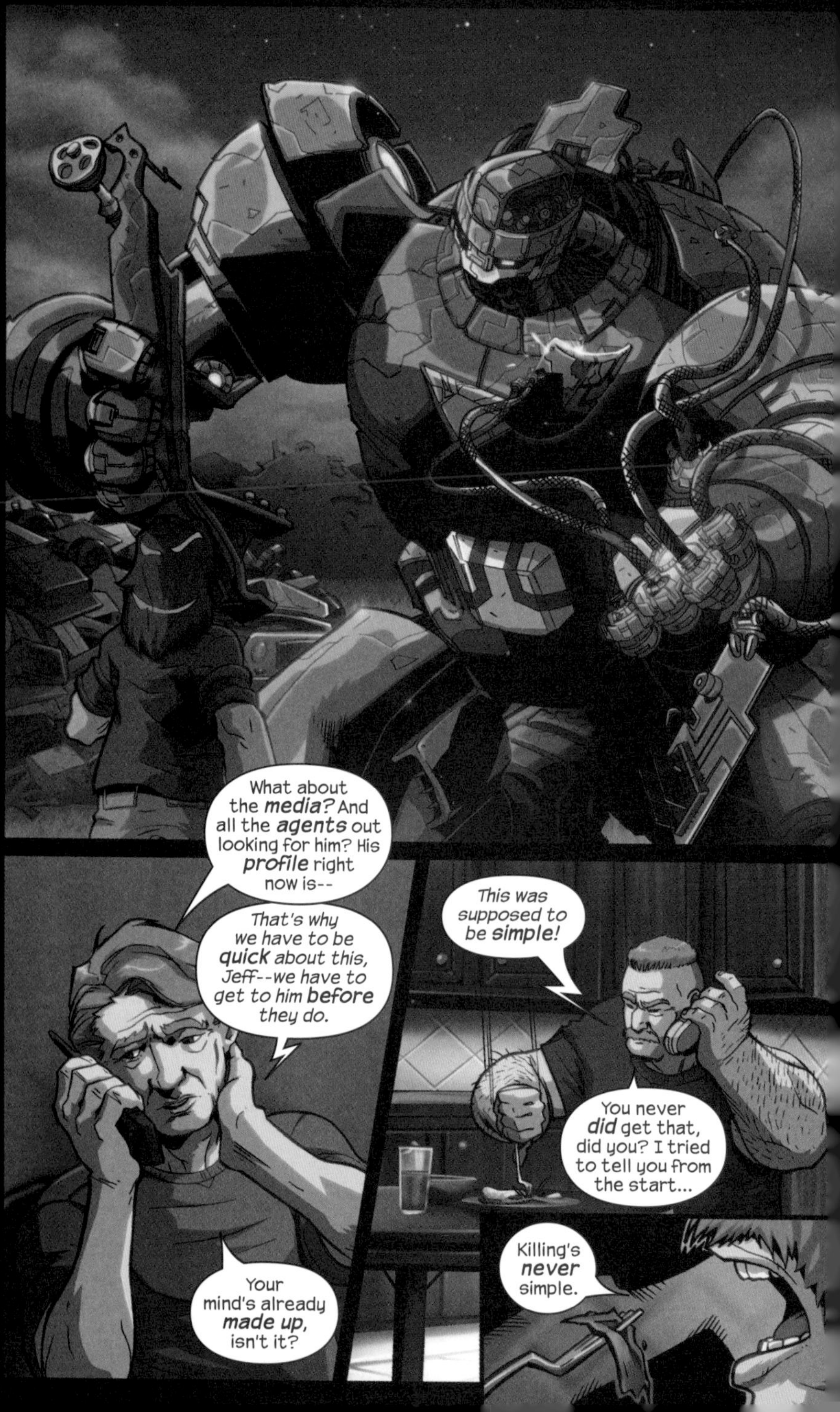
What about the *media?* And all the *agents* out looking for him? His *profile* right now is--
That's why we have to be ***quick*** *about this, Jeff--we have to get to him* ***before*** *they do.*
This was supposed to be ***simple!***
You never *did* get that, did you? I tried to tell you from the start...
Your mind's already *made up*, isn't it?
Killing's *never* simple.

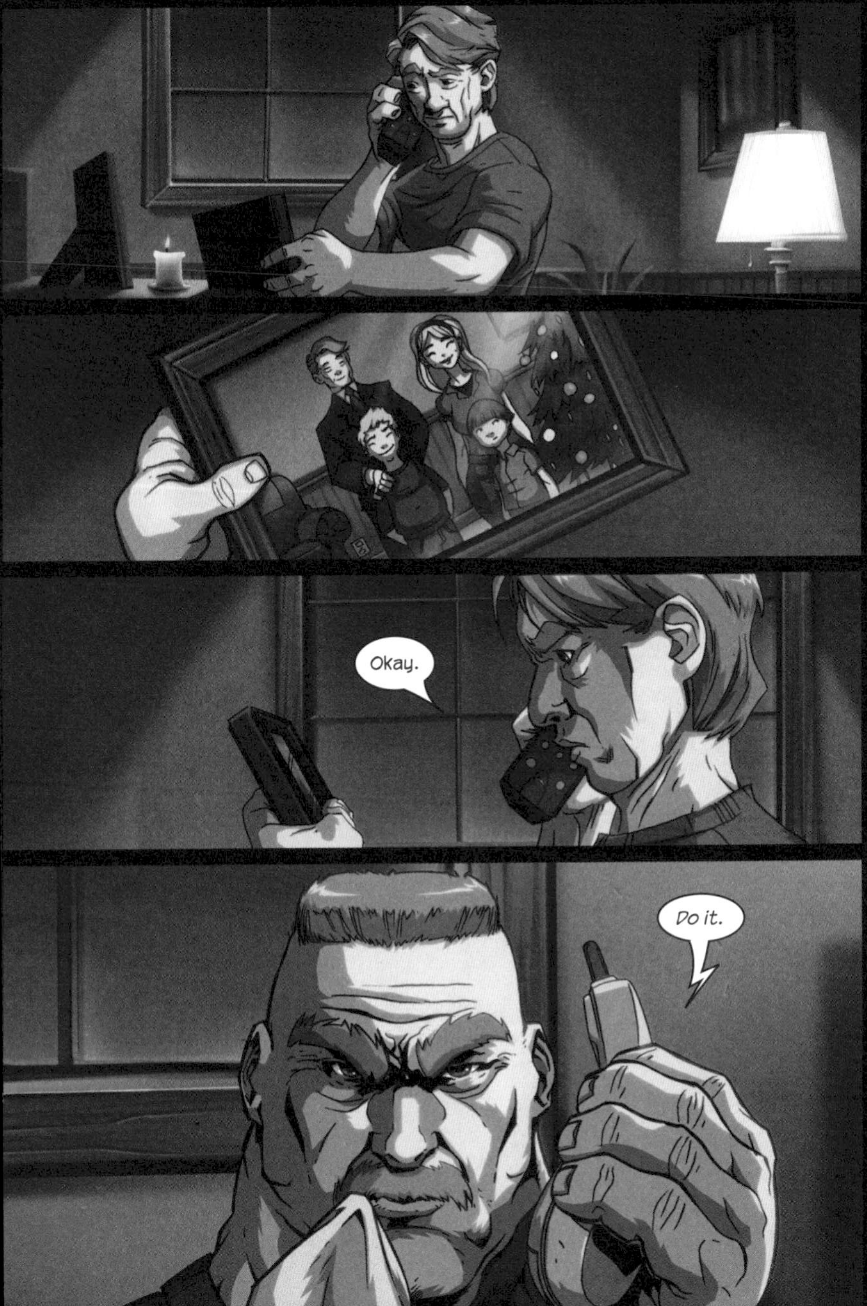
Okay.
Do it.

D A M A G E D

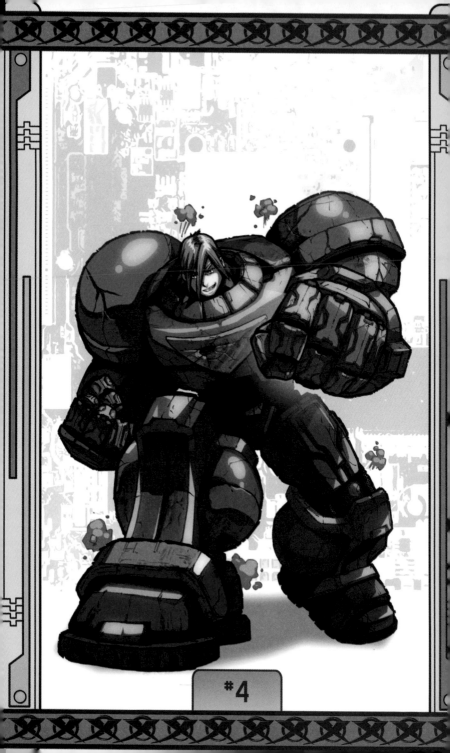

#4

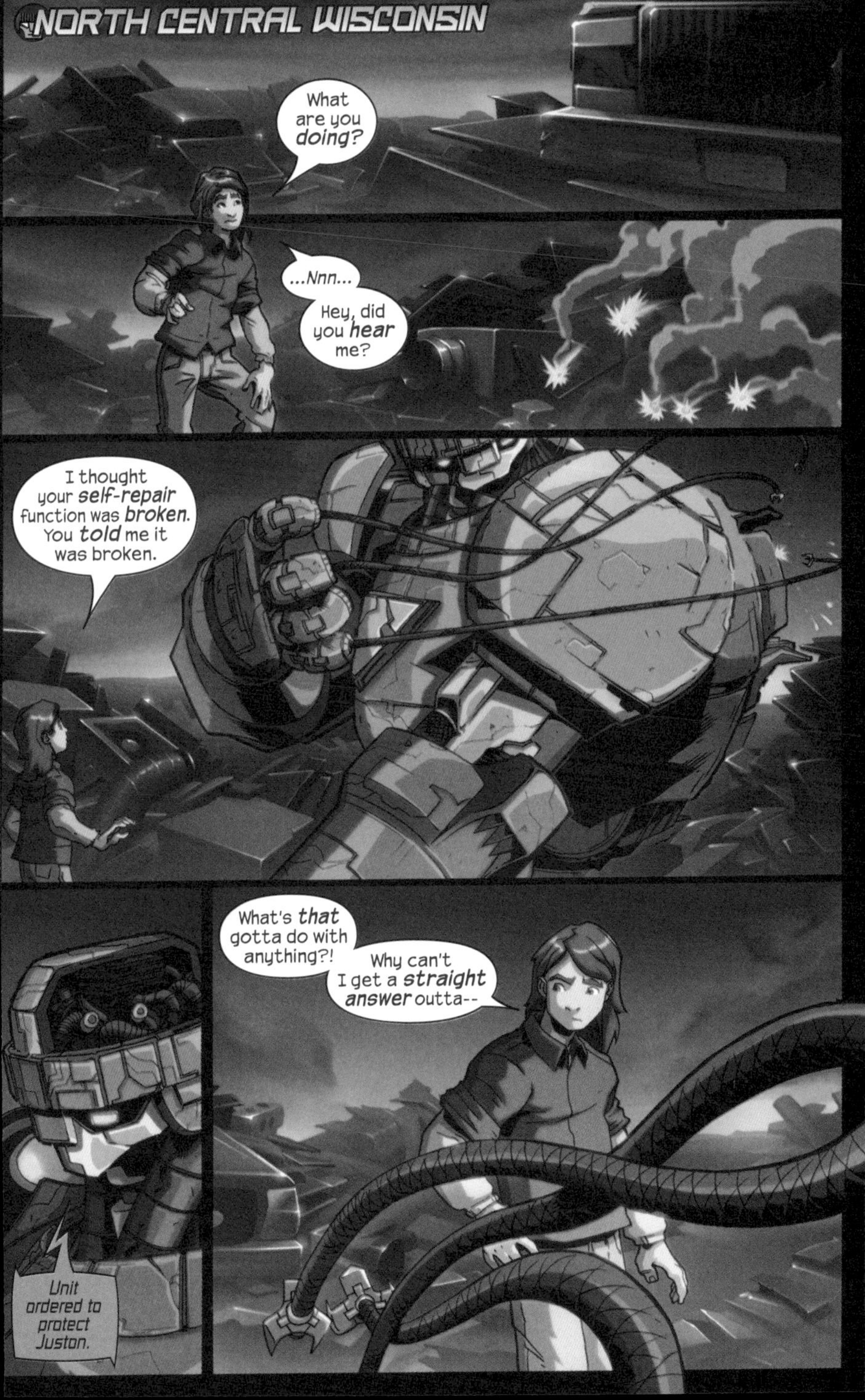

NORTH CENTRAL WISCONSIN
What are you doing?
...Nnn...
Hey, did you hear me?
I thought your self-repair function was broken. You told me it was broken.
Unit ordered to protect Juston.
What's that gotta do with anything?!
Why can't I get a straight answer outta--

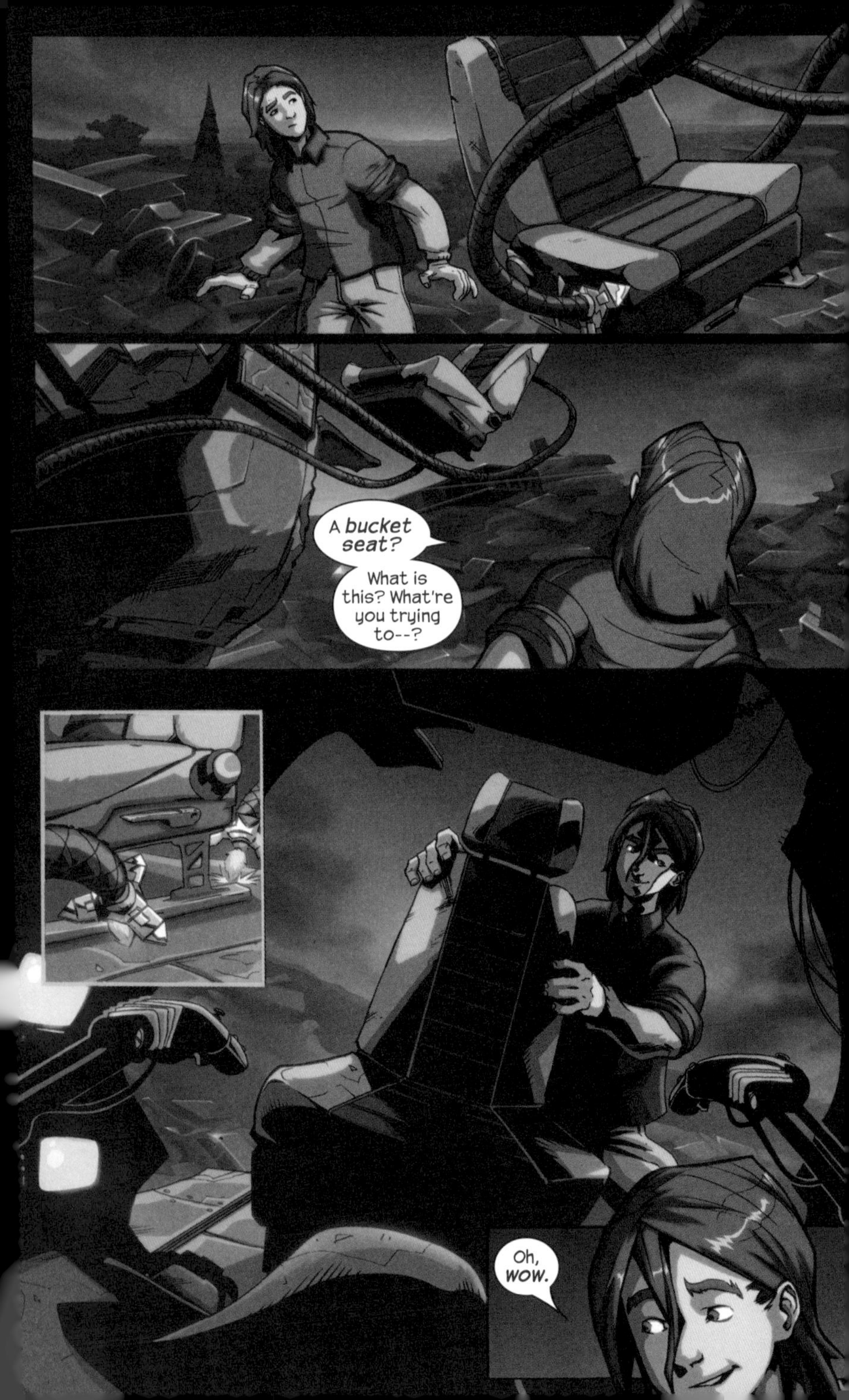
A *bucket seat?*
What is this? What're you trying to--?
Oh, *WOW.*

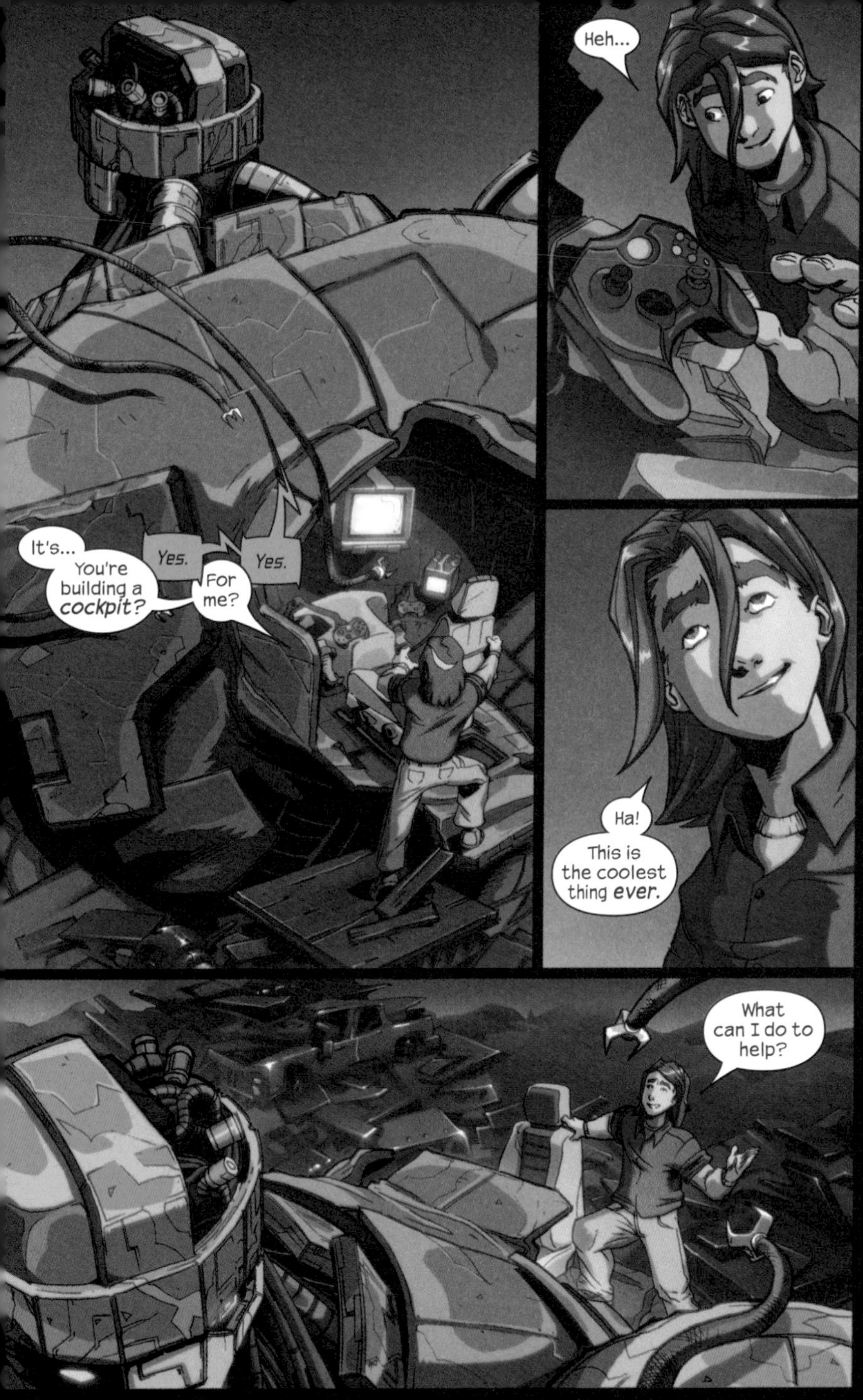
It's...
You're building a cockpit?
Yes.
Yes.
For me?
Heh...
Ha!
This is the coolest thing ever.
What can I do to help?

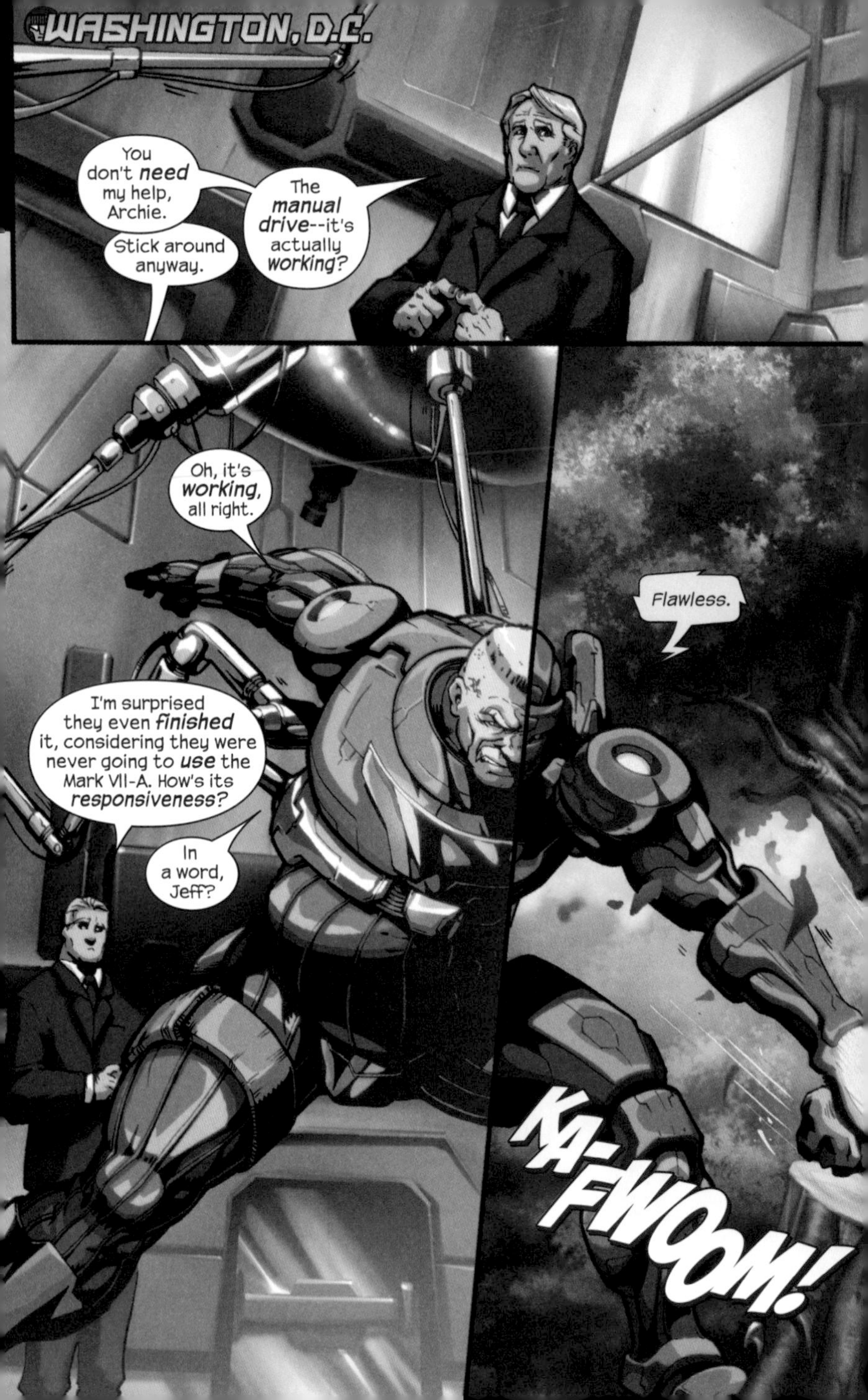
WASHINGTON, D.C.
You don't *need* my help, Archie.
Stick around anyway.
The *manual drive*--it's actually *working*?
Oh, it's *working*, all right.
I'm surprised they even *finished* it, considering they were never going to *use* the Mark VII-A. How's its *responsiveness*?
In a word, Jeff?
Flawless.
KA-FWOOM!

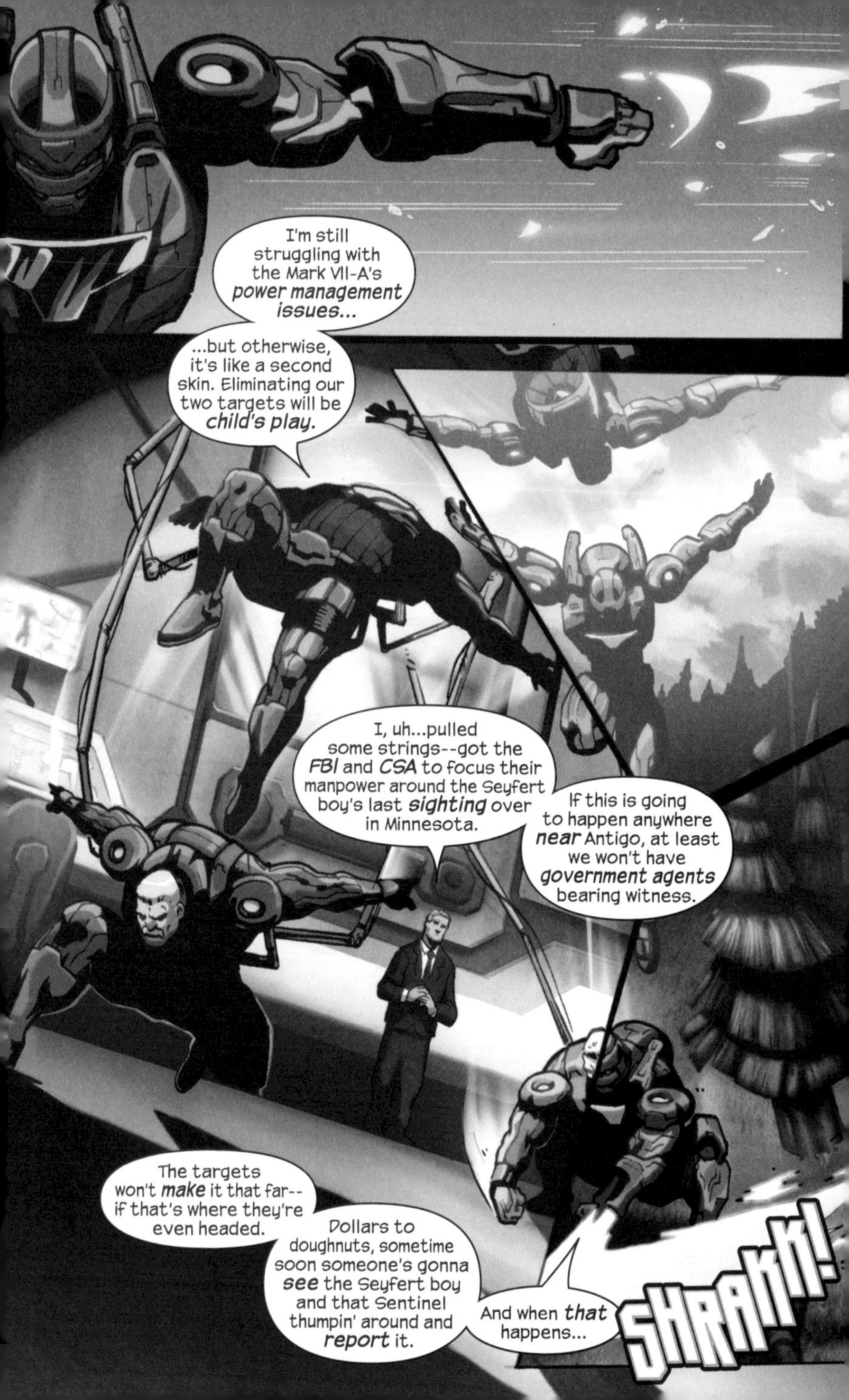
I'm still struggling with the Mark VII-A's *power management issues...*
...but otherwise, it's like a second skin. Eliminating our two targets will be *child's play.*
I, uh...pulled some strings--got the *FBI* and *CSA* to focus their manpower around the Seyfert boy's last *sighting* over in Minnesota.
If this is going to happen anywhere *near* Antigo, at least we won't have *government agents* bearing witness.
The targets won't *make* it that far--if that's where they're even headed.
Dollars to doughnuts, sometime soon someone's gonna *see* the Seyfert boy and that Sentinel thumpin' around and *report* it.
And when *that* happens...
SHRAKK!

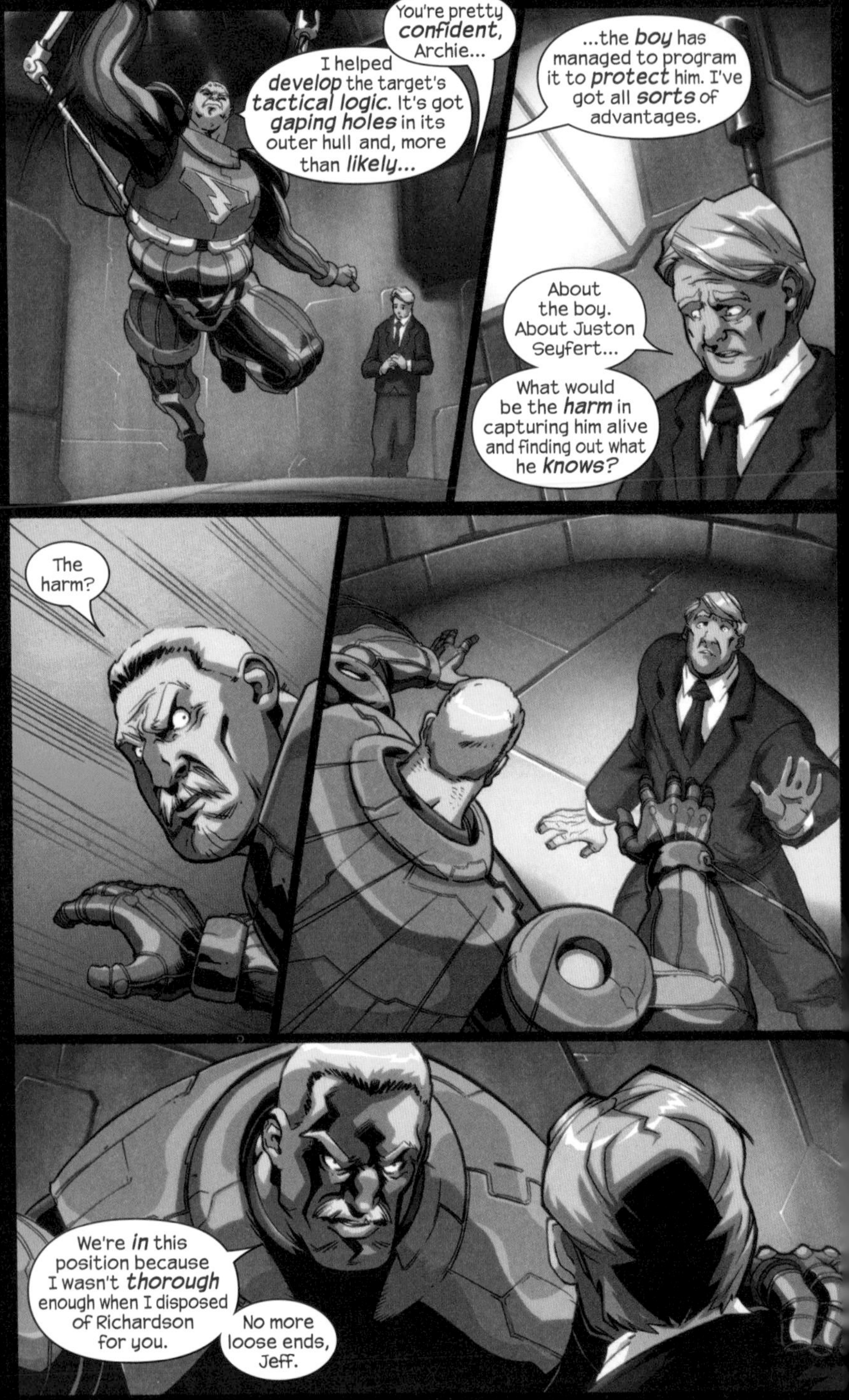
You're pretty *confident*, Archie...
I helped *develop* the target's *tactical logic*. It's got *gaping holes* in its outer hull and, more than *likely*...
...the *boy* has managed to program it to *protect* him. I've got all *sorts* of advantages.
About the boy. About Juston Seyfert...
What would be the *harm* in capturing him alive and finding out what he *knows?*
The harm?
We're *in* this position because I wasn't *thorough* enough when I disposed of Richardson for you.
No more loose ends, Jeff.

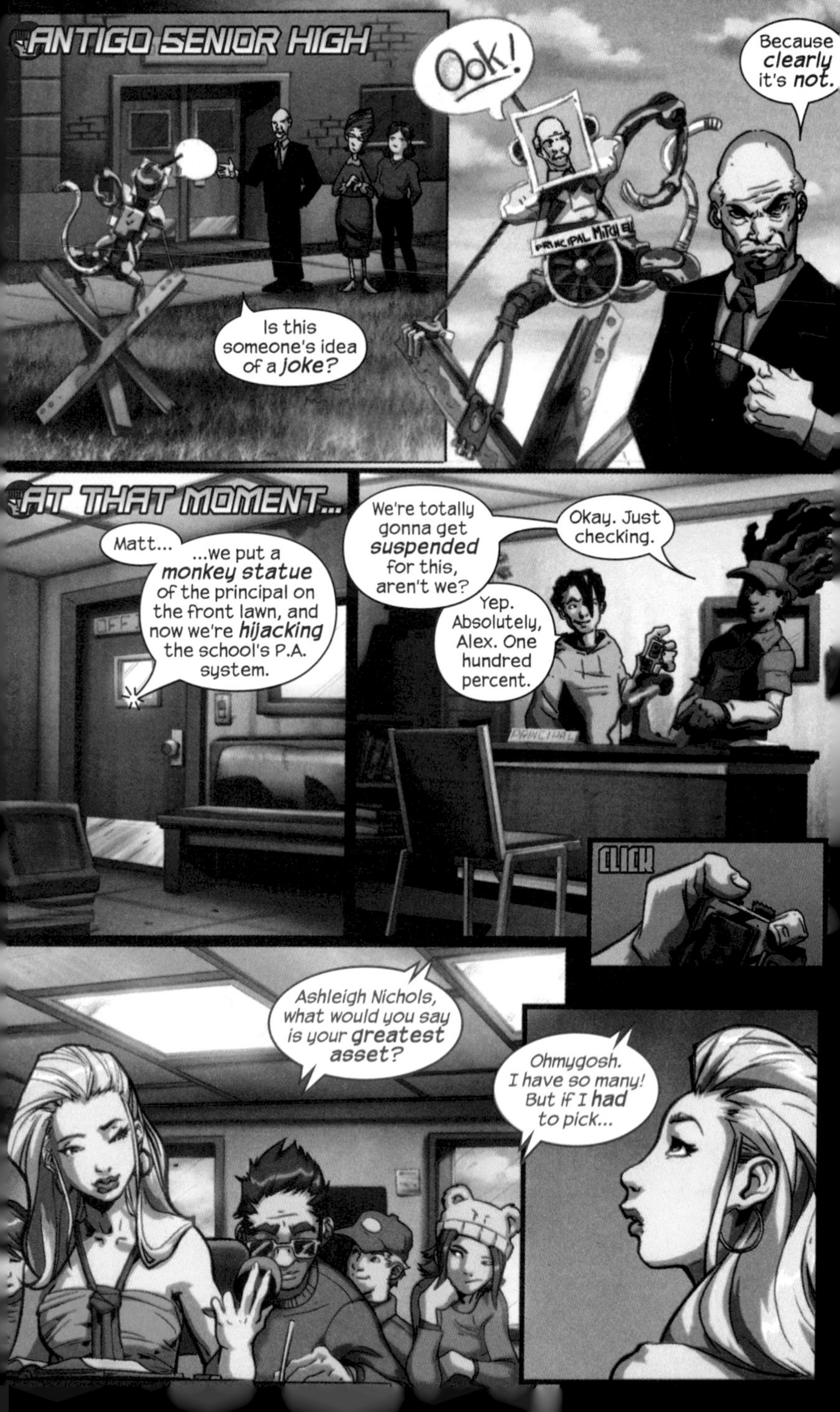

ANTIGO SENIOR HIGH
Is this someone's idea of a joke?
Ook!
PRINCIPAL MITCHELL
Because clearly it's not.
AT THAT MOMENT...
Matt...
...we put a monkey statue of the principal on the front lawn, and now we're hijacking the school's P.A. system.
We're totally gonna get suspended for this, aren't we?
Yep. Absolutely, Alex. One hundred percent.
Okay. Just checking.
PRINCIPAL
CLICK
Ashleigh Nichols, what would you say is your greatest asset?
Ohmygosh. I have so many! But if I had to pick...

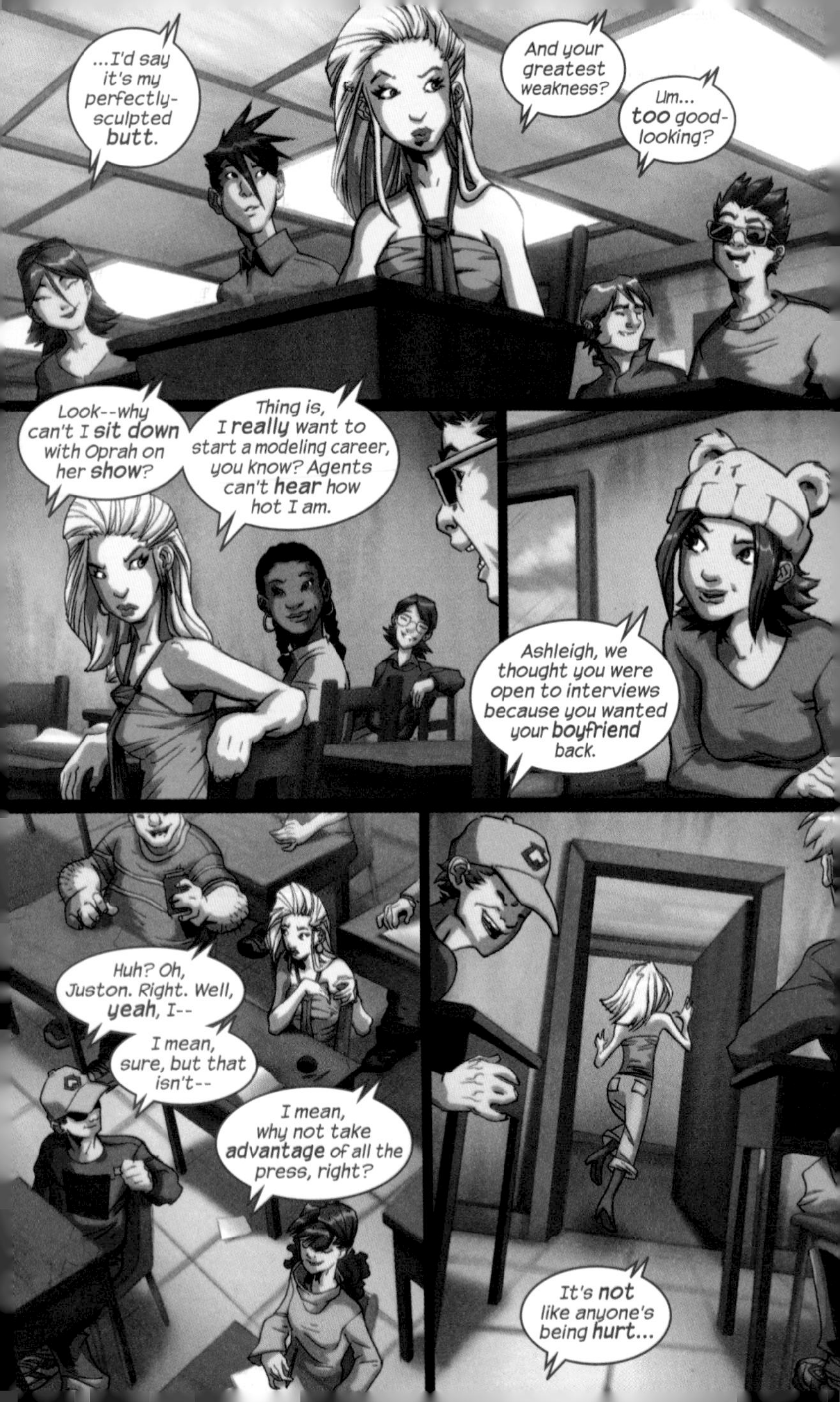
...I'd say it's my perfectly-sculpted butt.
And your greatest weakness?
Um... too good-looking?
Look--why can't I sit down with Oprah on her show?
Thing is, I really want to start a modeling career, you know? Agents can't hear how hot I am.
Ashleigh, we thought you were open to interviews because you wanted your boyfriend back.
Huh? Oh, Juston. Right. Well, yeah, I--
I mean, sure, but that isn't--
I mean, why not take advantage of all the press, right?
It's not like anyone's being hurt...

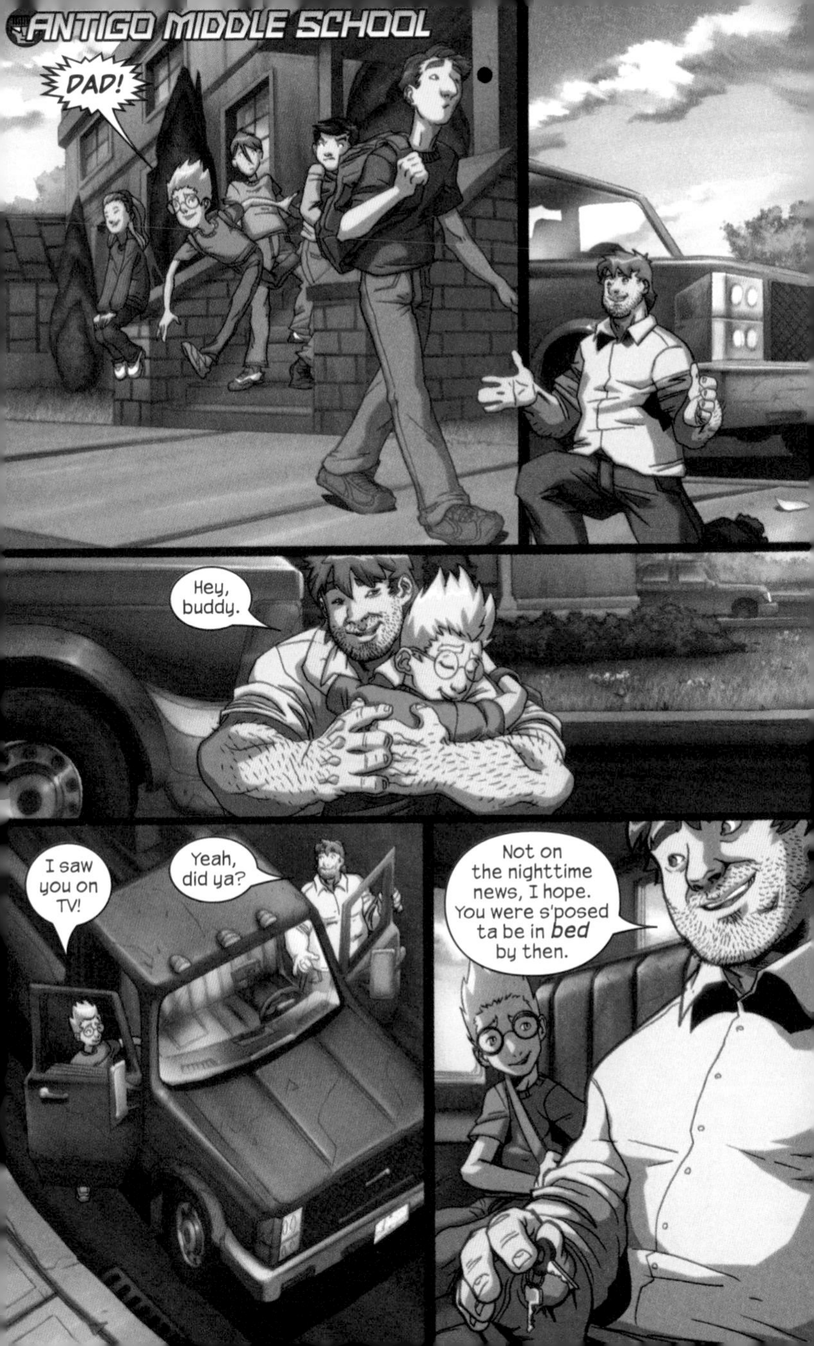
ANTIGO MIDDLE SCHOOL
DAD!
Hey, buddy.
I saw you on TV!
Yeah, did ya?
Not on the nighttime news, I hope. You were s'posed ta be in *bed* by then.

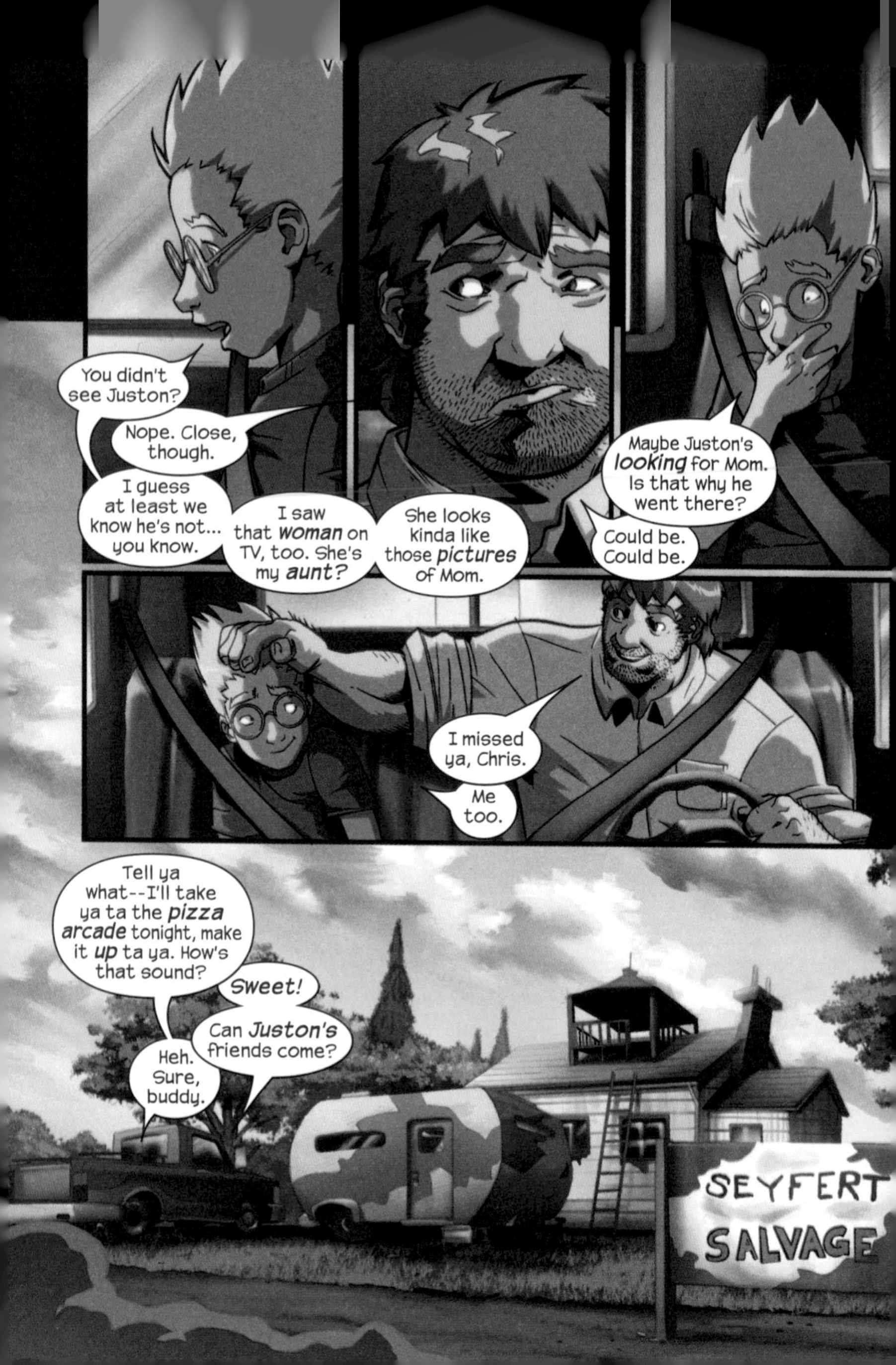
You didn't see Juston?
Nope. Close, though.
I guess at least we know he's not... you know.
I saw that woman on TV, too. She's my aunt?
She looks kinda like those pictures of Mom.
Maybe Juston's looking for Mom. Is that why he went there?
Could be. Could be.
I missed ya, Chris.
Me too.
Tell ya what--I'll take ya ta the pizza arcade tonight, make it up ta ya. How's that sound?
Sweet!
Can Juston's friends come?
Heh. Sure, buddy.
SEYFERT SALVAGE

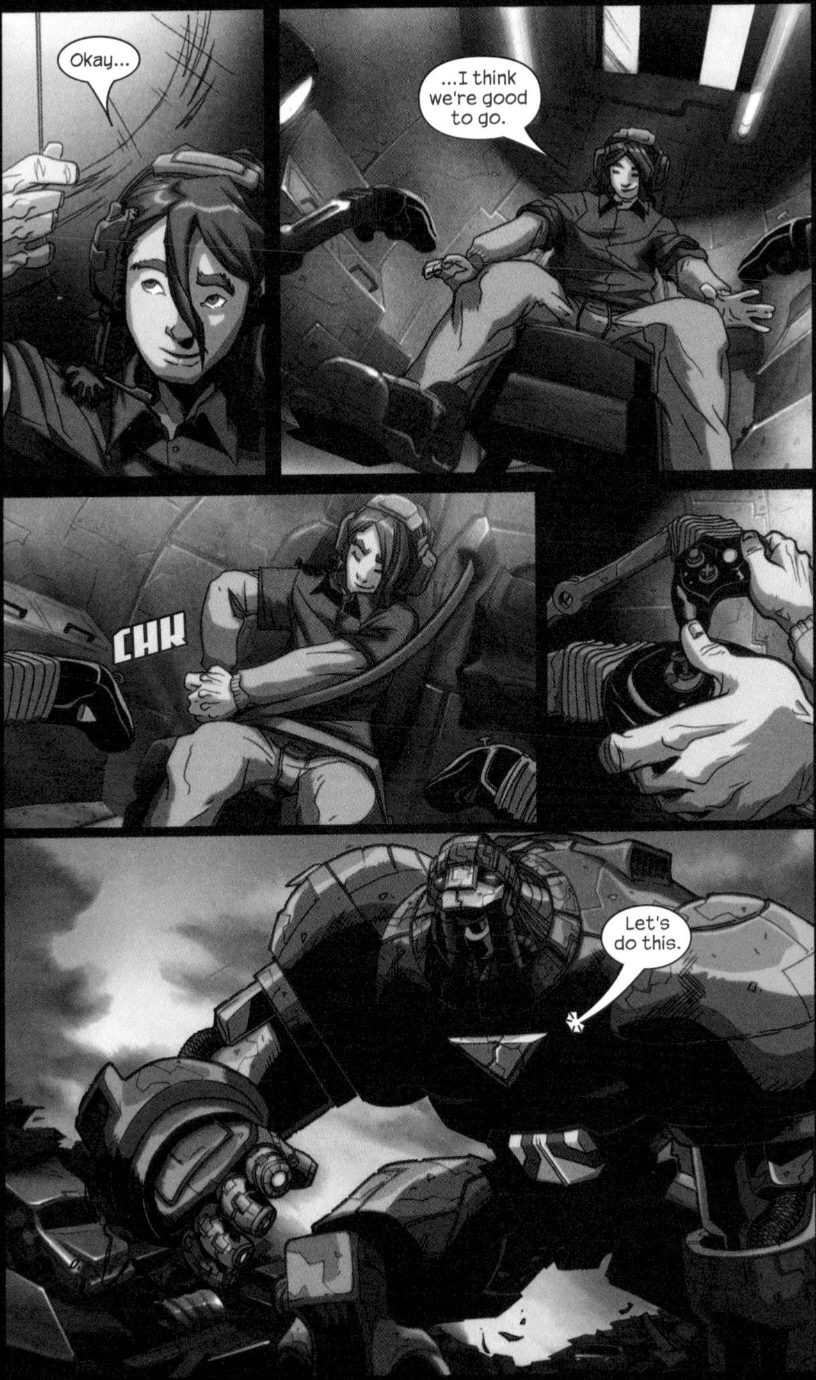

Okay...
...I think we're good to go.
CHK
Let's do this.

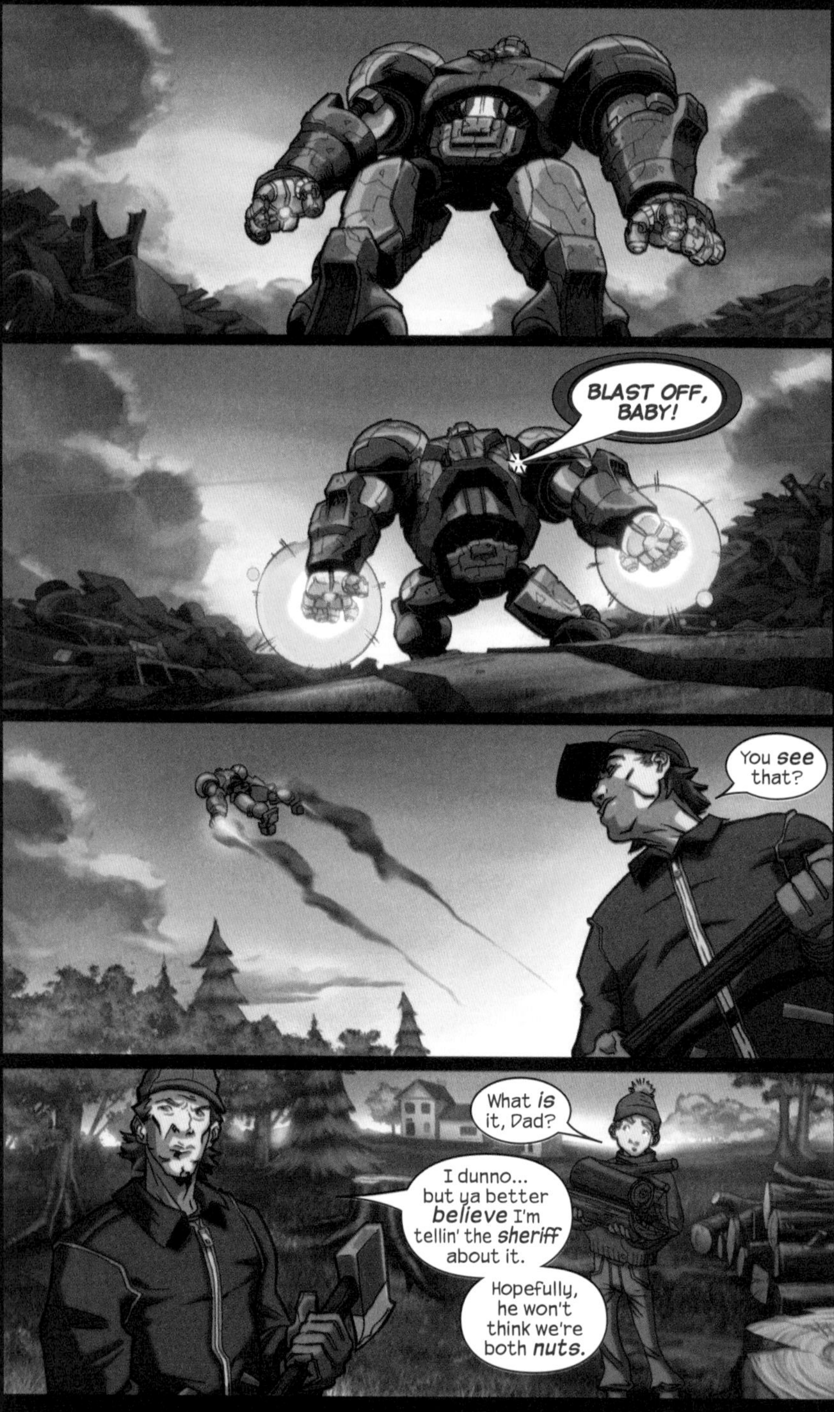
BLAST OFF, BABY!
You *see* that?
What *is* it, Dad?
I dunno... but ya better *believe* I'm tellin' the *sheriff* about it.
Hopefully, he won't think we're both *nuts.*

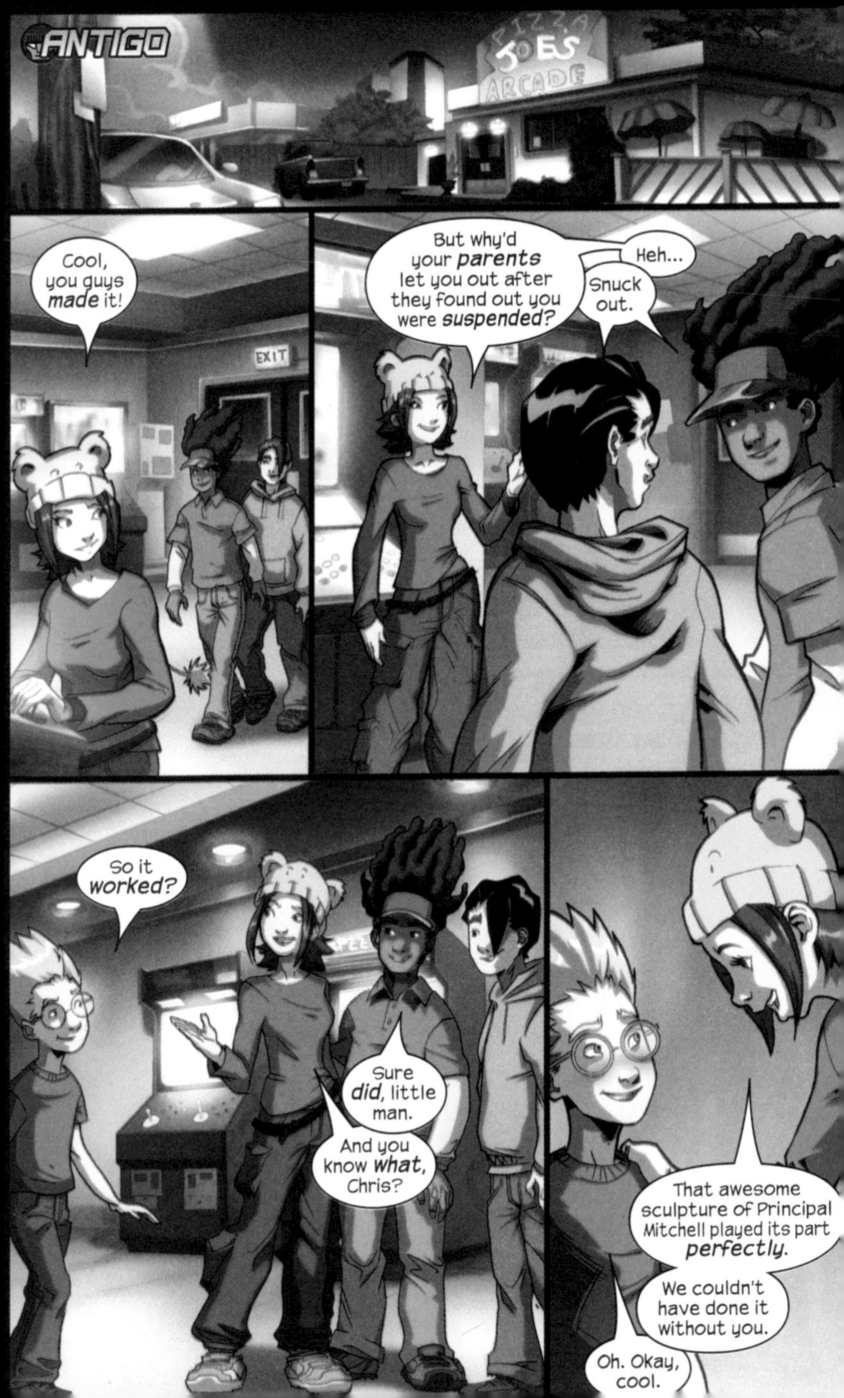
ANTIGO
PIZZA JOE'S ARCADE
Cool, you guys made it!
EXIT
But why'd your parents let you out after they found out you were suspended?
Snuck out.
Heh...
So it worked?
Sure did, little man.
And you know what, Chris?
That awesome sculpture of Principal Mitchell played its part perfectly.
We couldn't have done it without you.
Oh. Okay, cool.

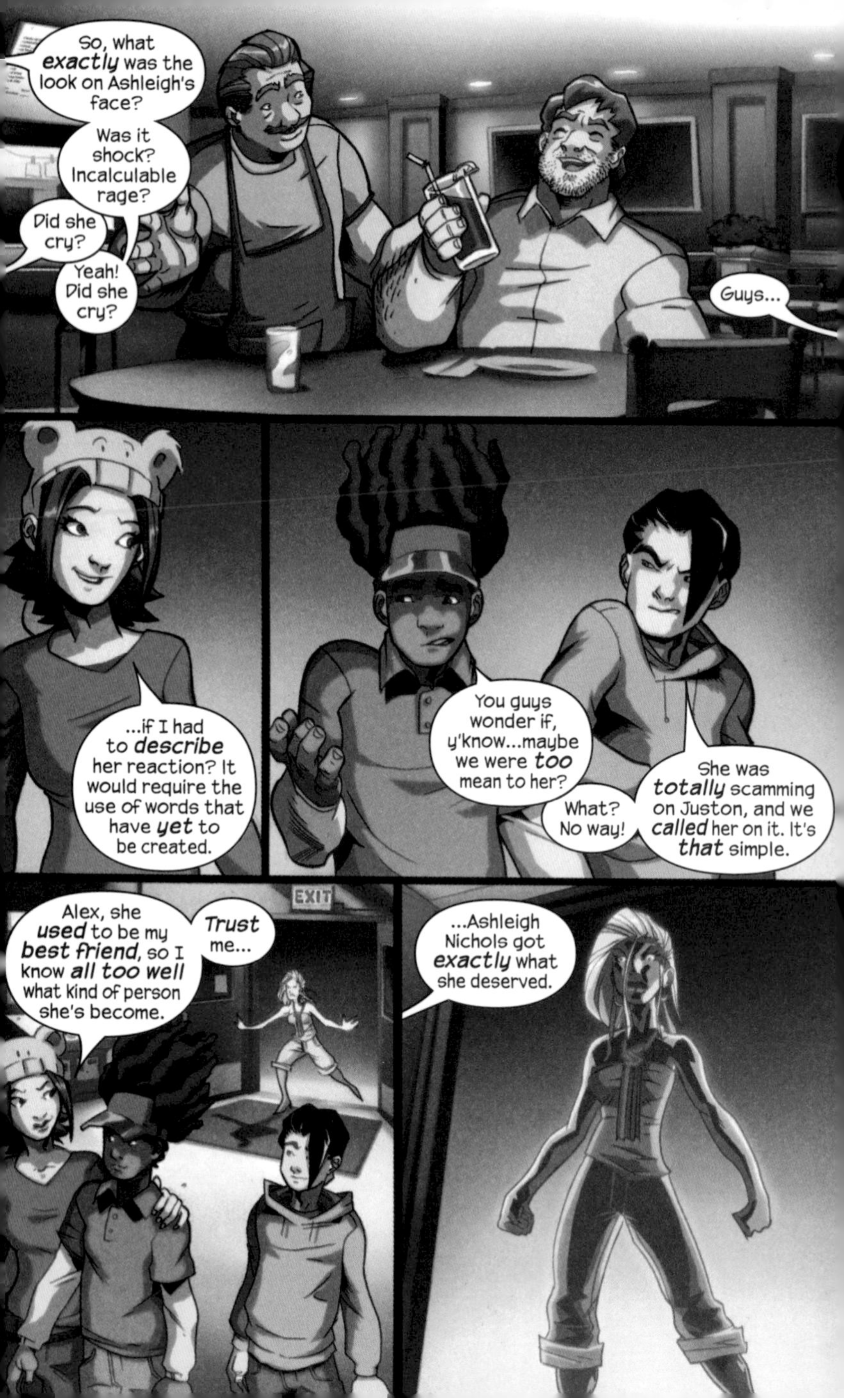
So, what *exactly* was the look on Ashleigh's face?
Was it shock? Incalculable rage?
Did she cry?
Yeah! Did she cry?
Guys...
...if I had to *describe* her reaction? It would require the use of words that have *yet* to be created.
You guys wonder if, y'know...maybe we were *too* mean to her?
What? No way!
She was *totally* scamming on Juston, and we *called* her on it. It's *that* simple.
EXIT
Alex, she *used* to be my *best friend*, so I know *all too well* what kind of person she's become.
Trust me...
...Ashleigh Nichols got *exactly* what she deserved.

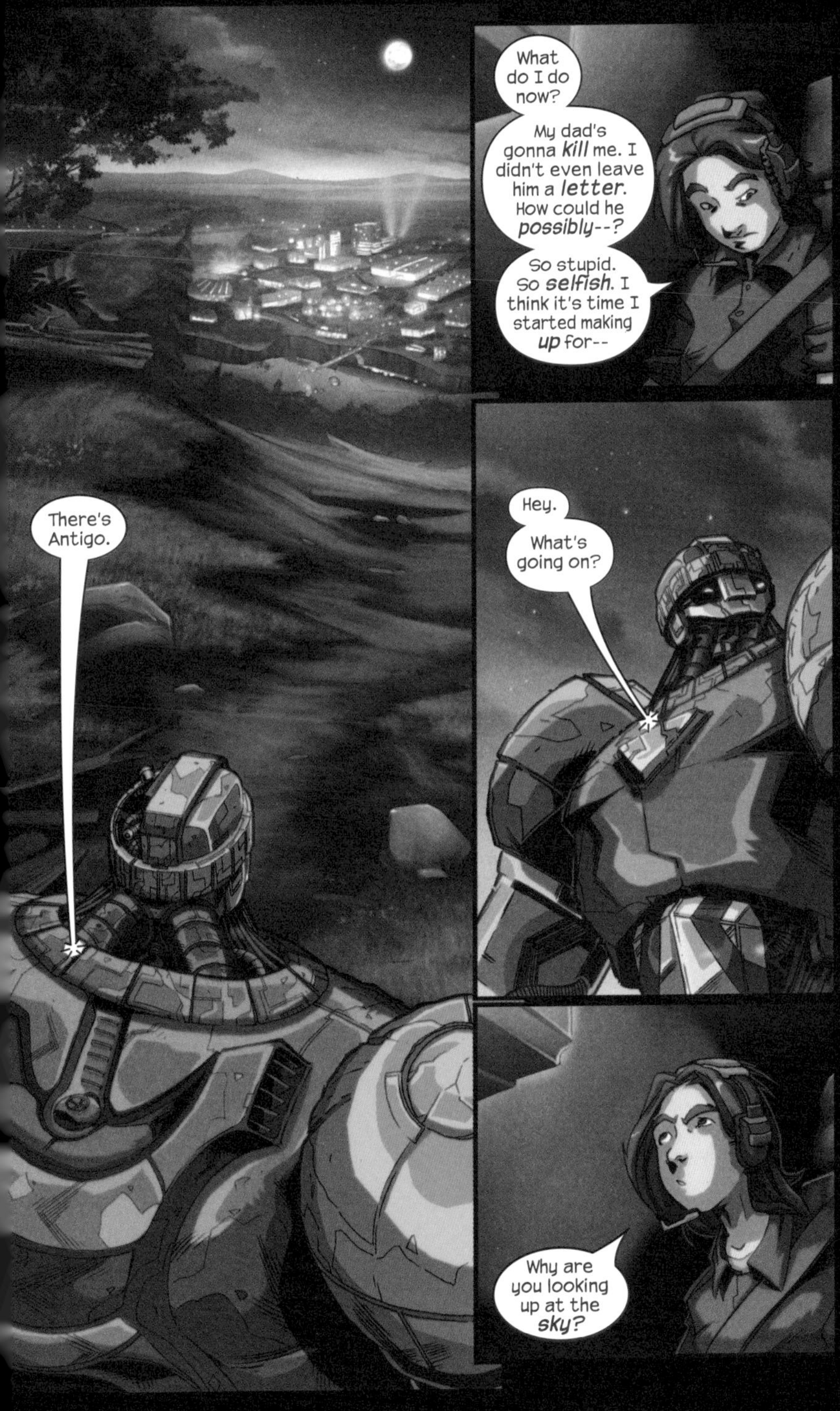
What do I do now?
My dad's gonna kill me. I didn't even leave him a letter. How could he possibly--?
So stupid. So selfish. I think it's time I started making up for--
There's Antigo.
Hey.
What's going on?
Why are you looking up at the sky?

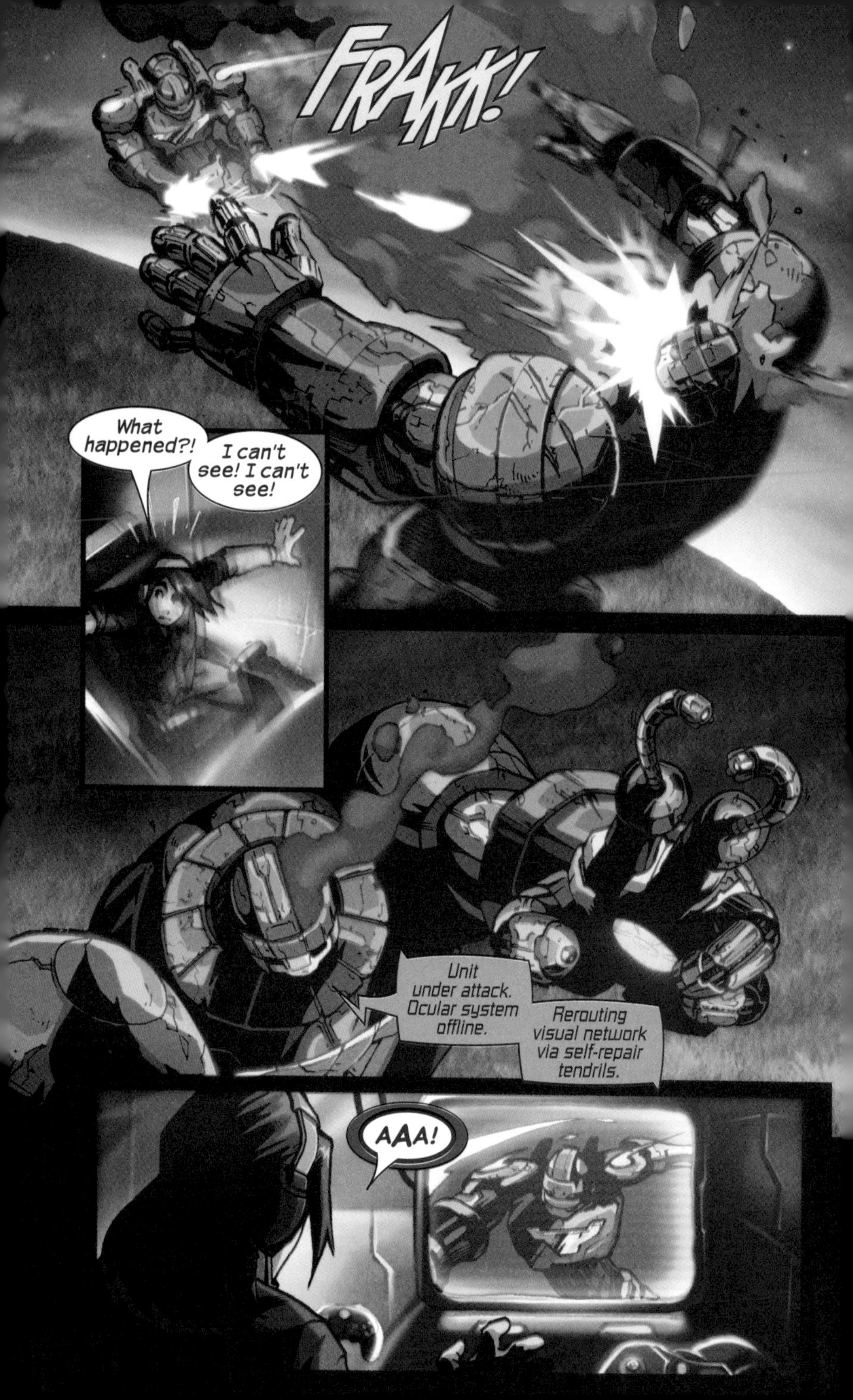
FRAKK!
What happened?!
I can't see! I can't see!
Unit under attack. Ocular system offline.
Rerouting visual network via self-repair tendrils.
AAA!

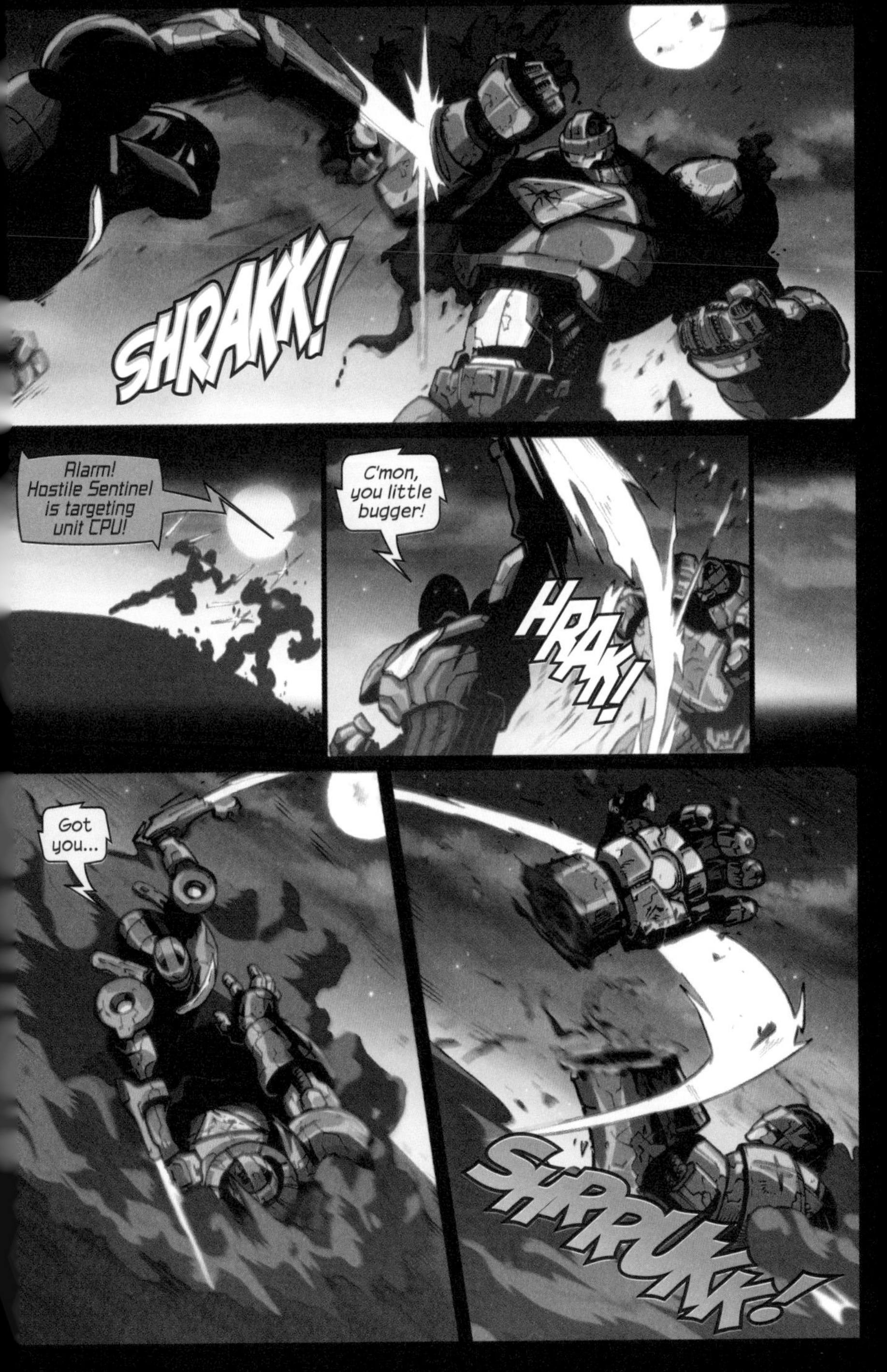
SHRAKK!
Alarm! Hostile Sentinel is targeting unit CPU!
C'mon, you little bugger!
HRAK!
Got you...
SHRUNK!

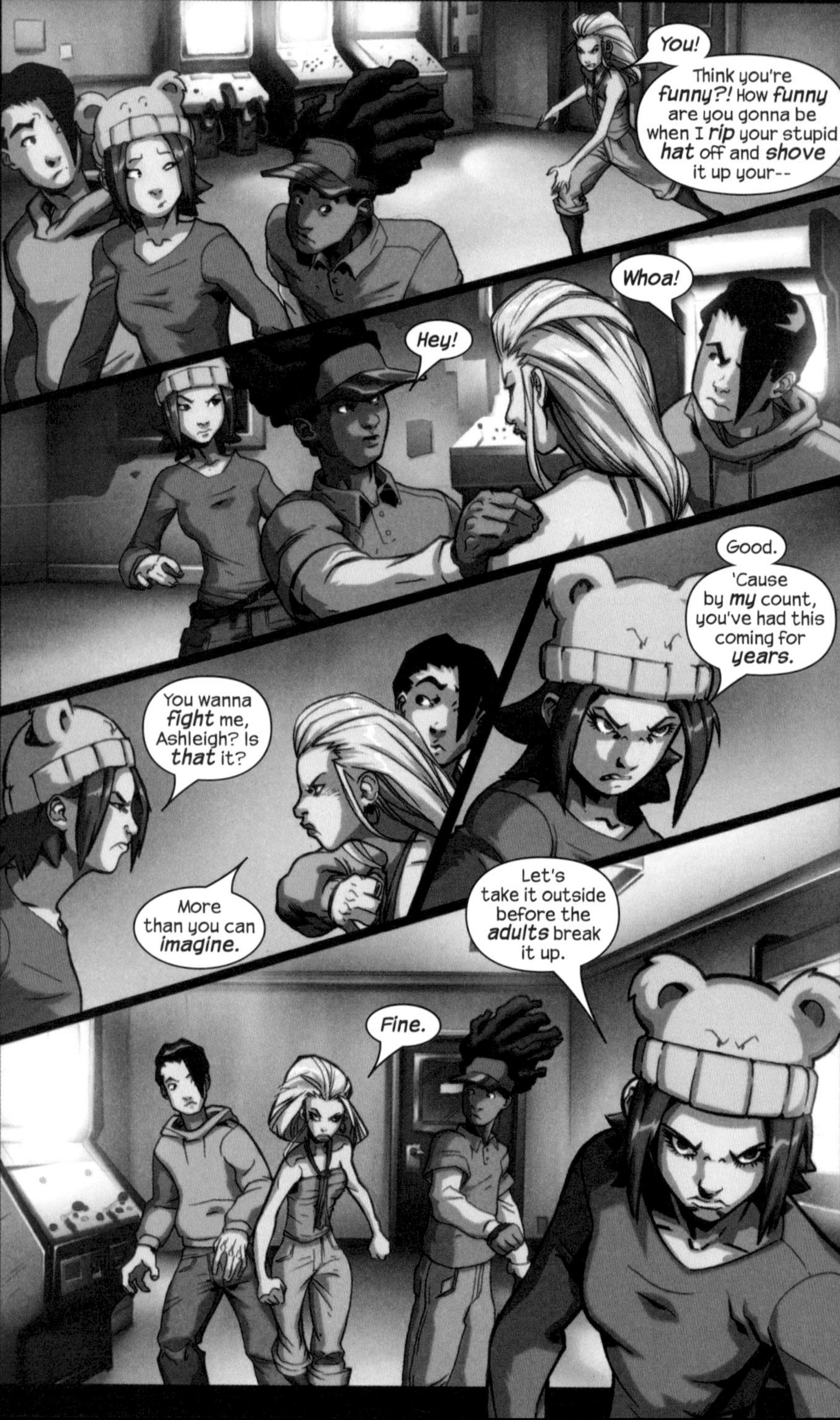
You!
Think you're funny?! How funny are you gonna be when I rip your stupid hat off and shove it up your--
Whoa!
Hey!
Good.
'Cause by my count, you've had this coming for years.
You wanna fight me, Ashleigh? Is that it?
More than you can imagine.
Let's take it outside before the adults break it up.
Fine.

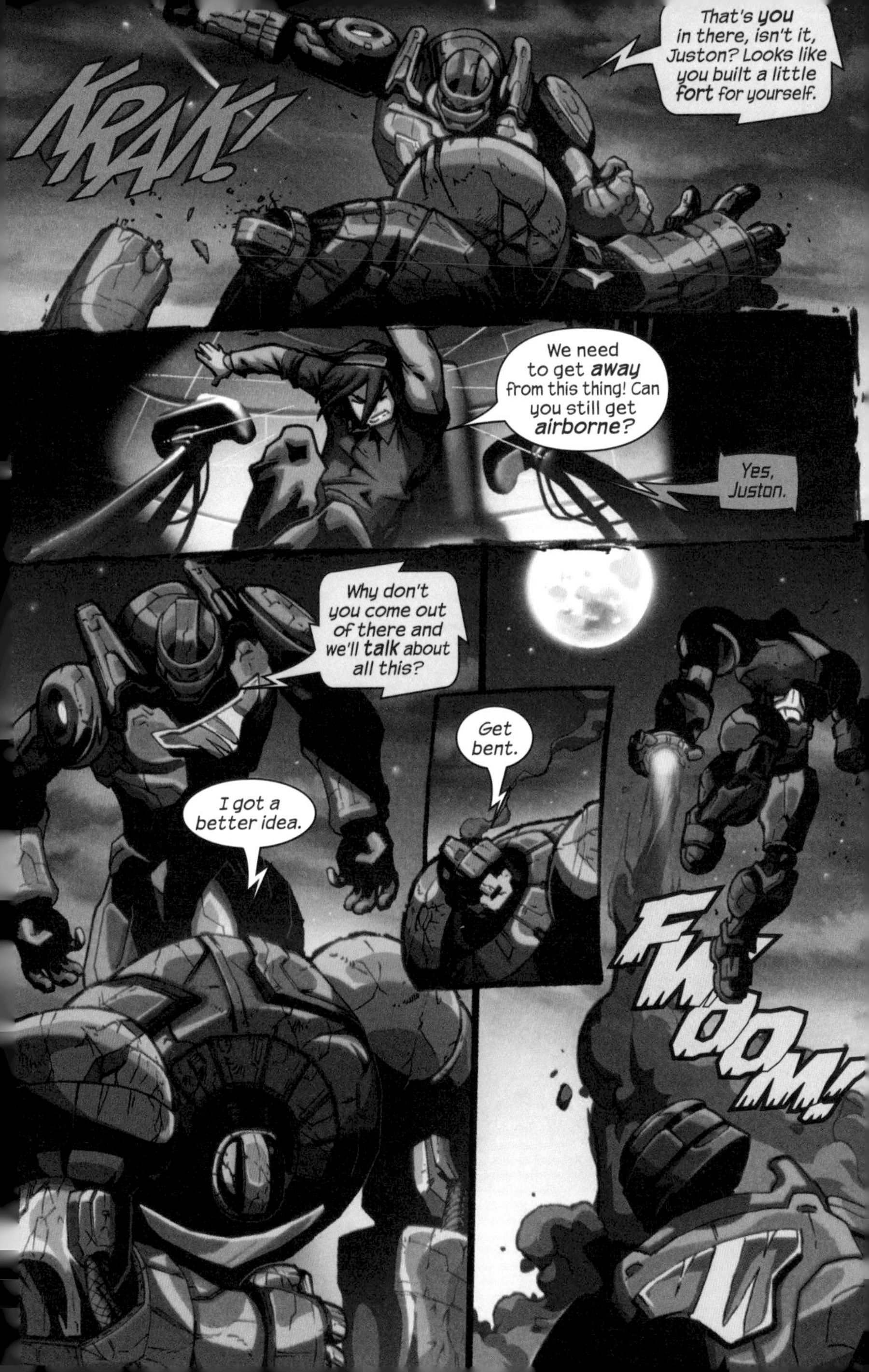
KRAK!
That's you in there, isn't it, Juston? Looks like you built a little fort for yourself.
We need to get away from this thing! Can you still get airborne?
Yes, Juston.
Why don't you come out of there and we'll talk about all this?
I got a better idea.
Get bent.
FWOOM!

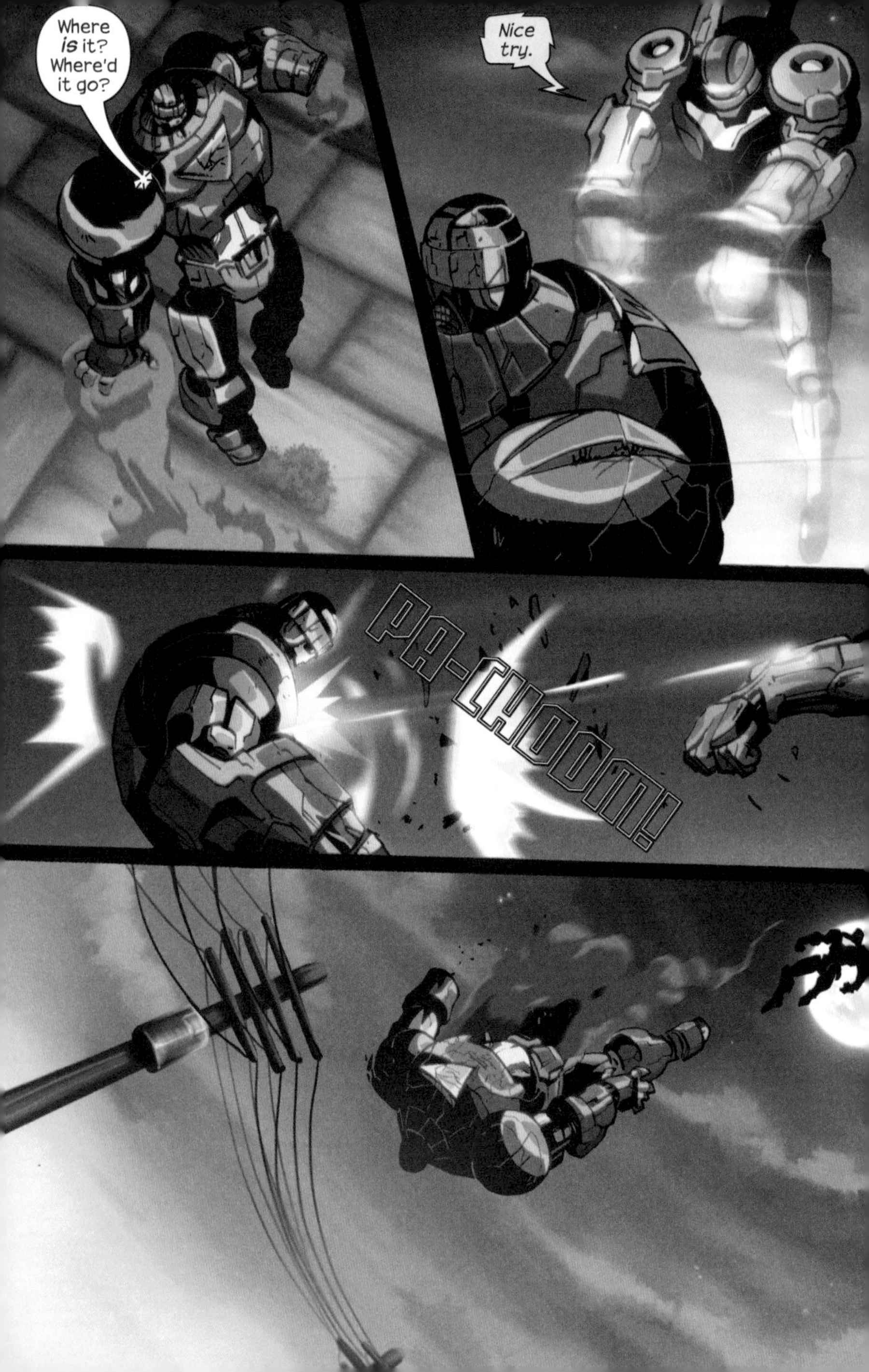
Where *is* it? Where'd it go?
Nice try.
PA-CHOOM!

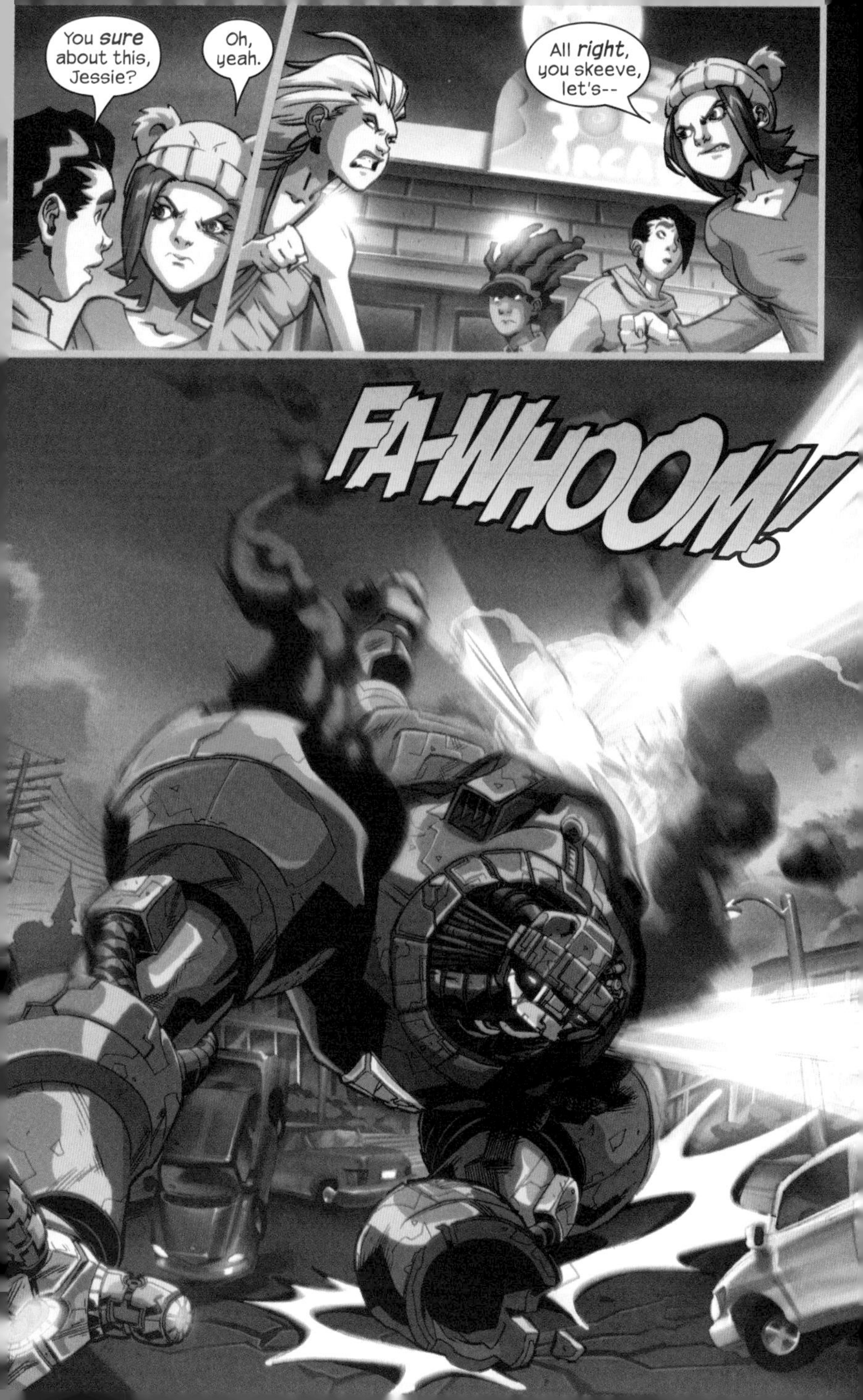
You *sure* about this, Jessie?
Oh, yeah.
All *right*, you skeeve, let's--
FA-WHOOM!

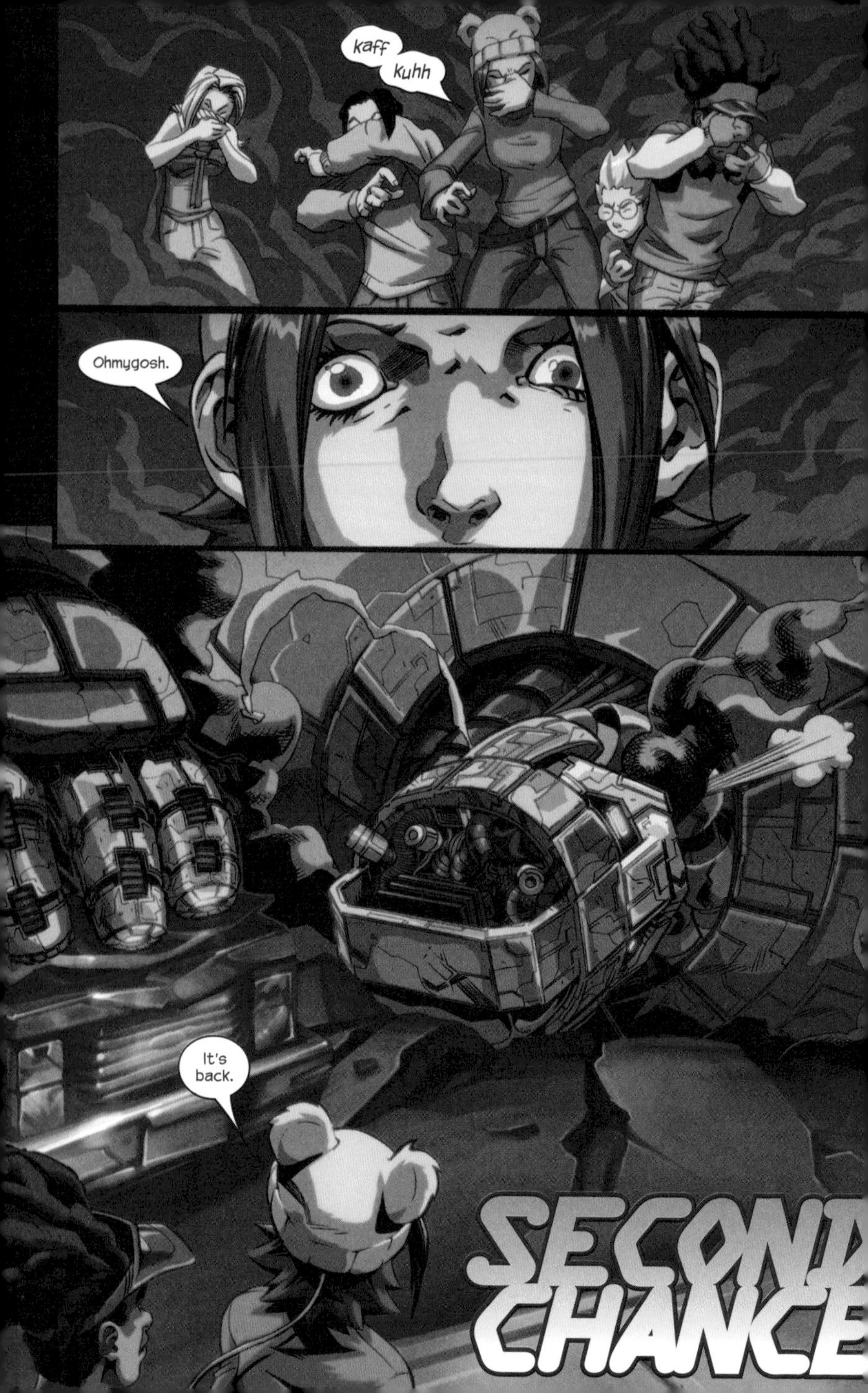
kaff
kuhh
Ohmygosh.
It's back.
SECOND CHANCE

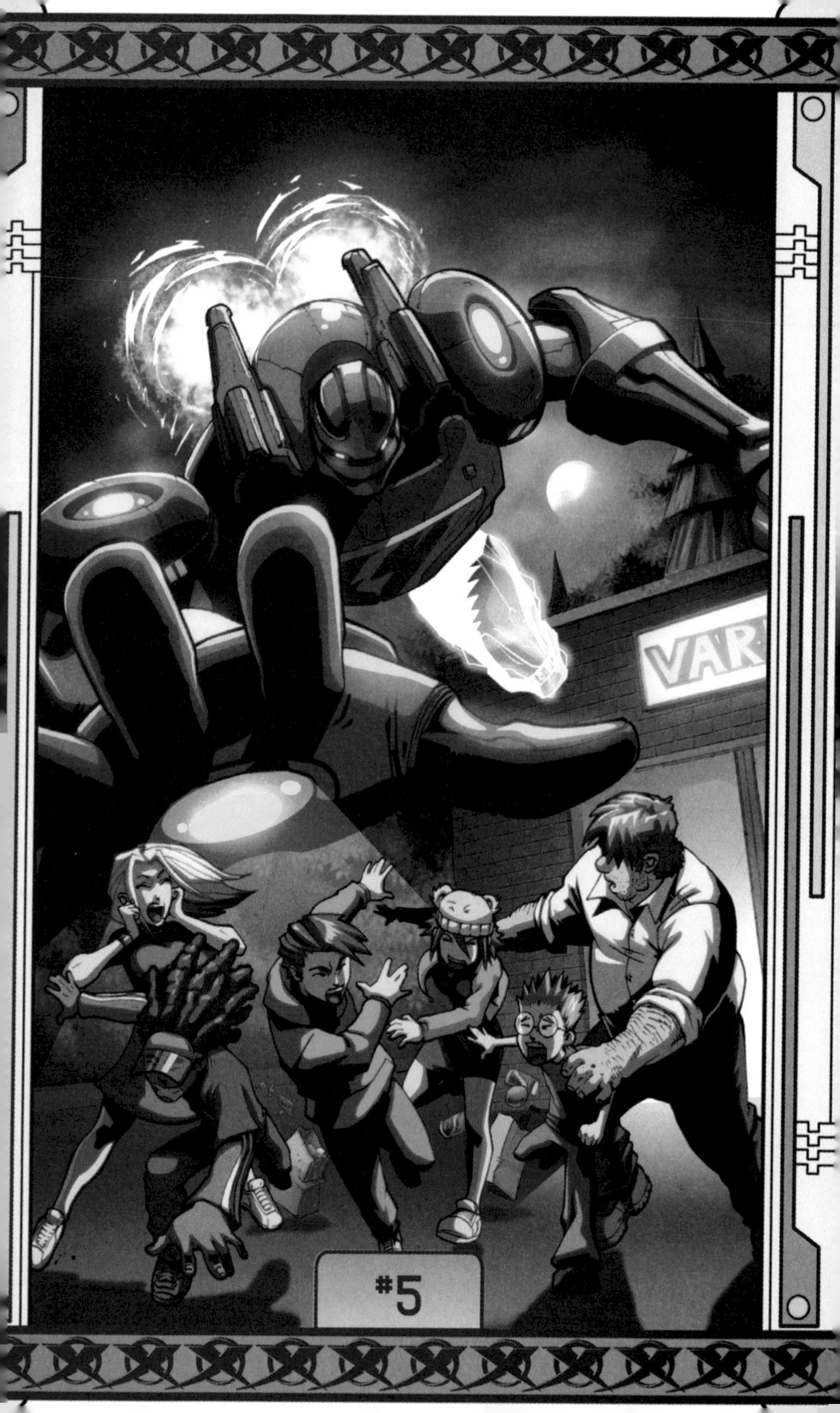
VAR
#5

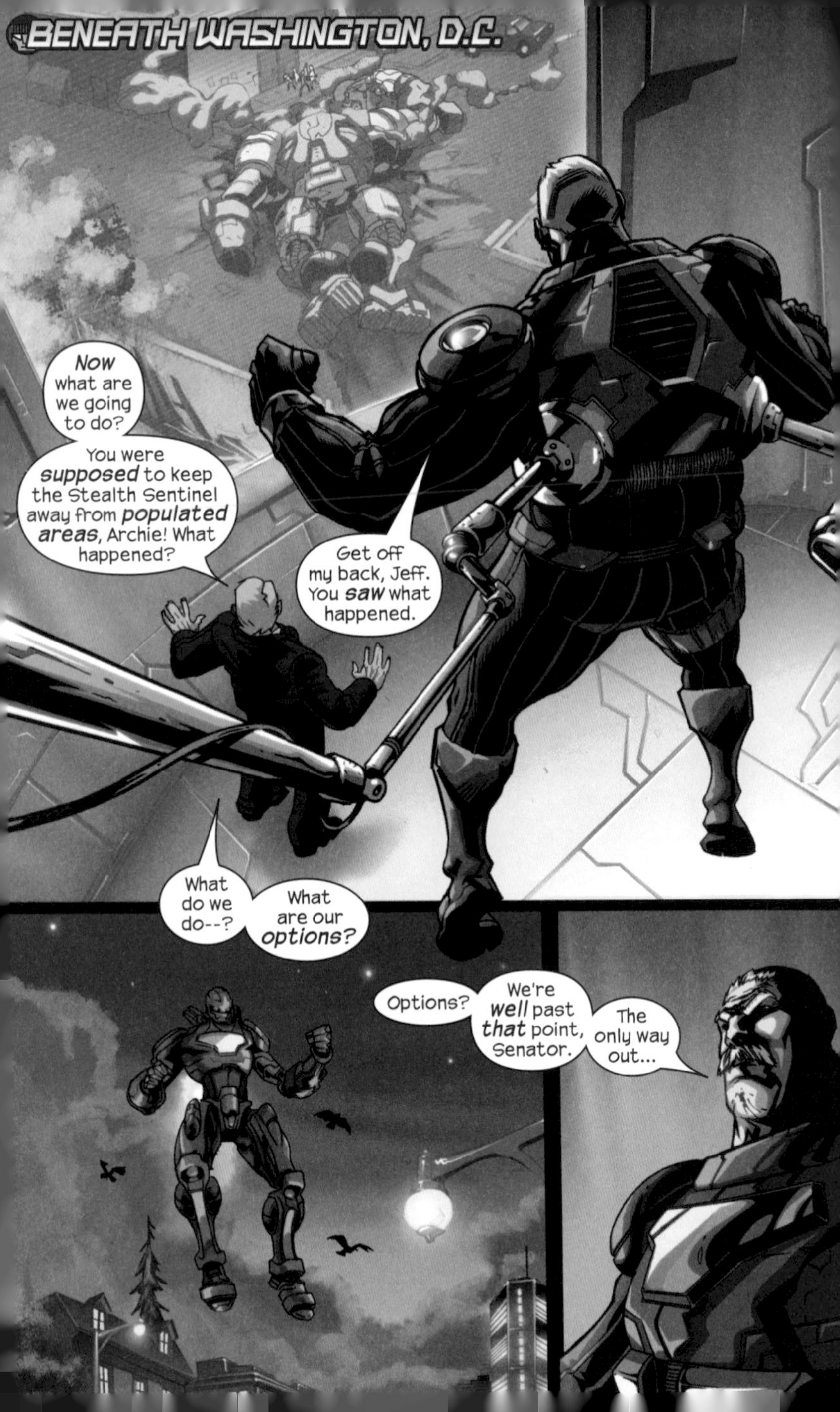
BENEATH WASHINGTON, D.C.
Now what are we going to do?
You were supposed to keep the Stealth Sentinel away from populated areas, Archie! What happened?
Get off my back, Jeff. You saw what happened.
What do we do--?
What are our options?
Options?
We're well past that point, Senator.
The only way out...

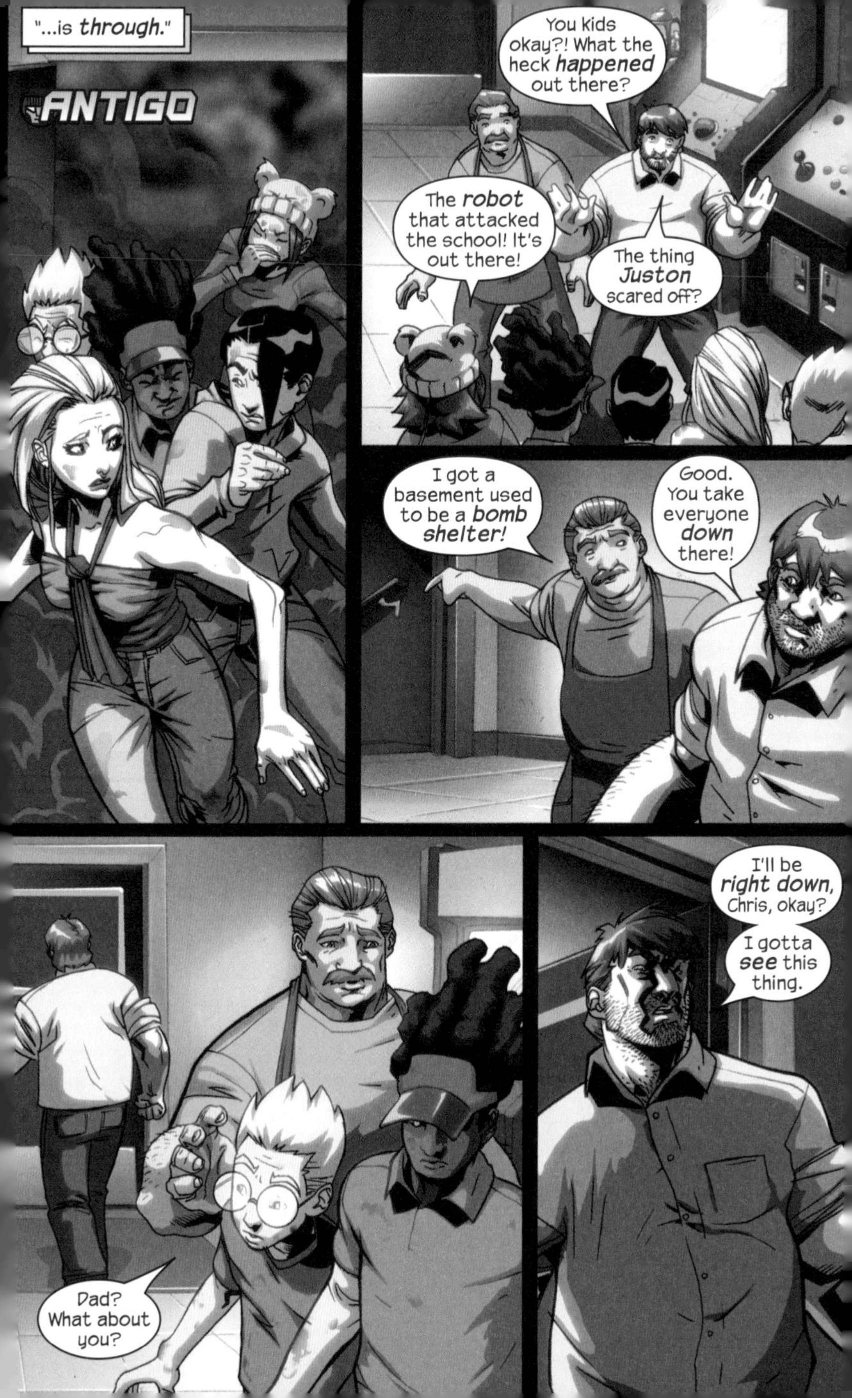
"...is through."
ANTIGO
You kids okay?! What the heck happened out there?
The robot that attacked the school! It's out there!
The thing Juston scared off?
I got a basement used to be a bomb shelter!
Good. You take everyone down there!
Dad? What about you?
I'll be right down, Chris, okay?
I gotta see this thing.

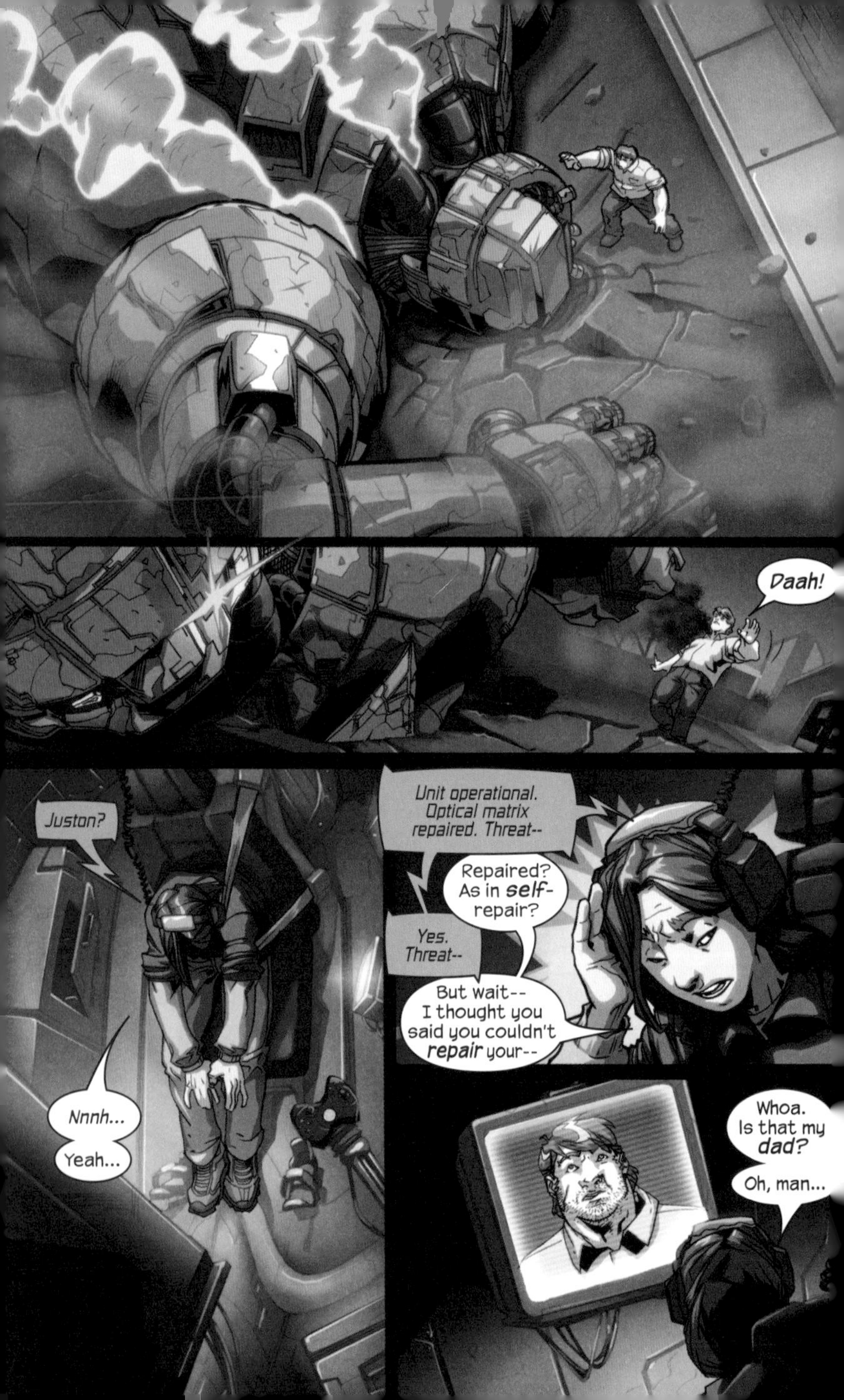
Daah!
Juston?
Nnnh...
Yeah...
Unit operational. Optical matrix repaired. Threat--
Repaired? As in *self*-repair?
Yes. Threat--
But wait-- I thought you said you couldn't *repair* your--
Whoa. Is that my *dad?*
Oh, man...

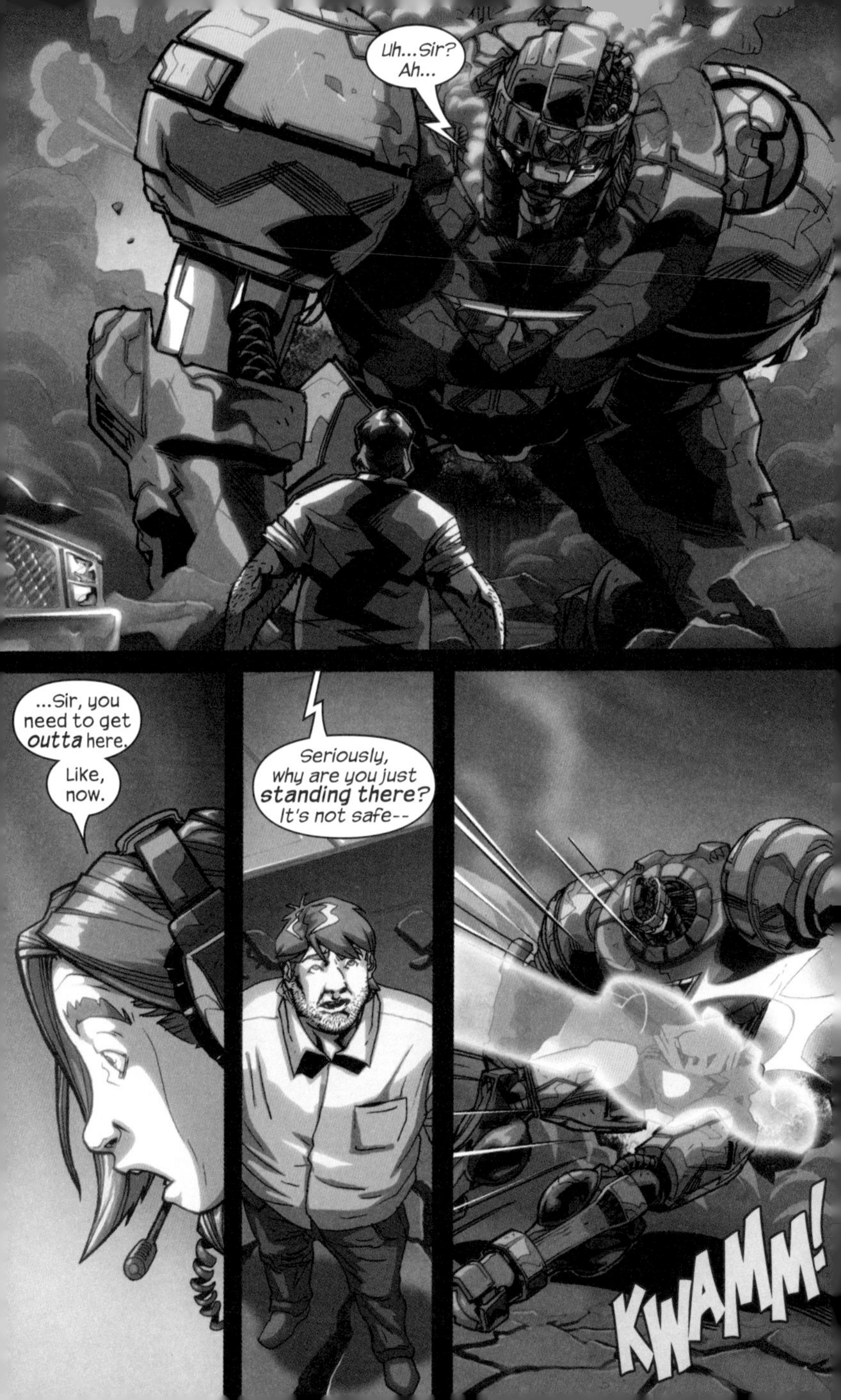
Uh...Sir? Ah...
...Sir, you need to get outta here.
Like, now.
Seriously, why are you just standing there? It's not safe--
KWAMM!

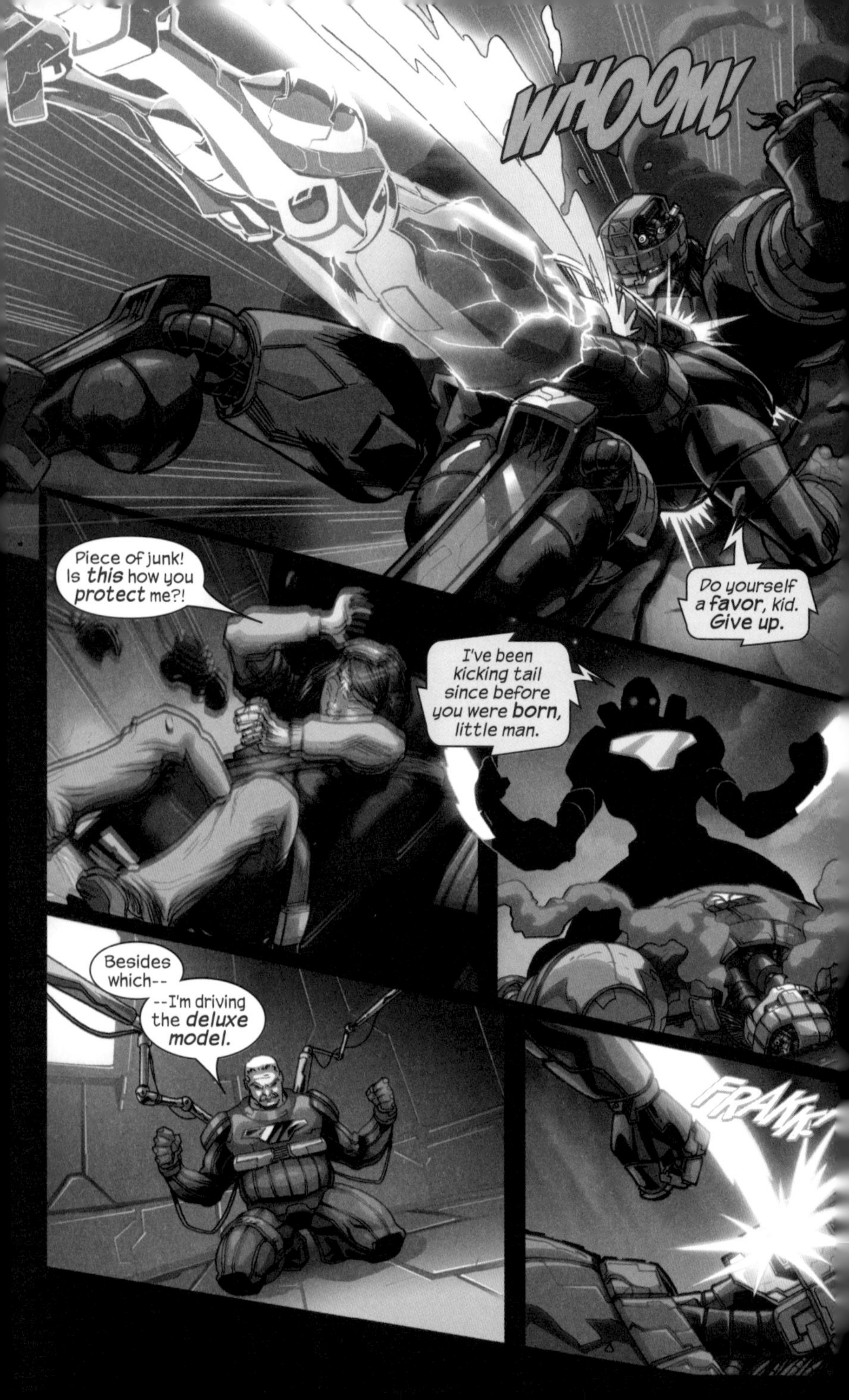
WHOOM!
Do yourself a favor, kid. Give up.
Piece of junk! Is this how you protect me?!
I've been kicking tail since before you were born, little man.
Besides which--
--I'm driving the deluxe model.
FRAKK!

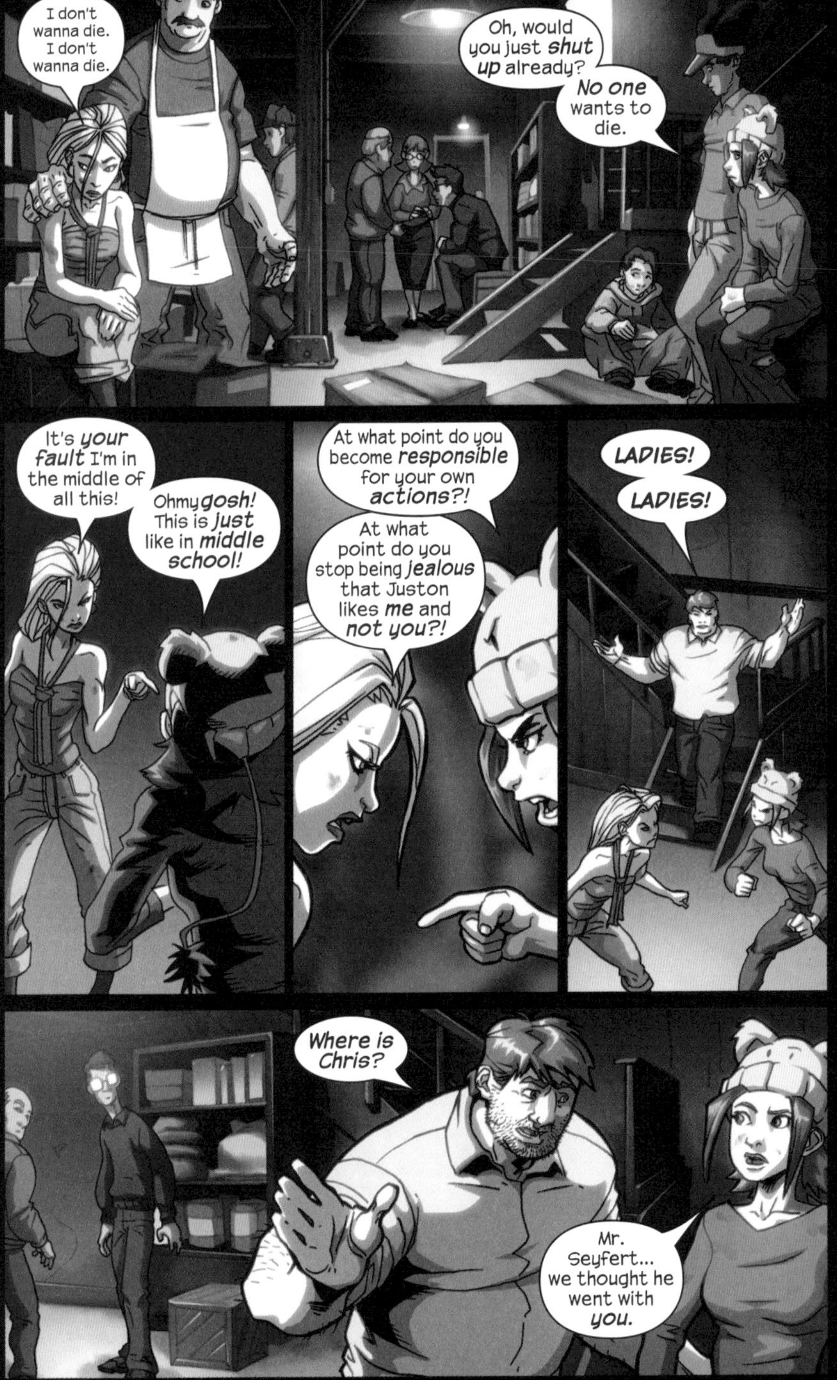
I don't wanna die. I don't wanna die.
Oh, would you just shut up already?
No one wants to die.
It's your fault I'm in the middle of all this!
Ohmygosh! This is just like in middle school!
At what point do you become responsible for your own actions?!
At what point do you stop being jealous that Juston likes me and not you?!
LADIES!
LADIES!
Where is Chris?
Mr. Seyfert... we thought he went with you.

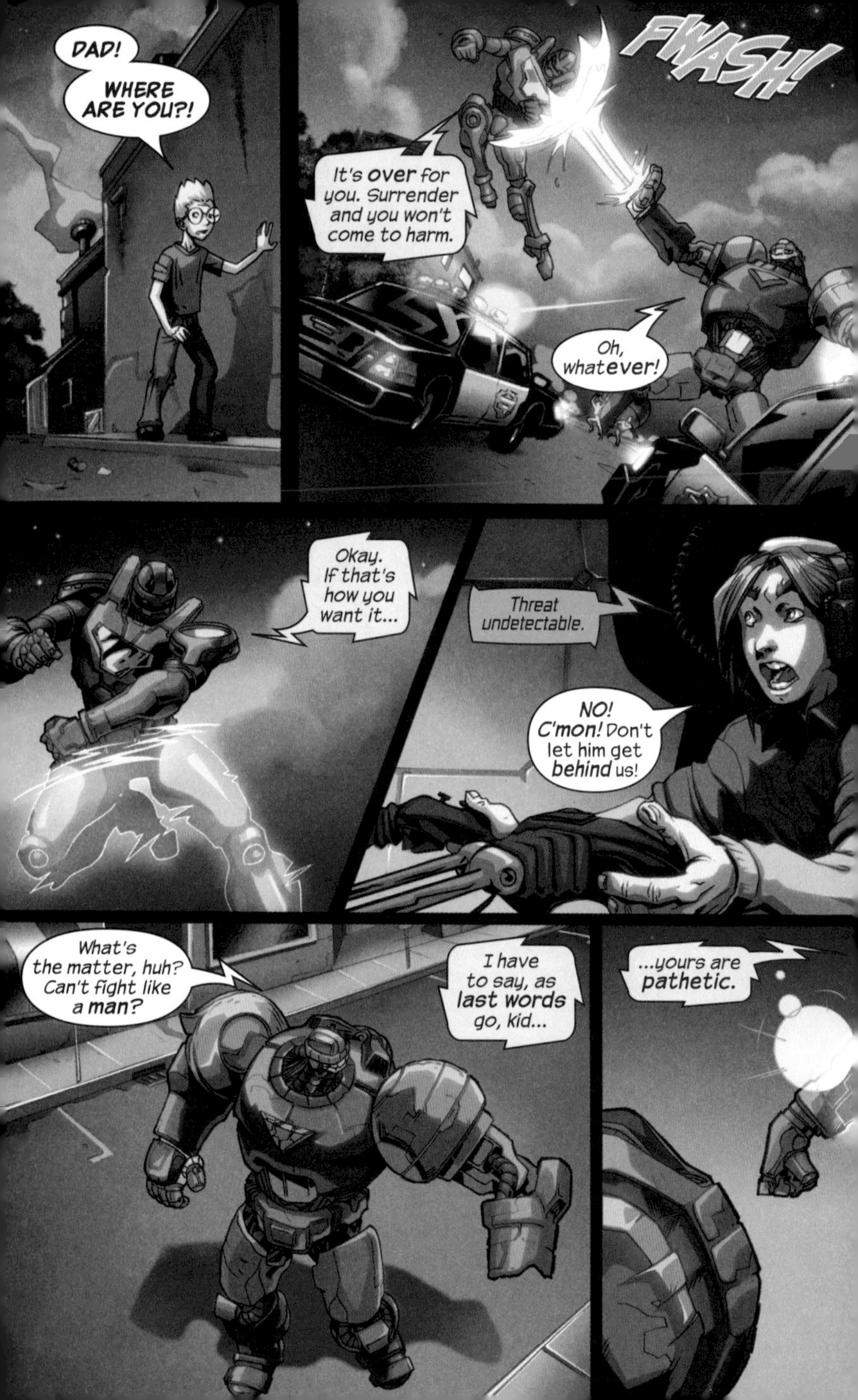
DAD!
WHERE ARE YOU?!
FWASH!
It's over for you. Surrender and you won't come to harm.
Oh, whatever!
Okay. If that's how you want it...
Threat undetectable.
NO! C'mon! Don't let him get behind us!
What's the matter, huh? Can't fight like a man?
I have to say, as last words go, kid...
...yours are pathetic.

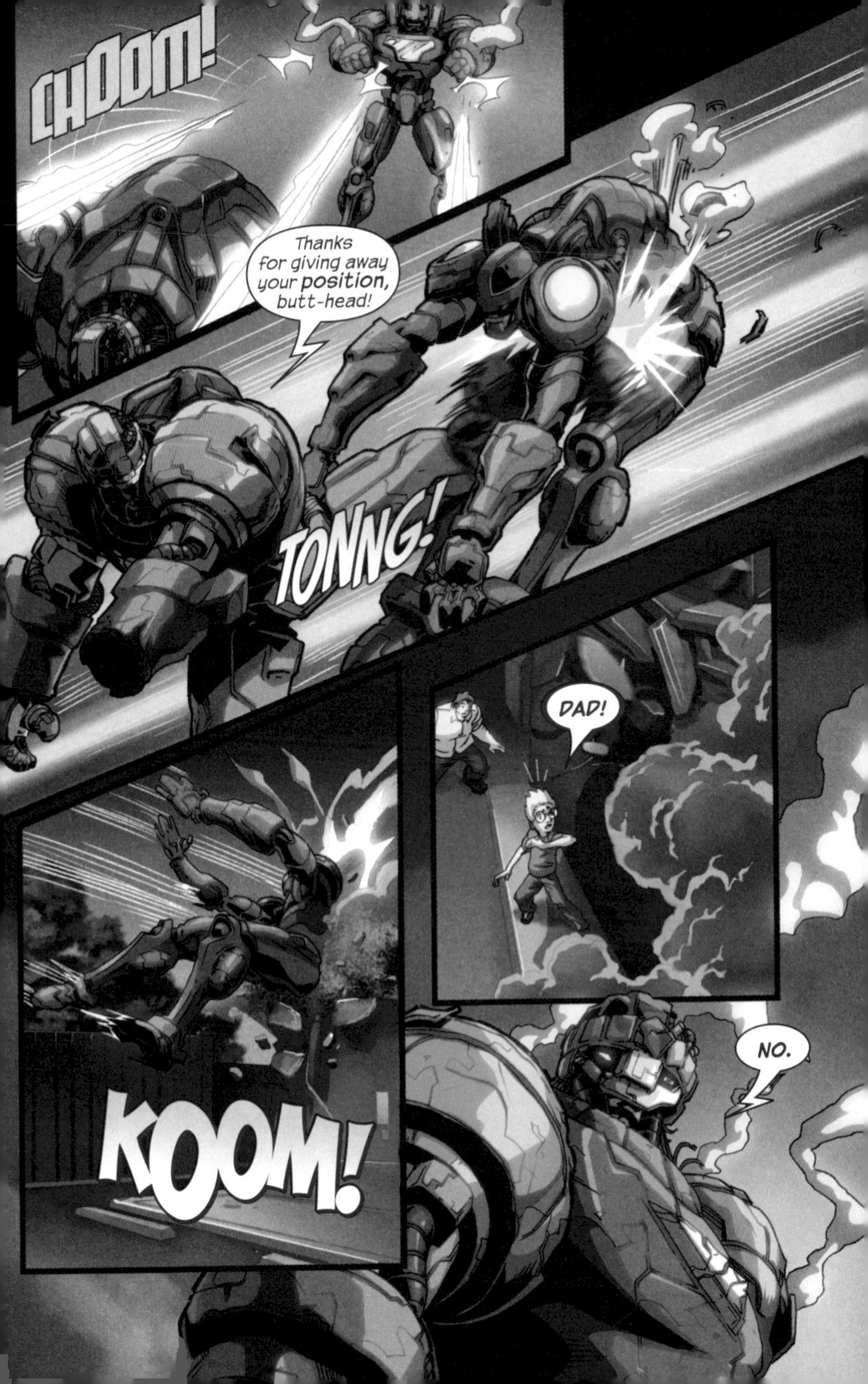
CHOOM!
Thanks for giving away your position, butt-head!
TONNG!
DAD!
KOOM!
NO.

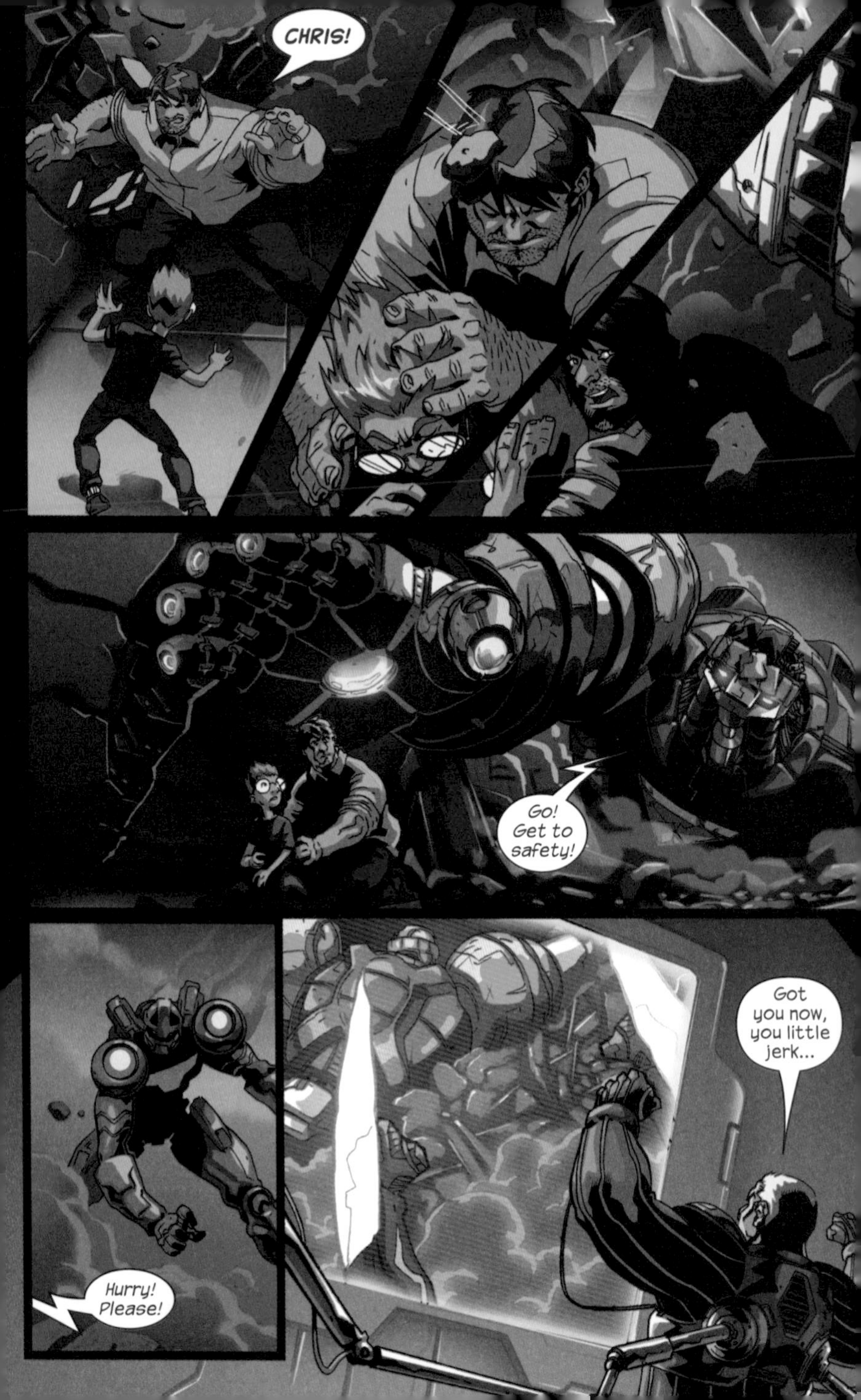
CHRIS!
Go! Get to safety!
Hurry! Please!
Got you now, you little jerk...

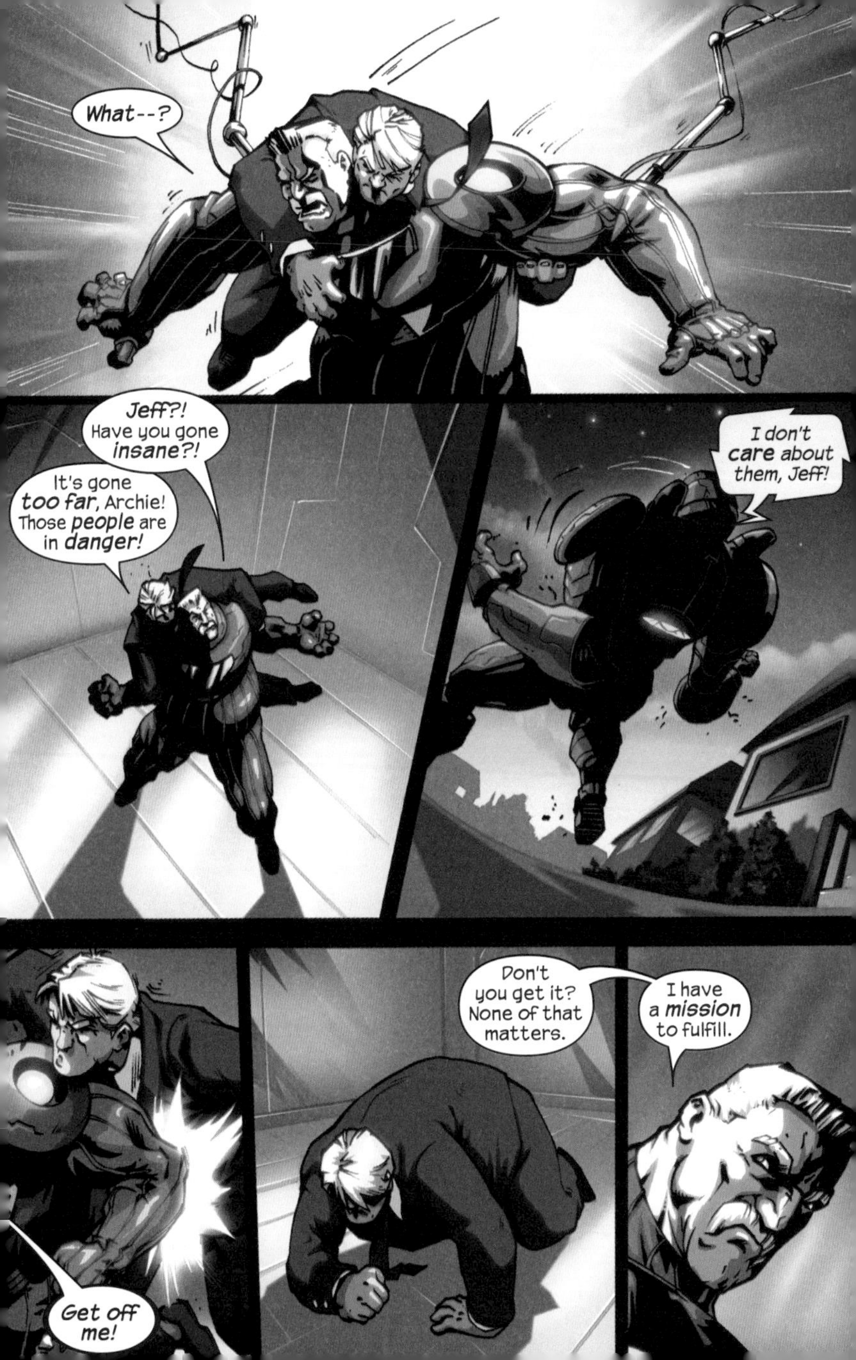
What--?
Jeff?! Have you gone insane?!
It's gone too far, Archie! Those people are in danger!
I don't care about them, Jeff!
Get off me!
Don't you get it? None of that matters.
I have a mission to fulfill.

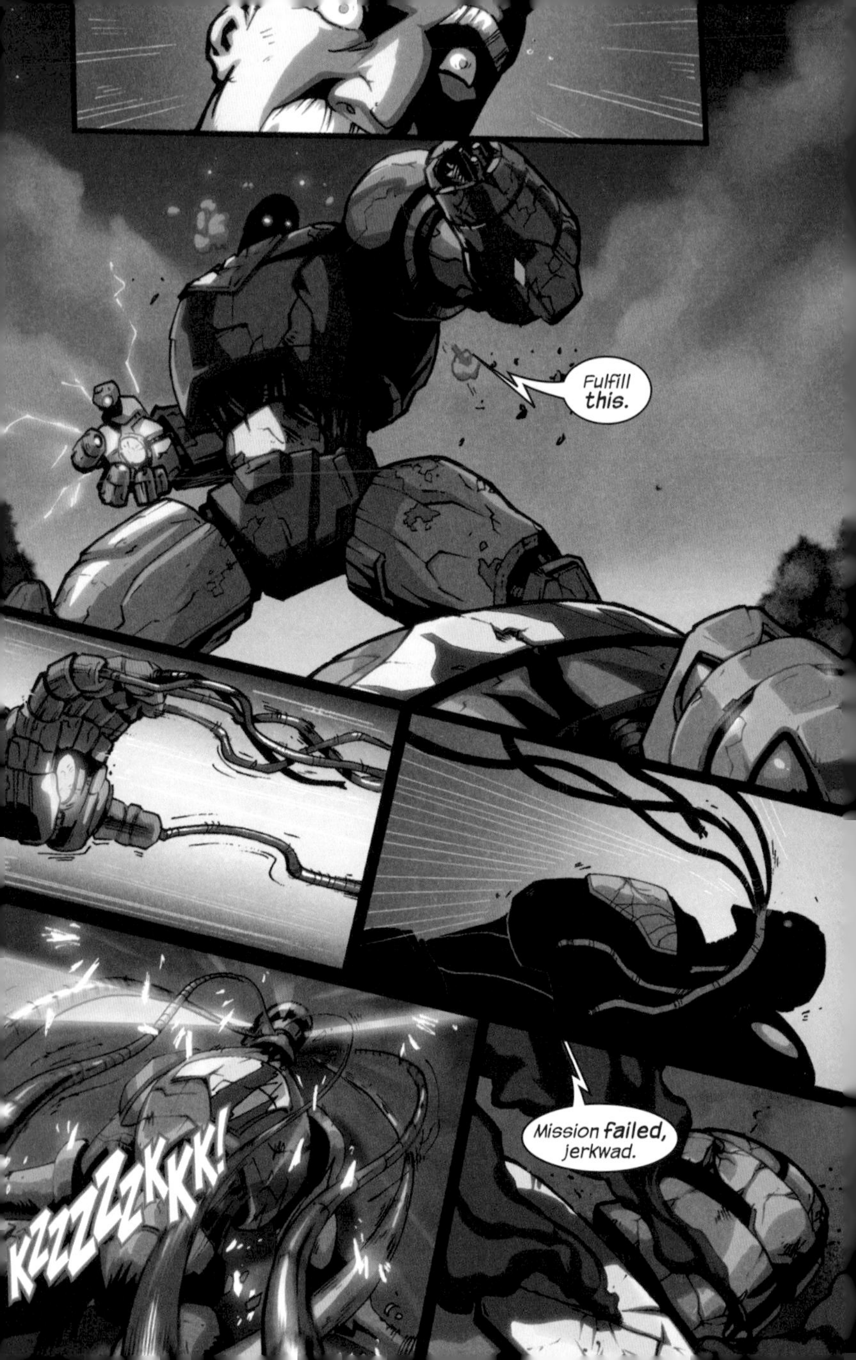
Fulfill this.
Mission failed, jerkwad.
KZZZZZKKK!

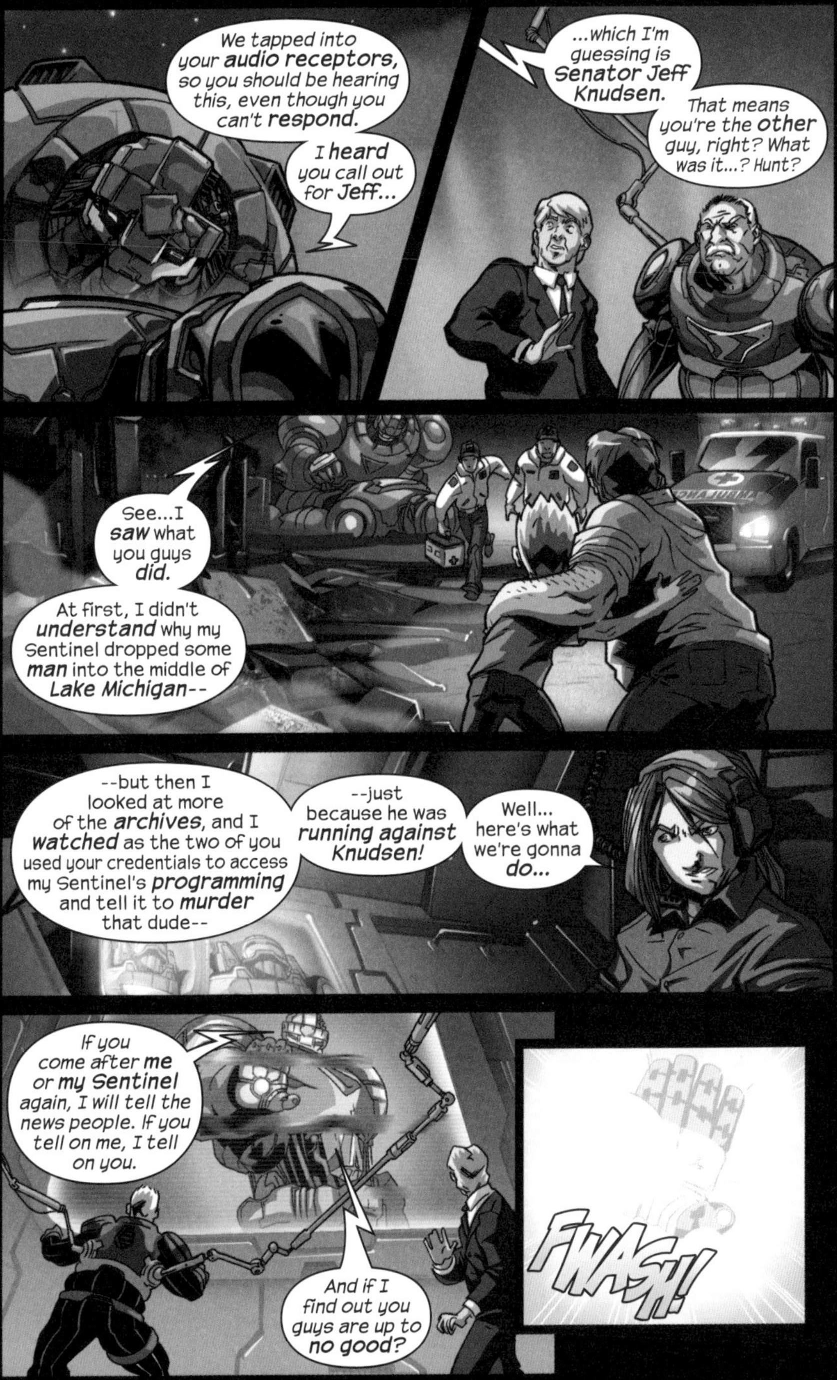

We tapped into your audio receptors, so you should be hearing this, even though you can't respond.
I heard you call out for Jeff...
...which I'm guessing is Senator Jeff Knudsen.
That means you're the other guy, right? What was it...? Hunt?
See...I saw what you guys did.
At first, I didn't understand why my Sentinel dropped some man into the middle of Lake Michigan--
--but then I looked at more of the archives, and I watched as the two of you used your credentials to access my Sentinel's programming and tell it to murder that dude--
--just because he was running against Knudsen!
Well... here's what we're gonna do...
If you come after me or my Sentinel again, I will tell the news people. If you tell on me, I tell on you.
And if I find out you guys are up to no good?
FWASH!

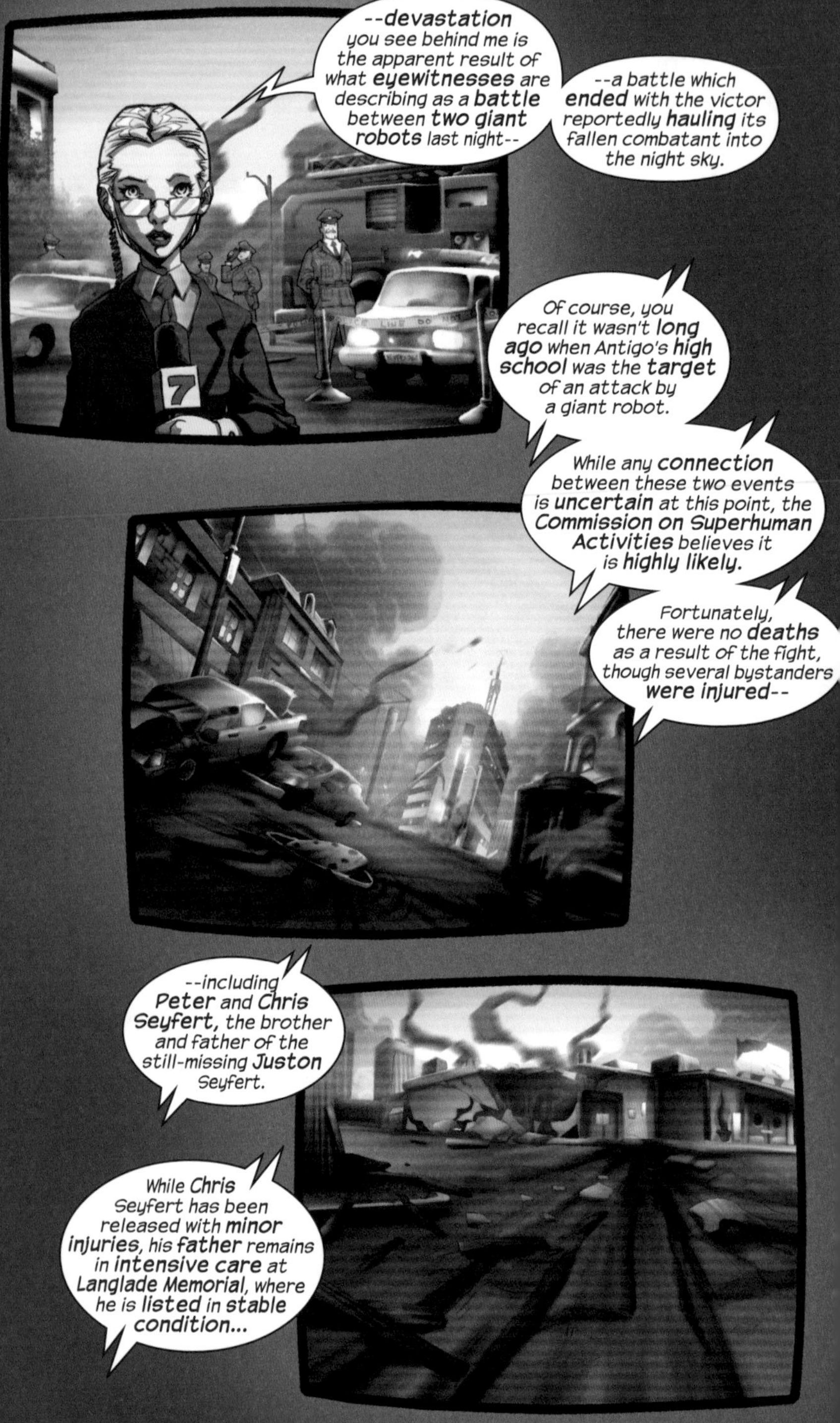
--devastation you see behind me is the apparent result of what eyewitnesses are describing as a battle between two giant robots last night--
--a battle which ended with the victor reportedly hauling its fallen combatant into the night sky.
Of course, you recall it wasn't long ago when Antigo's high school was the target of an attack by a giant robot.
While any connection between these two events is uncertain at this point, the Commission on Superhuman Activities believes it is highly likely.
Fortunately, there were no deaths as a result of the fight, though several bystanders were injured--
--including Peter and Chris Seyfert, the brother and father of the still-missing Juston Seyfert.
While Chris Seyfert has been released with minor injuries, his father remains in intensive care at Langlade Memorial, where he is listed in stable condition...

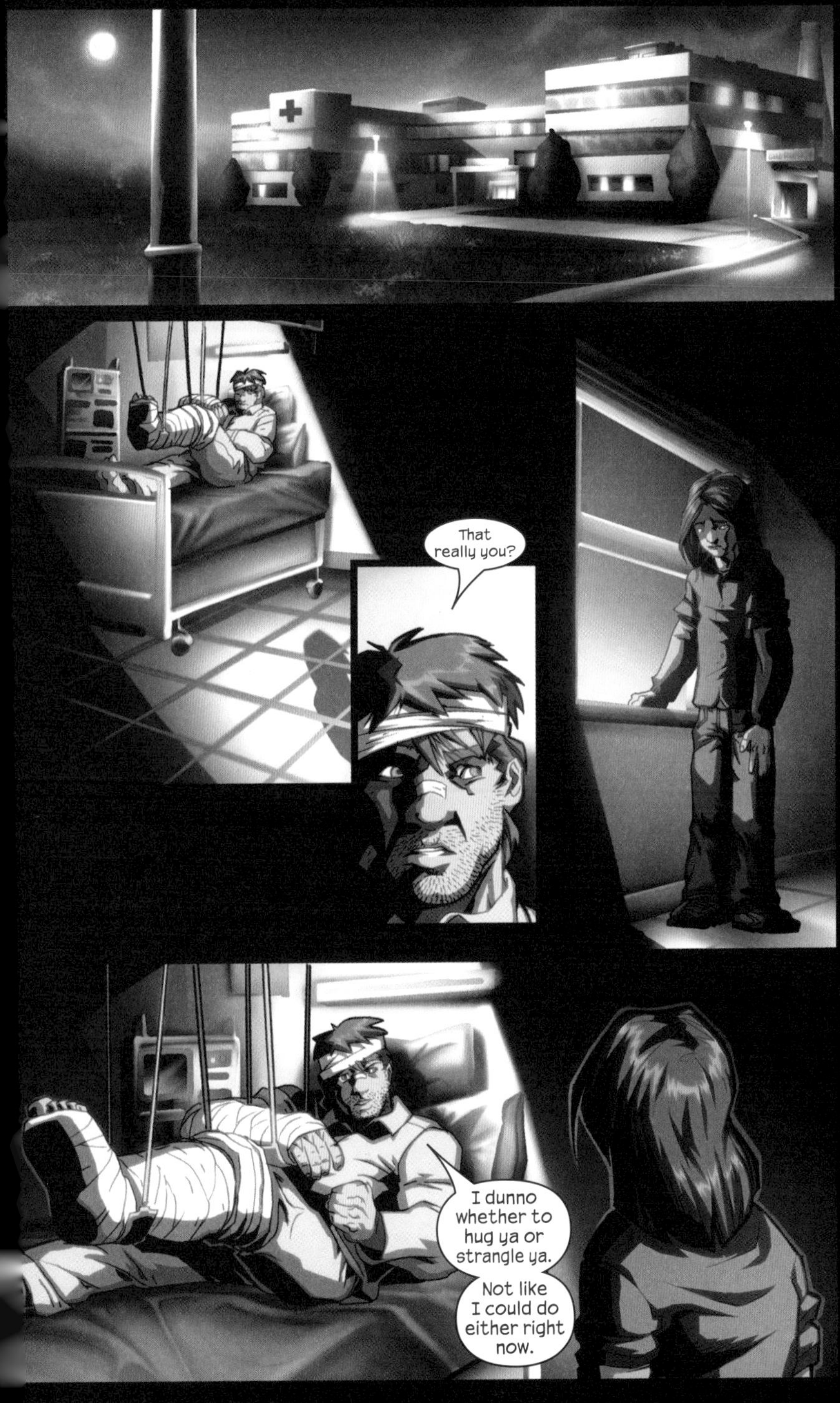
That really you?
I dunno whether to hug ya or strangle ya.
Not like I could do either right now.

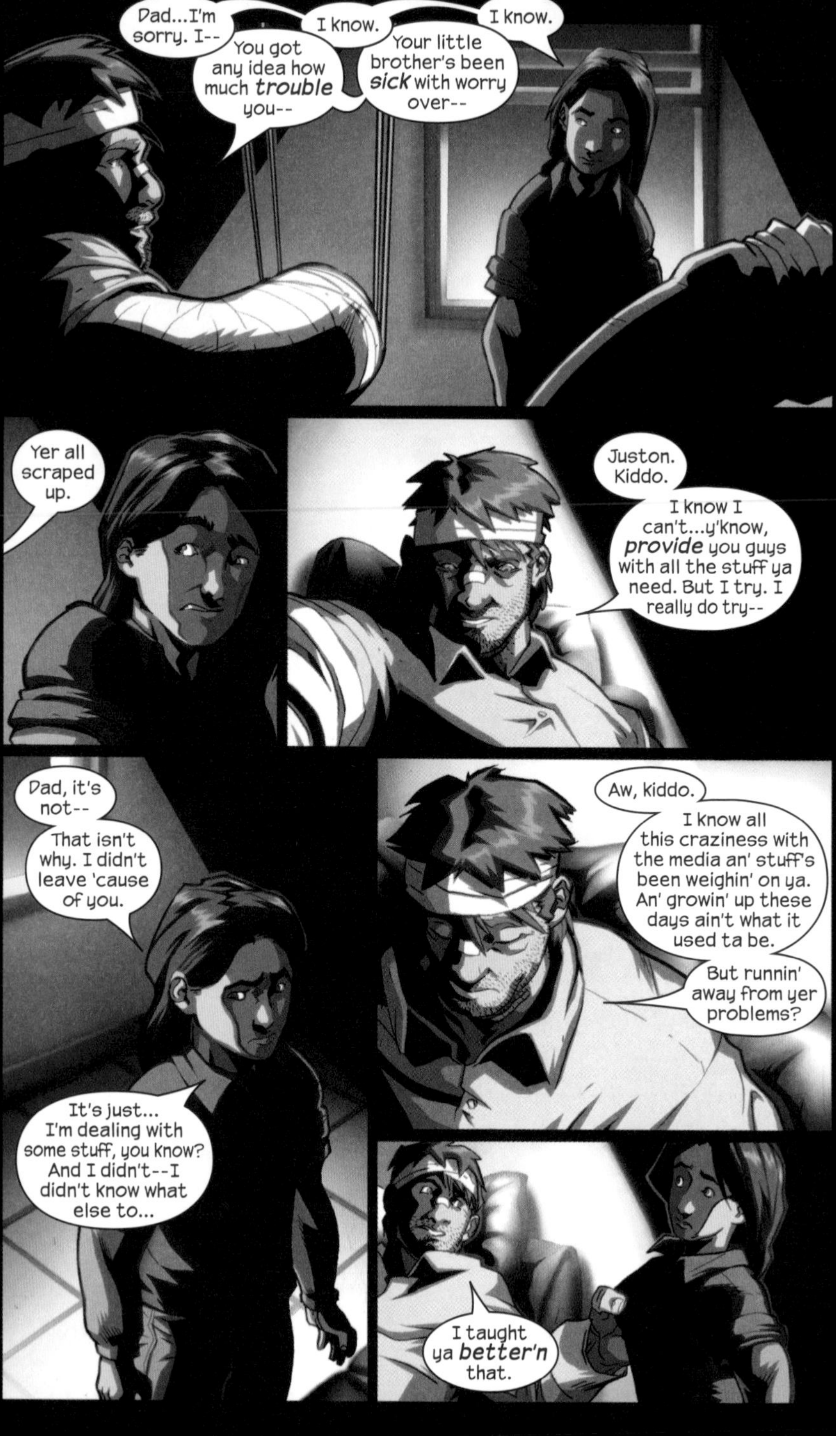

Dad...I'm sorry. I--
I know.
You got any idea how much *trouble* you--
I know.
Your little brother's been *sick* with worry over--
Yer all scraped up.
Juston. Kiddo.
I know I can't...y'know, *provide* you guys with all the stuff ya need. But I try. I really do try--
Dad, it's not--
That isn't why. I didn't leave 'cause of you.
Aw, kiddo.
I know all this craziness with the media an' stuff's been weighin' on ya. An' growin' up these days ain't what it used ta be.
But runnin' away from yer problems?
It's just... I'm dealing with some stuff, you know? And I didn't--I didn't know what else to...
I taught ya *better'n* that.

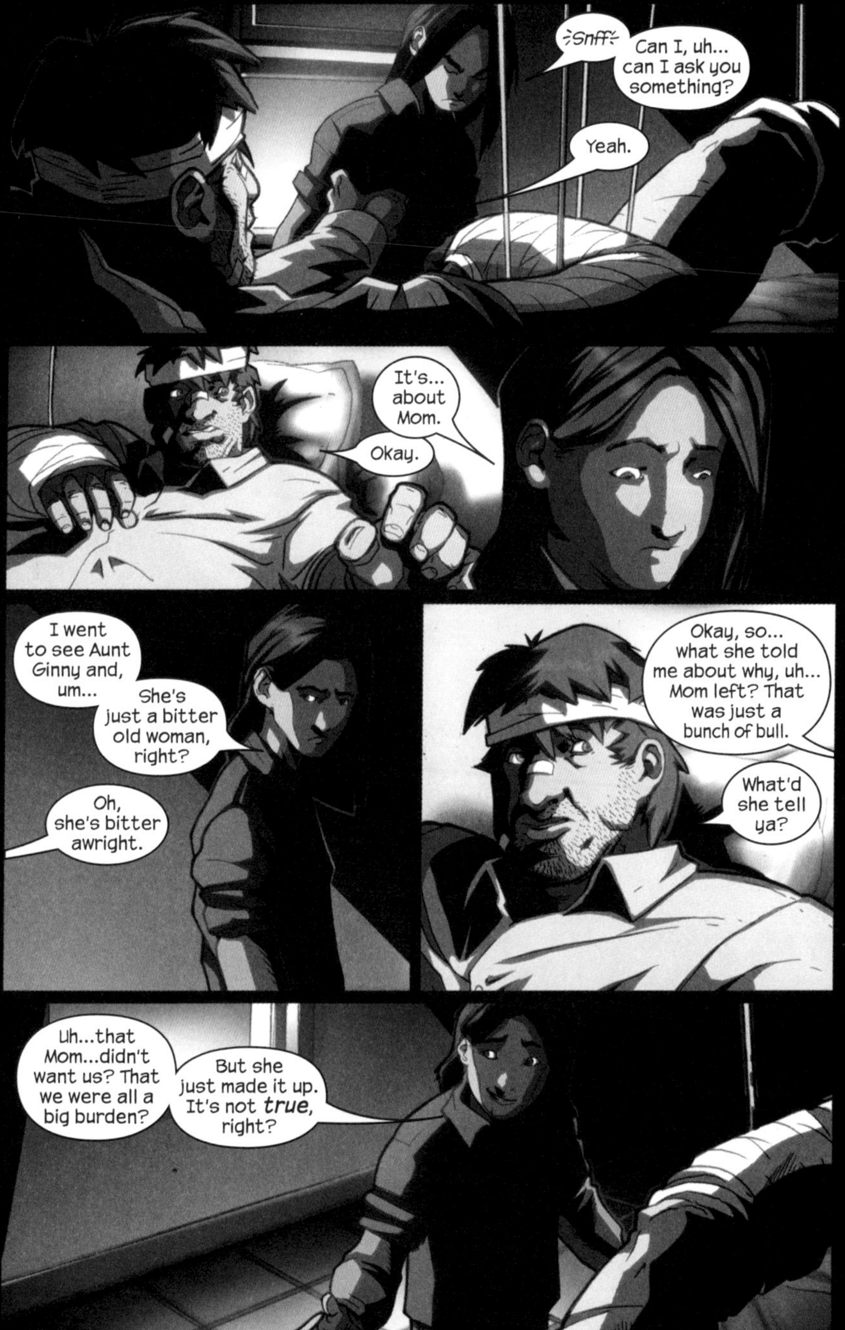
Snff
Can I, uh... can I ask you something?
Yeah.
It's... about Mom.
Okay.
I went to see Aunt Ginny and, um...
She's just a bitter old woman, right?
Oh, she's bitter awright.
Okay, so... what she told me about why, uh... Mom left? That was just a bunch of bull.
What'd she tell ya?
Uh...that Mom...didn't want us? That we were all a big burden?
But she just made it up. It's not *true*, right?

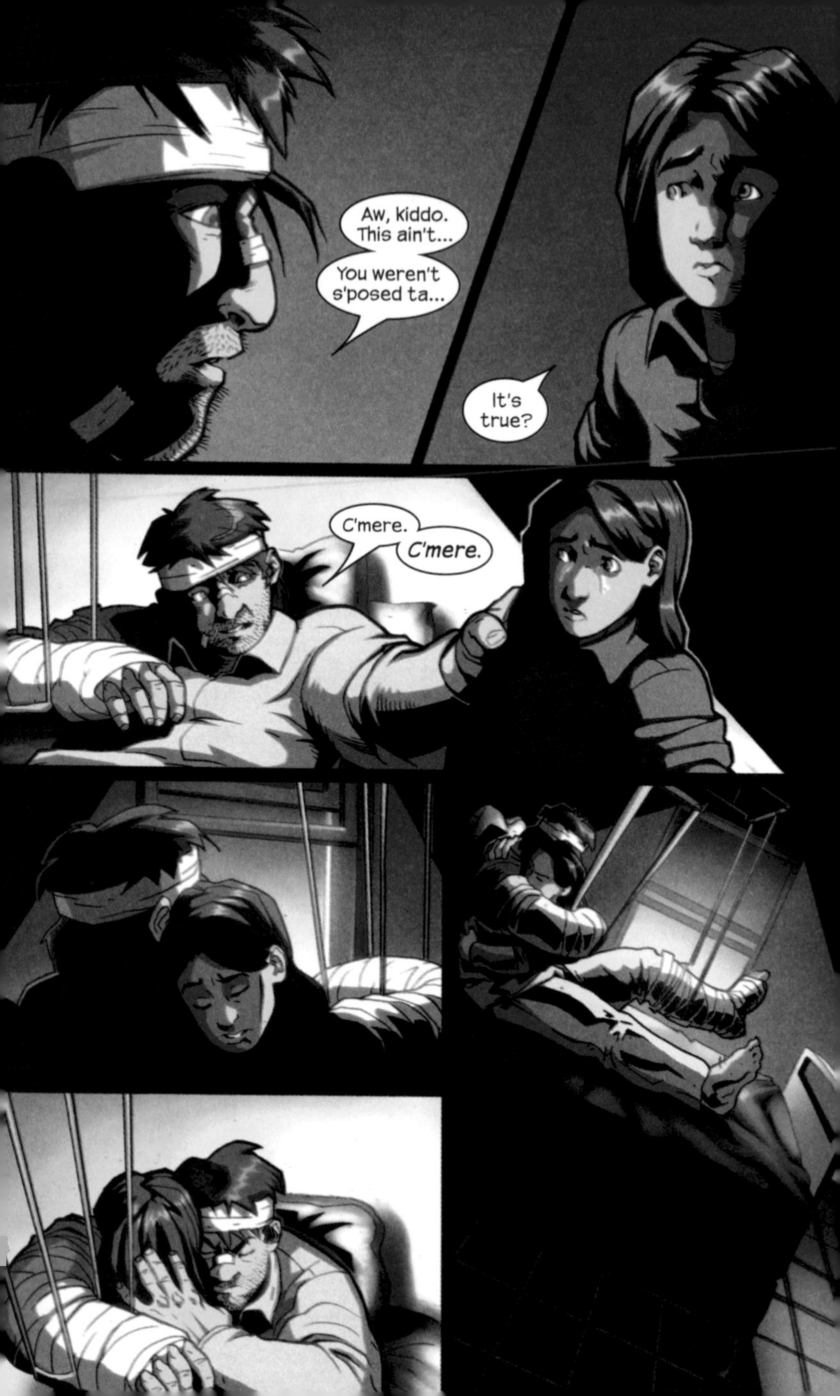

Aw, kiddo. This ain't...
You weren't s'posed ta...
It's true?
C'mere.
C'mere.

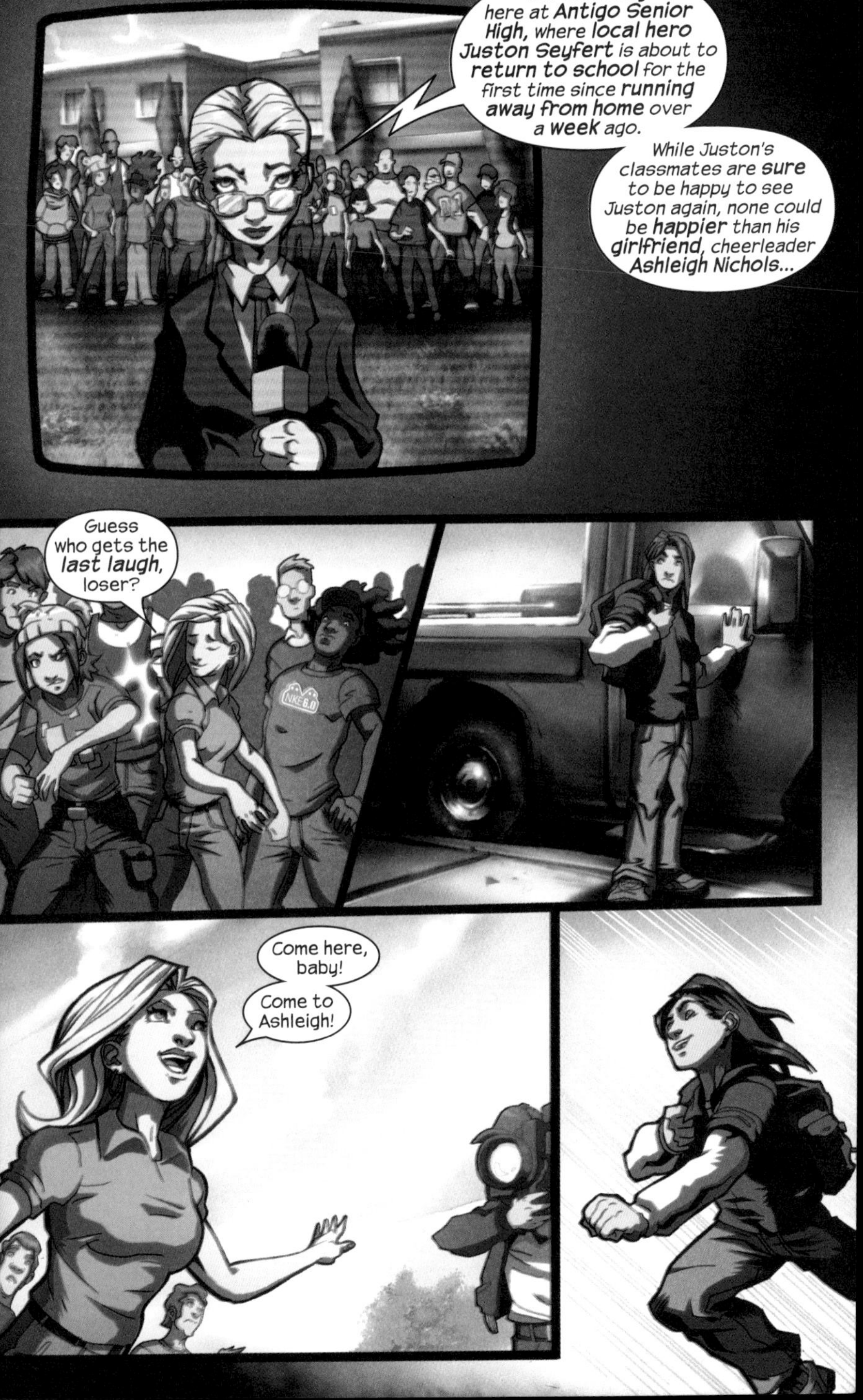
I'm standing here at Antigo Senior High, where local hero Juston Seyfert is about to return to school for the first time since running away from home over a week ago.
While Juston's classmates are sure to be happy to see Juston again, none could be happier than his girlfriend, cheerleader Ashleigh Nichols...
Guess who gets the last laugh, loser?
NKE 6.0
Come here, baby!
Come to Ashleigh!

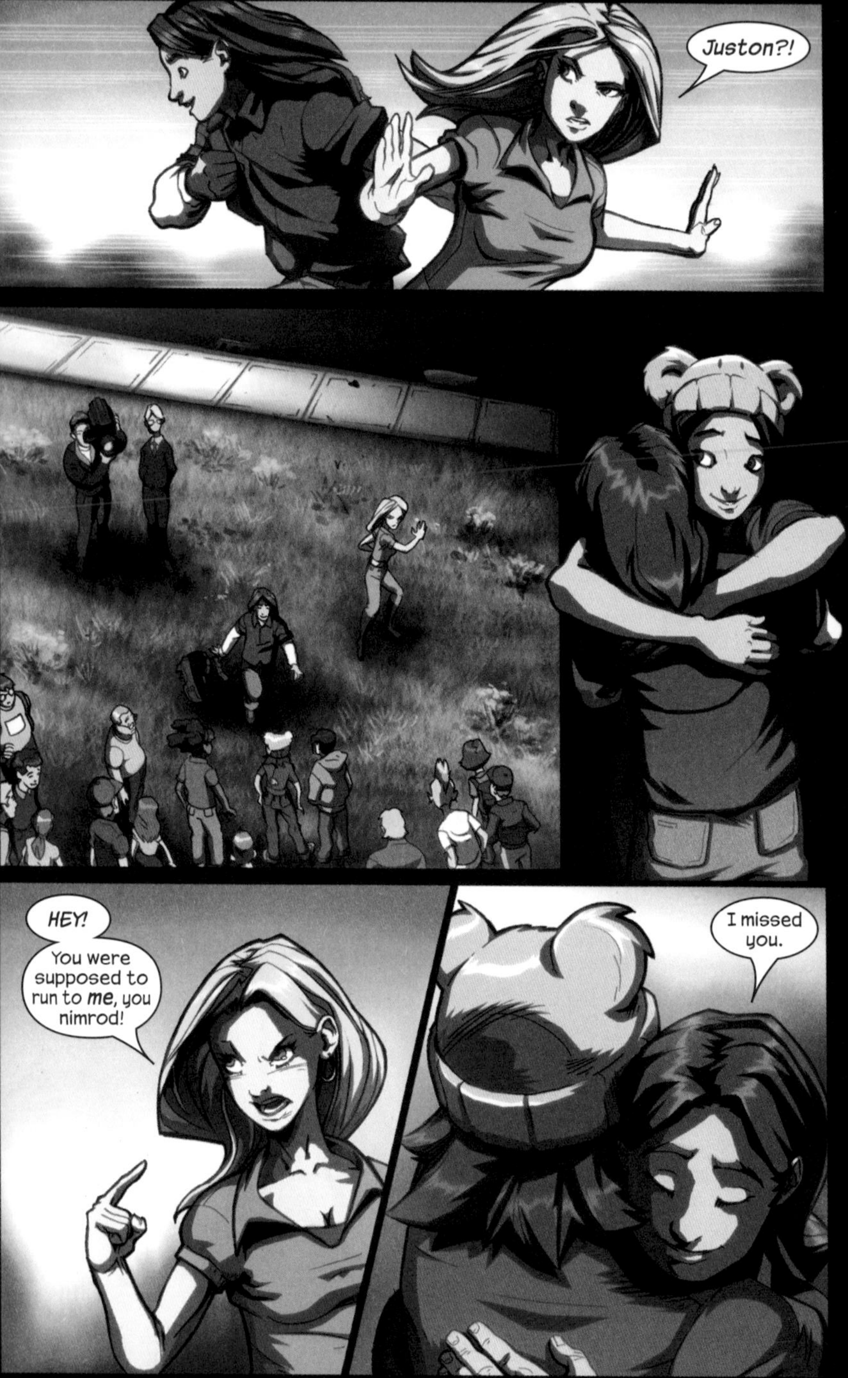
Juston?!
HEY!
You were supposed to run to *me*, you nimrod!
I missed you.

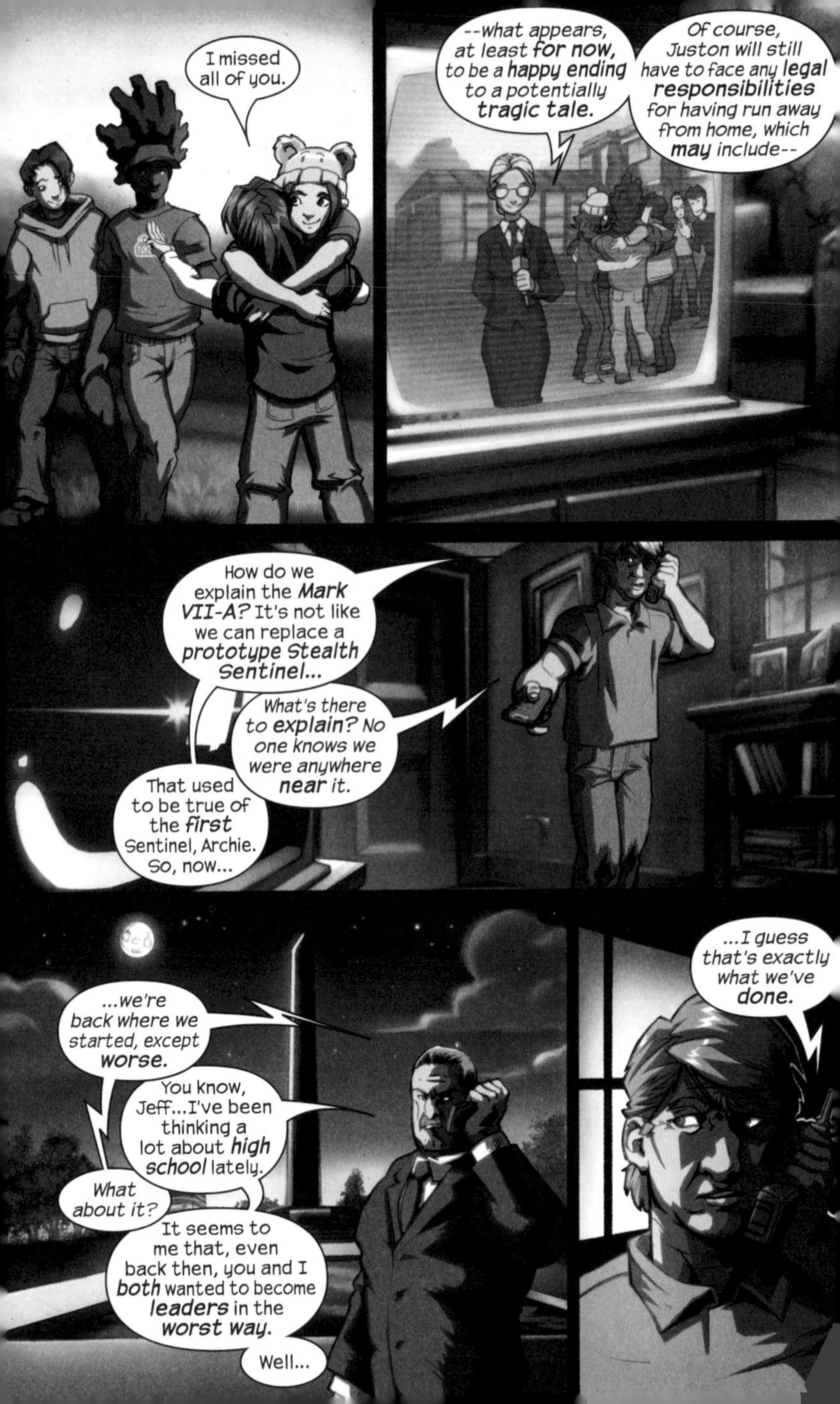
I missed all of you.
--what appears, at least for now, to be a happy ending to a potentially tragic tale.
Of course, Juston will still have to face any legal responsibilities for having run away from home, which may include--
How do we explain the Mark VII-A? It's not like we can replace a prototype Stealth Sentinel...
What's there to explain? No one knows we were anywhere near it.
That used to be true of the first Sentinel, Archie. So, now...
...we're back where we started, except worse.
You know, Jeff...I've been thinking a lot about high school lately.
What about it?
It seems to me that, even back then, you and I both wanted to become leaders in the worst way.
Well...
...I guess that's exactly what we've done.

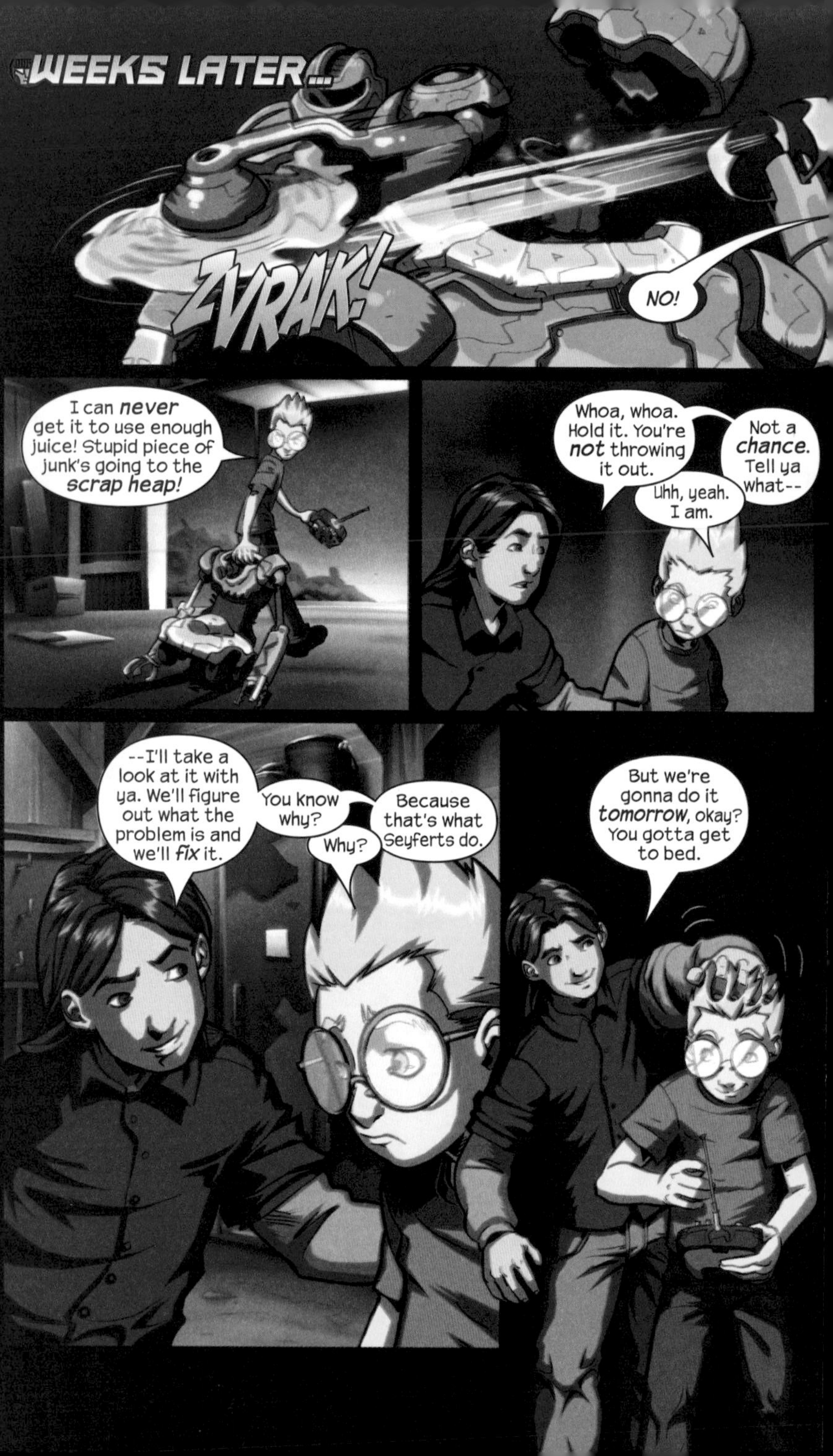
WEEKS LATER...
ZVRAK!
NO!
I can never get it to use enough juice! Stupid piece of junk's going to the scrap heap!
Whoa, whoa. Hold it. You're not throwing it out.
Uhh, yeah. I am.
Not a chance. Tell ya what--
--I'll take a look at it with ya. We'll figure out what the problem is and we'll fix it.
You know why?
Why?
Because that's what Seyferts do.
But we're gonna do it tomorrow, okay? You gotta get to bed.

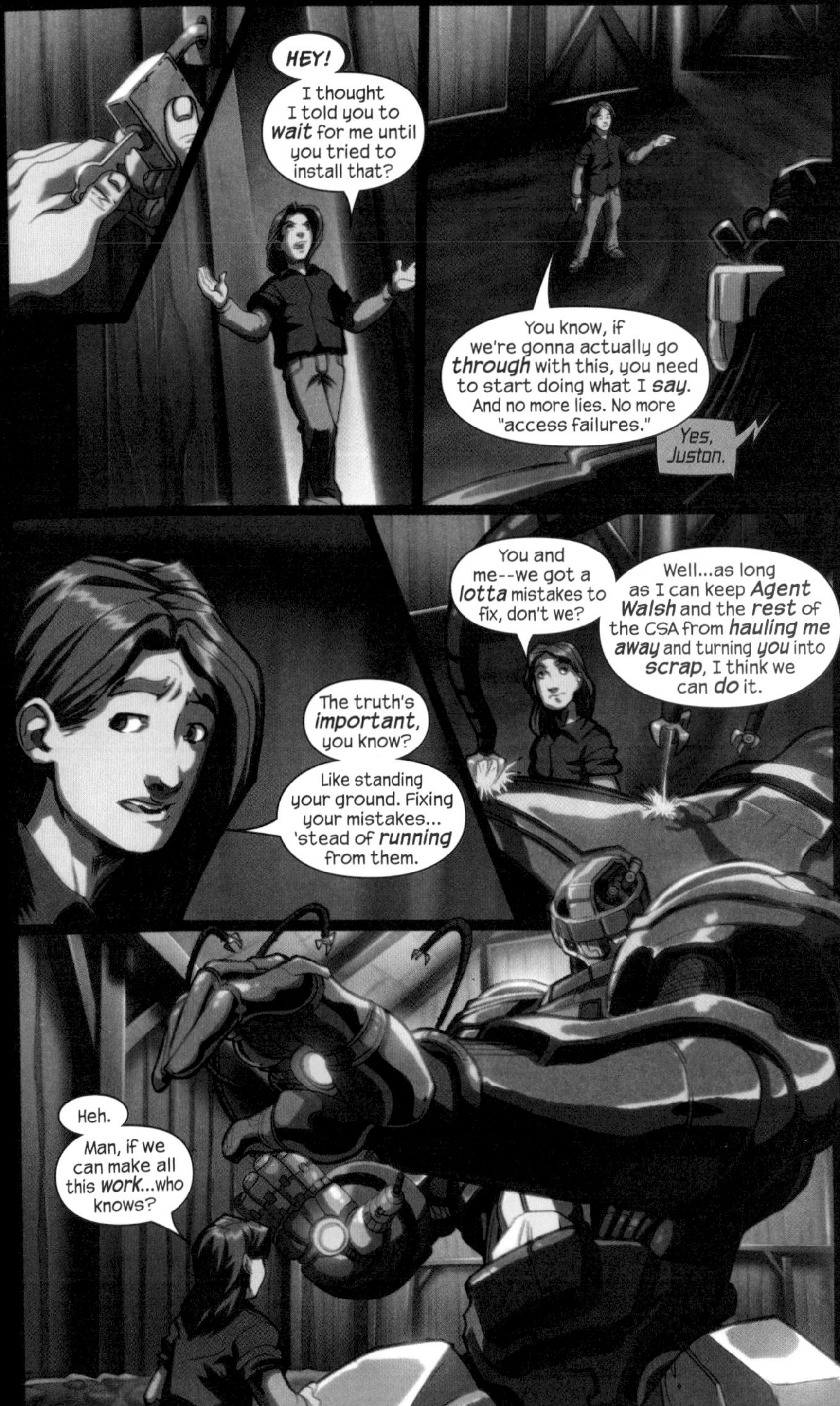
HEY!
I thought I told you to *wait* for me until you tried to install that?
You know, if we're gonna actually go *through* with this, you need to start doing what I *say*. And no more lies. No more "access failures."
Yes, Juston.
The truth's *important*, you know?
Like standing your ground. Fixing your mistakes... 'stead of *running* from them.
You and me--we got a *lotta* mistakes to fix, don't we?
Well...as long as I can keep *Agent Walsh* and the *rest* of the CSA from *hauling me away* and turning *you* into *scrap*, I think we can *do* it.
Heh.
Man, if we can make all this *work*...who knows?

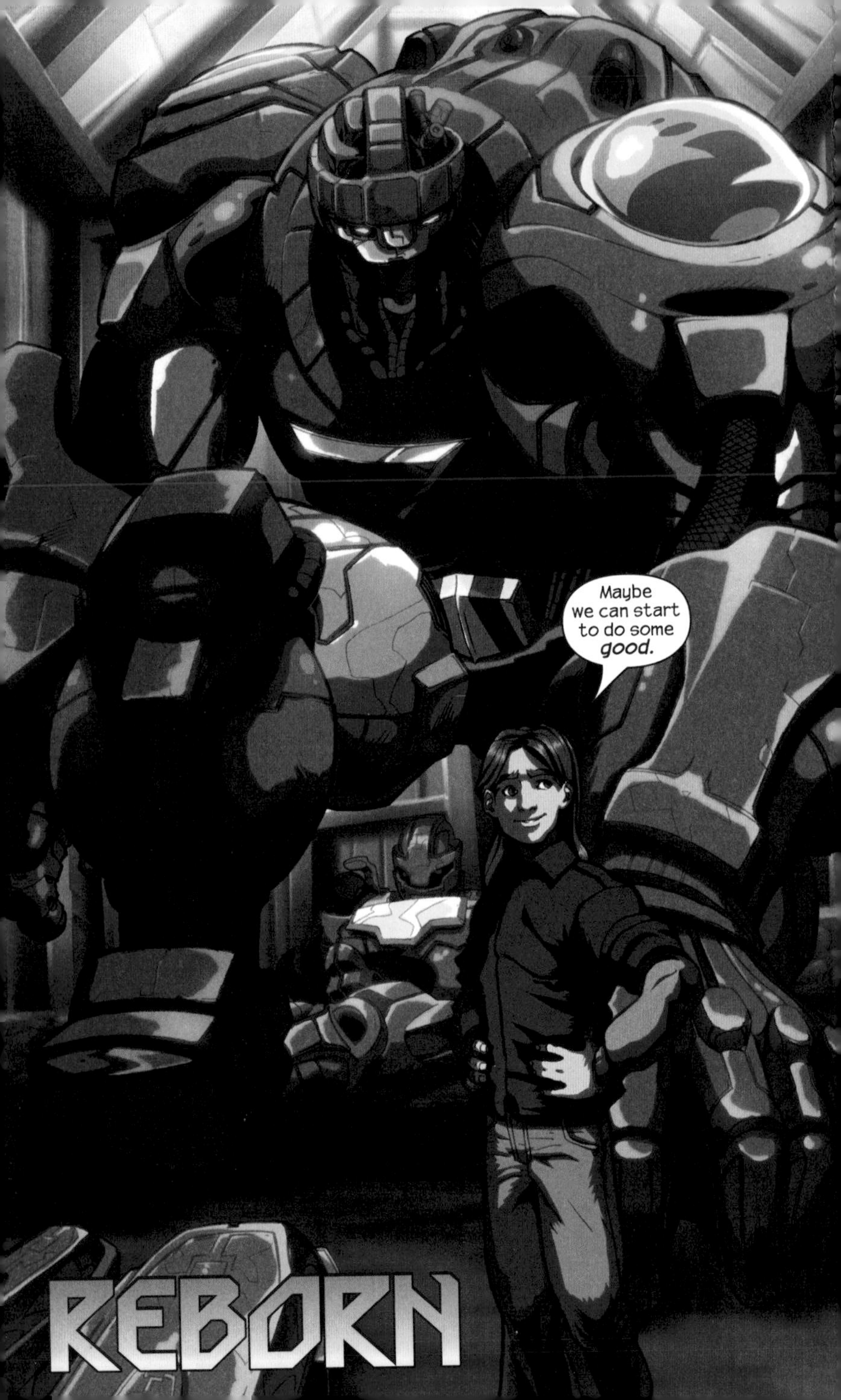

Maybe we can start to do some good.
REBORN